THE DEMOCRATS

THOMAS JEFFERSON

When John Trumbull painted this portrait, Thomas Jefferson was serving in France as the American minister and longing for a relief from official duties. Instead of retiring to become a gentleman farmer, Jefferson soon found himself in the vortex of partisan politics, destined to found the Democratic party as a means of preserving republican government in the new nation.

The
Democrats
From Jefferson to Carter

Robert A. Rutland

Louisiana State University Press
Baton Rouge and London

Designer: Patricia Douglas Crowder
Typeface: VIP Sabon
Typesetter: LSU Press
Printer: Thomson Shore, Inc.
Binder: John Dekker & Sons, Inc.

LIBRARY OF CONGRESS CATALOGING IN PUBLICATION DATA

Rutland, Robert Allen, 1922–
  The Democrats, from Jefferson to Carter.

  Bibliography: p.
  Includes index.
  1. Democratic Party—History. I. Title.
JK2316.R93   329.3'09   79–10326
ISBN 0–8071–0574–0

to
Dumas Malone
a genuine Jeffersonian Democrat

Contents

Illustrations

Preface

Is there a discernible difference between the major political parties in the United States? Idle chatter at cocktail parties insists there is not; but political science professors make charts and punch computer tapes in search of a sophisticated answer. Most Americans can agree that third parties are foredoomed to fail, but they are uncertain about the reasons why Americans have been limited to two major political parties throughout most of their national existence. This book attempts to show the lay reader how the oldest party reached its present ground, after nearly two centuries of landslide victories, close shaves, and humbling defeats. Anything which survives that long deserves some credit, and although political parties are a mixed blessing, they have served our republic well enough for the nation to be one of only two survivors among all the governments existing in 1776. Such a record deserves serious study, which scholars are hard at work to provide. But the voters also need to be more aware of the ideas and men who have breathed life into their parties. The democracy of Jefferson and Jackson set the nation's course for half a century, only to lie almost dormant for another fifty years. Was Franklin D. Roosevelt's impact on the Democratic party of lasting value? And what of substance lies behind the slogans and the 30-second television commercials?

A quick survey is in some ways a treading on dangerous ground, for some facts are beyond simplification and some interpretations are still disputed by historians whose grandfathers thought the issues settled. All I have tried to provide is an overview that may not comfort but will at least point out the philosophical goals, the major issues, and the men who stood out. A companion work on the Republicans is needed, and I plan to write it. For the moment, I hope readers of both parties will find some useful information here and can stop wondering about the differences that separate the Democrats from the Republicans. Honest clashes of opinion, resolved by the majority vote, are the heart and soul of the democratic process and were the *raison d'être* of the Democratic party at the time of its founding. I hope it becomes clear that our best citizens have always placed the good of the country at the top of their list of priorities. Above all parties, there must be a faith in the democratic spirit as intoned by Thomas Jefferson, "the most authentic genius yet produced by America," who "never lost an affection and respect for the common people."*

*J. Harvie Wilkinson, "The Place of a University," *Virginia Quarterly Review*, LIII (Spring, 1977), 200.

Acknowledgments

Sometimes the writing of a book is more ordeal than pleasure. This little work has been a labor of love, carried forward by the friendship of many concerned citizens of both persuasions (Democratic and Republican) and by the patience of valued colleagues. The first category includes friends ranging from Eric Johnson to Bob Haldeman, and the list of the latter group is headed by Jeanne K. Sisson, for she can parse a sentence with the best of them. Staige D. Blackford, Jr., of the University of Virginia, gave the manuscript a careful reading and made many helpful suggestions for its improvement. Finally, the enthusiasm and skills of the editorial staff of the Louisiana State University Press have been major factors in the making of this book.

The care of human life and happiness, and not their destruction, is the first and only legitimate object of good government.

Thomas Jefferson, 1809

THE DEMOCRATS

ONE

The Jeffersonian Genesis

I am not a member of an organized political party—I'm a Democrat."

Will Rogers said it, and laughed. But as it sometimes happens, the joke was on the nation. Rogers spoke in the 1920s, when it seemed that the Democrats loved to fight each other more than they wanted to win a national election. Astounding losses in the 1920 and 1924 presidential campaigns had left the party in disarray. The great goals enunciated by the party founder, Thomas Jefferson, seemed remote. In the South the blacks were not able to vote, owing to a variety of strategems to keep white Democrats in power (while white Republicans in Washington looked the other way). In the North, black Republican votes helped offset the inevitable Solid South returns every four years, and informal historians within the Democratic party ranks bemoaned the embarrassing fact that Grover Cleveland and Woodrow Wilson were their only White House occupants over a 68-year span.

Indeed, so beleaguered were the Democrats in 1928, as they faced a ruinous campaign pitched on religious bigotry and sanctimonious moralizing, that a spokesman sought solace in reflecting that while "there is less practical sense in the Democratic party . . . there is more human emotion. It may be that it has less gumption, but it certainly has more soul." In the debacle that followed the Hoover-Smith contest, however, the Democrats showed enough gumption to reestablish two-party government in the United States. The party Jefferson said he did not want, but which he founded, weathered one more crisis. In fact, the history of the Democratic party is a series of crises—surmounted and unsurmounted. Any nation that survives with its political machinery more or less intact after two hundred years must weather many devastating storms. In America the political parties have furnished the sails for the ship of state, and only once were the sails torn from their rigging. The Democrats of 1860 used flimsy cloth and they forfeited their right to exercise power for most of the next two generations. Yet the party of Jefferson and Andrew Jackson was capable of coming back. Why? Were there basic principles that could sustain a political party after savage attacks by the opposition had brought it to the brink of extinction?

Jefferson thought so, and he nourished that belief until the first Democrats were firmly entrenched as the dominant national party with control of the presidency and the Congress. Labeled "Republicans," and so called from about 1796 until 1828, these Democrats came into being almost in spite of themselves. The title grudgingly bestowed on their party was a direct outgrowth of the American Revolution and its aftermath, for the Founding Fathers believed that the Revolution had been fought to establish a republican government in a sovereign nation. Learned in ancient history and disgusted with recent British politics, they agreed that creating a republican form of government was the best way to keep power in the hands of the people. In a republic, aristocratic pretensions based on hereditary power counted for nothing, and Americans of all persuasions agreed in 1787–1788 that they had perfected a constitution which set limits on power and made the government responsive to the will of the people. Their handiwork, framed at Philadelphia after a series of troublesome compromises, was based on the assumption (and hope) that organized political parties would not develop in the new republic. Not for them the decadent British example of Whig and Tory, which they perceived as a system of corruption incarnate. "There is nothing I dread so much as the division of the Republic into two great parties," John Adams sighed in 1789. Such a circumstance, the vice-president insisted, "is to be feared as the greatest political evil under our Constitution." Jefferson put it another way. "If I could not go to Heaven but with a party," he wrote in 1789, "I would not go there at all."

George Washington, James Madison, and virtually all the men in charge of the new government in 1789 agreed. Perhaps Alexander Hamilton, always painfully frank, knew better, but for a time the fashion in republican circles was to look upon political parties as instruments of the devil. Moreover, the Constitution nailed down the nonpartisan ideal in its method of choosing a president. The electoral college was to be a gathering of the good and wise, principled men who kowtowed to no party allegiance; and obviously the system good enough to elect the president would be adequate for state and local elections. Citizens of good character and high motives (well, most of the time—but not always—as Madison had conceded in *The Federalist* 10) would be candidates for office; and they would be elected by virtuous, or at least well-informed, voters. "Faction" was an evil that had to be avoided, else the new nation would go the way of ancient Rome and modern England, both hateful examples of the ruin induced by luxury and corruption. "The public good is disregarded in the conflicts of rival parties," Madison acknowledged. But he went on to say that the "latent causes of faction" were "sown in the nature of man" and the most common of the causes was the "unequal distribution of property."* "Those who

---

*As to what a faction was, Madison made it clear that he was talking about "a number of citizens . . . who are united and actuated by some common impulse of passion, or of interest, adverse to the rights of other citizens, or to the permanent and aggregate interests of the community."

hold and those who are without property have ever formed distinct interests in society." Fortunately, Madison concluded, the Constitution promised the cure for the duplicity and venality that flourished in political parties. The frequent elections of the people's representatives, brought together from all parts of the Union, would control the main vices of party politics, he said. If some men lacked virtue, or wanted to run roughshod over the rights of others, the Constitution had safeguards to keep parties of them from taking the shape of those detested factions which had destroyed Rome and plagued Mother England at that very moment.

The breezes of the Revolution were still blowing, but Madison and Jefferson were more committed to the republican ideals than most of their comrades from the heady days of '76. There had been early signs of disenchantment in the postwar years when, in the aftermath of paper-money legislation and low commodity prices, a handful of angry Massachusetts farmers had scared the wits out of the Boston bankers and lawyers. One consequence of that tempest in a teapot, known in history as Shays's Rebellion, had been hushed talk that what the country really needed was a king. Even the suggestion that an American monarchy might solve the nation's problems made Jefferson bristle. Looking firsthand at the effects of monarchy in France, he wrote that he was "astonished at some people's considering a kingly government as a refuge. If all the evils which can arise among us from the republican form of our government from this day to the day of judgment could be put into a scale against what this country suffers from its monarchical form in a week, or England in a month, the latter would preponderate." To the end of his days, Jefferson feared any political movement in America that the favored few supported, for he believed that a powerful clique considered the Constitution only a stopgap measure.

The founder of the Democratic party had his first hint of a

4

strong antirepublican sentiment when he returned from France to become Washington's secretary of state. "I was much astonished, indeed, at the mimicry I found established of royal forms and . . . by the monarchical sentiments I heard expressed and openly maintained in every company." Washington, Jefferson noted, was not a party to such talk. However, the president was surrounded by men who maintained that the Constitution was "in fact, only a stepping stone to something better." Madison shared Jefferson's disappointment in the shallowness of the commitment to republican institutions they discerned in Washington's most trusted advisers, particularly Alexander Hamilton, the secretary of the treasury. Hamilton, of course, denied the existence of "a Monarchial party" and hastened to assure a close friend of both Jefferson and Madison that the charge was absurd: "I assure you on my *private faith* and *honor* as a Man that there is not in my judgment a shadow of foundation of it."

There was truth, however, in the charge that Hamilton was enamored with the British way of running a country. As early as 1781 he had diagnosed the young nation's financial problem and called for a British remedy. "A national debt, if it is not excessive, will be to us a national blessing," he ventured. A decade later, when Hamilton was attempting to activate his plans, Madison took the opposite view: "I go on the principle that a Public Debt is a Public curse, and in a Rep[ublican] Govt a greater than in any other." Such diverging views heralded a bitter clash. Then as the cabinet meetings grew more tense, Jefferson's antipathy to Hamilton's financial program was spelled out in an emerging philosophy that became the bedrock tenet of the republicans. Hamilton wanted the new government to weave two English ideas into the fabric of the new nation: a national debt (which would provide a secure form of investment in gilt-edged securities) and a counterpart to the Bank of England. Old-time republicans, including most of Jefferson's friends in Virginia, had favored the sale of public lands in the West as a means of eliminating the national debt of about $40 million left from the Revolution. This fitted their idea of low taxes (just enough to pay the bills for a small-scale government). And of course these republicans wanted only a housekeeping force for an army and navy. Hamilton and his followers were not interested in exploiting the western lands, except in private speculations, but favored a tariff that would create a permanent force of collectors and agents who would constitute a loyal civil service. And, if a sizable army and navy were needed, the Federalists agreed that there was no harm in an army larger than any token force. The revolutionary cry "No standing army!" had, to the Federalists, become a shopworn cliché.

When Jefferson looked back on his cabinet battles with Hamilton, he summarized their relationship as being like that of "two cocks in a pit." Though no blood was shed, Hamilton began to see Madison and Jefferson as holding an attitude toward France "unsound & dangerous. *They have a womanish attachment to France and a womanish resentment against Great Britain.*" In domestic matters Hamilton thought the two democrats equally misguided. *"Mr. Madison cooperating with Mr. Jefferson is at the head of a faction decidedly hostile to me,"* and, what was worse, the pair's goals were *"dangerous to the union, peace and happiness of the country."* *

The Jeffersonians had a different view. They looked to the secretary of state as their champion who had more than a sentimental attachment to the shibboleths of '76. A national revenue system and its handmaiden, a federally chartered bank, created jobs and incomes for city dwellers of means. Farmers made up over 95 percent of the population and would ultimately pay the tariffs, which would be passed on to them on the imported goods they bought. America had few factories, which meant that most tools, paints, wallpaper, dry goods, textiles, glass, and hardware came from

*Alexander Hamilton to Edward Carrington, May 26, 1792.

abroad. Merchants and shippers would make money sending the farmers' wheat and pork to the Caribbean and Europe, and then make more profit selling the farmers English calicoes and scythes. So the farmers and planters not only conquered insects and bad weather but had to pay twice to the city-dwelling commercial crowd, who also owned most of the government securities. Thus it seemed that the farmers were being discriminated against through the Federalist program, and Jefferson was only voicing a common complaint when he said that America's cities were "the strongholds of Federalism." "The inhabitants of the commercial cities," he said, "are as different in sentiment and character from the country people as any two distinct nations, and are clamorous against the order of things established by the agricultural interest." The collision between the Federalists and Republicans was a clash between the cash box and the corncrib, Jeffersonians believed. The mismatch would go to the townsmen in their countinghouses if their avarice was abetted by the national government.

At the root of their differences lay a key issue: whether an energetic or a loose-reined federal government was needed. The hard-line Federalists believed that the more the nation adhered to a system imitative of the English Constitution, the better off the country would be, while the democratic republicans (as one told Madison) thought "the English Constitution is a vicious one pretty well patched up & corrected." A hint of troubles to come fell during the first session of Congress, when the senators favored high-sounding titles for the new president and were overruled by Madison and his friends in the House who ridiculed their pretensions. When Jefferson learned of the proposed presidential title ("His Highness, the President of the United States of America, and Protector of the Rights of the Same"), he called it "the most superlatively ridiculous thing I ever heard of." Not surprisingly, the Jeffersonians considered this near-miss from the "aristocratic Junto" more than a warning shot that there were men in high places who would love to see aristocratic titles conferred on well-to-do Federalists. No matter that the Constitution forbade such tomfoolery.

Although Washington tried to steer clear of the two political forces that were taking shape in his cabinet meetings, Hamilton pushed his fiscal program, and the president more and more sided with him. With the Federalist plan for a national bank, tariffs, excise taxes, a military force, and a funded debt in full swing by 1793, Jefferson adopted Hamilton's tactic of going to the people through the newspapers. To spread Federalist doctrine, Hamilton's friends supported the *Gazette of the United States*. Jefferson counterattacked through the columns of the *National Gazette*, edited by Madison's classmate from Princeton days, Philip Freneau. The debate slid into a morass of invective when war broke out between England and France. The Federalists whooped it up for England, while Jefferson and his supporters sided with republican France. In Europe most people were illiterate and left the conduct of state business to their betters, but Americans had a republican curiosity to learn what was going on. A friend of Madison's traveling to the capital noted, "At the Inns on the Road I was surprised to find the knowledge, which the Land Lords, and the Country People who were at some of them, had acquired, of the Debates and Proceedings of Congress." Small wonder that the printers increasingly took sides. "The salvation of America depends on our alliance with France," the Philadelphia *General Advertiser* insisted, while the *Columbian Centinel* lambasted the pro-French crowd as "Jacobinical minions."

Discouraged by Hamilton's domination of the Washington administration, Jefferson resigned from the cabinet. By January, 1794, he was back at his mountaintop retreat, leaving Madison in charge of the hemmed-in Republican command post in Philadelphia. Meanwhile, Madison had fallen out of grace with Washington. During the last years of Washington's second term, the Federalists consolidated their power, although such incidents as the Whiskey Rebellion focused attention on the growing gap between the Federalist and Republican schools of thought. If the Republican approach to government seemed negative, that was because of the prevailing theory among them that government itself was negative. "What is government itself but the greatest of all reflections on human nature?" Madison asked. "If men were angels, no government would be necessary." Madison's archadversary, Hamilton, did not think men were angelic, but he believed that government could be a positive force for an expanding nation dominated by "thinking men"—lawyers, bankers, merchants, and shipowners. The inherent conservatism of the farmer-planter fixed Republican ideas about what the American Revolution had been fought to achieve: stability and self-government, with the states rather than the federal government left to deal with a variety of local concerns, and low taxes and low prices on foreign goods for the farmers. For the government to intervene in the affairs of men by making profits almost certain for one class and hazardous for another, offended the Democratic Republicans mightily.

Although some historians see in Hamilton's program a positive approach to government, and consequently deem Jefferson's negative, another viewpoint stresses Jefferson's belief that the natural tendency of government was to interfere and become meddlesome, thus creating more problems than it could solve. After the Paris bread riots in 1789 Jefferson summed up his ideas in a sentence, as he commented on the crisis brought on by the royal government: "Never was there a country where the practice of governing too much had taken deeper root & done more mischief." But with this native distrust of government—and here was Jefferson's secret—he linked an almost unlimited faith in the tillers of the soil who made up most of the population in every country. Next to an overbearing government, Jefferson feared the specter of British power, for the Revolution had only been half-won as long as the "monarchists" held places of power. Thus Jefferson's basic brand of republicanism came to the fore. "Here was indeed a statesman who believed that most farmers, whether great or small, are honest and that most other people are not, and, moreover, that England is not to be trusted. This was the common point of union in every faction of Jeffersonian Republicanism."* "From the first arrival of our forefathers on the rock of Plymouth, to the present hour, Britain has been inimical to this country," a Republican newspaper observed in 1796. No good Republican argued otherwise, particularly after the storm caused by Jay's Treaty.

What had been a loose-jointed lot of dissenters moved toward some kind of an organized opposition during the Jay treaty debates in Congress. In simple terms, the Federalists wanted the treaty to preserve trade relations with England and were willing to postpone unfinished business in the West; their opponents wanted a tough stand on the frontier friction and no concessions to England whatever. The fight over the treaty in Congress proved that a deep-rooted philosophical difference existed between the two factions, and out of their bitter struggle for power the Democratic Republican party was born. The treaty was barely ratified, and in the aftermath Madison and his followers in the House of Representatives sought to derail the agreement by withholding the necessary funds to implement some of the treaty's provisions. They tried to rally state legislatures and key figures behind their opposition but were overwhelmed by Federalists who countered with petitions and steady pressure on congressmen. After Madison engineered a caucus, he could not hold a majority together. The Federalists triumphed, but the Jefferson-Madison coterie had learned a lesson. In the presidential election of 1796 they made their first bold move.

The race began the moment Washington took his hat out of

* Wilfred E. Binkley, *American Political Parties: Their Natural History* (New York: Knopf, 1963), 78.

the ring, as he warned in the same breath against "the baneful effects of the Spirit of Party." Washington had barely finished his farewell address before Adams had staked his claim as the general's successor. The Republicans, however, realized the superficiality of the vice-president's popularity and were determined to make a fight for the presidency. Jefferson had plenty of friends in Congress, for he had been pushing spokesmen of farmers and planters into elections to thwart the land speculators and stockjobbers he detested. Ultimately, a Jefferson-Burr ticket took rather lumpy shape; New York was a vital state and Aaron Burr gave the Republicans that balance which would never again be overlooked. Burr was well liked and a good friend of Madison, so he seemed safe enough. But the party lines were indistinct. "There was still much uncertainty as to who, if anybody, was running for anything and, if so, for what," historian Roy Nichols noted.

The outcome was not surprising. Adams had three more electoral votes than Jefferson (71 to 68), and so he became president; and under the Constitution as it then stood, Jefferson was chosen vice-president. Washington's dream of a nonpartisan national administration was about to crumble, but for the moment the choices seemed sensible. Here were the author and the promoter of the Declaration of Independence, back at doing what they did best—guiding the Republic—while England and France tore each other apart across the Atlantic.

Led by a dictator, republican France was winning over George III's England, and many active Americans were unable to watch the European wars dispassionately. To the differences already at work (the commercial and professional crowd lined up against the farmer-planter interest) there now came a hastening of the political metamorphosis. The Federalists tended to wish England well in her fight with Napoleon, while Jefferson and his adherents favored the French. Adams showed his statesmanship (and alienated the extremists in his party) when he would not allow the country to become an unwanted ally of the English, despite French provocations on American ships. To the disgust of the Federalist hotheads, Adams sent a peace mission to France that was almost bipartisan. The commissioners were ill used by the French diplomats and came home to expose the corruption in Napoleon's inner circle with the publication of the XYZ Papers. Charles Cotesworth Pinckney's reply to the devious Talleyrand, "No, not a sixpence; millions for defence, but not one penny for tribute," became a Federalist rallying cry. The Jeffersonians took slight solace from the honorable role Elbridge Gerry played in the farce. Meanwhile, a number of Democratic Republican societies sprang up across the nation as outposts to weave a web of opposition to pro-English Federalist policies.

In fact, most of the Democratic Republican societies had been founded in 1793 and 1794, when the French Revolution was beginning to heat up. Then, concerned Americans had formed groups somewhat akin to the committees of correspondence of revolutionary days, to consider courses of action if "the glorious efforts of France be eventually defeated," for in that unhappy event America, "the only remaining depository of liberty, will not long be permitted to enjoy in peace . . . the happiness of a republican government."* The waves of protest against Jay's Treaty gave the societies a shot in the arm, while Federalists denounced the groups as "French Jacobin clubs." Against a backdrop of Jay dummies hung in effigy, the societies helped reinforce the Jeffersonians' feeling that a majority of the people shared their fear of "monarchical ambition." Republican newspapers reported the doings of these societies, including their entertainments, at which much toasting had a political tinge. "May the patriots of '76 step forward with Jefferson their head and cleanse the country of degeneracy and

*Circular of the Philadelphia Democratic Society, quoted in Eugene P. Link, *Democratic-Republican Societies, 1790–1800* (New York: Columbia University Press, 1942), 11.

corruption," a New York Society toasted. Federalists fumed and fussed and fired back salvos in the *Gazette of the United States* and other partisan journals. Jefferson prodded his followers to reply in kind. If the Republicans did not support newspapers that could counterattack the pro-English party he said, then "republicanism will be entirely browbeaten."

Amidst the British impressment of Americans on the high seas and French attacks on Yankee ships in the Caribbean, the Federalists misread public opinion and concocted legislation that completed the polarization of political parties. Stung by the effronteries of the bumbling Citizen Edmond Genet, lashed by the acid paragraphs in Benjamin Franklin Bache's Philadelphia *Aurora*, and convinced that the Francophiles' comeuppance would have widespread approval, the Federalists whipped together a legislative package that was in reality a bombshell. First came a harsh naturalization law (requiring proof of fourteen years' residence with a five-year declaration period) in June, 1798, followed by the Alien Friends and Alien Enemies acts, and capped by the notorious Sedition Act, passed a month later. Intended to implant Federalists in solid control of the national government, the Alien and Sedition acts not only backfired, they gave the Jeffersonian Republicans the reason they had needed to become, unashamedly, a political party.

Sanctimoniously, the leading Federalists in Congress had insisted that plots and conspiracies were being hatched by foreigners (*i.e.*, Frenchmen and their friends) and that the underpinnings of law and order were jeopardized by a licentious press. John Adams lost control of his common sense and sided with the lawmakers who believed that their neat parcel of laws would strangle the Republicans and their scurrilous newspapers. "The spirit of disunion is much diminished," Adams conceded, "but unless the spirit of libelling and sedition shall be controlled by an execution of the laws, that spirit will again increase." Testy and tired, Adams signed the bills in the mistaken belief that Republican editors would soon recant or keep their silence. A flurry of prosecutions against newspaper printers followed (Bache cheated them by dying in a yellow fever epidemic), Congressman Matthew Lyon became a national hero when the Federalists tried to pillory him, and the Federalists somehow became a pure-and-simple nativist party.

The target of the Alien acts had been the Frenchmen either in America or about to emigrate here, but thousands of Irish Americans and more thousands of German Americans saw in the vindictive legislation a threat to their well-being. A New England Federalist visiting Pennsylvania wrote home complaining that the Irish he had encountered were "the most God provoking Democrats on this side of Hell." Federalist congressman Harrison Gray Otis defended the Alien laws on the ground that since French spies had infiltrated Holland and Switzerland, "may we not expect the same means to be employed against this country?" The stiff-necked New England Federalists may have believed they were voting to save the country, but a dark page was torn out of their political catechism and handed to the opposition. The Jeffersonians knew what to do.

Plainly, Jefferson perceived, the acts were meant to stifle the opposition. The arrest of only Republican editors proved that much. To Jefferson it was incredible that Americans languished in jails for printing attacks on Adams and the other "monarchists." Already there was some talk of giving weapons to the yeomen farmers who could show that the embers of '76 were still alive, whenever tyranny threatened. These chilling rumors only convinced Jefferson of the need to counter the Federalists' strategy with a republican weapon. From his vantage point Jefferson scanned the Blue Ridge and came up with an answer that he shared first with Madison, then with the whole country—the Kentucky Resolutions. Sent to the people anonymously, the Kentucky resolves declared that when an unconstitutional act was passed by

Congress, the states could "interpose" and nullify the offending law. The doctrine was laden with danger, but it was a peaceable means of protesting an obnoxious, unconstitutional law. Madison agreed to work up a similar argument for the Virginia legislature and to press for the joint cooperation of all the fifteen states. Both the Kentucky and Virginia resolutions fitted the mold of classic propaganda pieces, for they captured the nation's attention, pointed the way to solving a problem of enormous magnitude, and yet upheld the spirit of the Constitution by proposing to work within the system. In a sense, the resolutions were the first party platform in American history. Still, only seven states responded, and the issue of whether the Alien and Sedition acts violated the First Amendment never even came before the Supreme Court. But the election of 1800 now loomed large, for the Republicans had a clear shot at the newly occupied White House in the swampy "Federal District."

Jefferson realized that merely being against the Federalists and their suppressive legislation was not an adequate basis for asking to be elected president. He needed to have his political philosophy spelled out, for the Republicans had moved over much ground in less than a decade. "The Republican party who wish to preserve the government in its present form, are fewer in number than the monarchical Federalists," he had confessed in 1792. By 1799 Jefferson was convinced the Republicans were in the majority. The next step was to formulate a party creed, and this Jefferson did through a series of letters to friends who (he knew) would let their friends see his ideas.

First, Jefferson said, the republican Constitution had to be preserved to check the Federalists' sliding toward a hereditary tenure for the president and senators, which would "worm out the elective principle." He was "for preserving to the States the powers not yielded by them to the Union . . . and I am not for transferring all the powers of the States to the General Government, and all those of that government to the executive branch." Jefferson went on to say: "I am for a government rigorously frugal and simple, applying all the possible savings of the public revenue to the discharge of the national debt; and not for a multiplication of officers and salaries merely to make partisans, and for increasing, by every device, the public debt, on the principle of its being a public blessing." Here was the kind of talk farmers liked to hear. Instead of an expensive army and navy, Jefferson explained, he favored a reliance upon "our militia solely, till actual invasion, and for such a naval force only as may protect our coasts and harbors" from a marauding enemy. "I am for free commerce with all nations; political connection with none; and little or no diplomatic establishment." He subscribed to Washington's advice concerning entangling alliances with other nations and wanted no American link "with the quarrels of Europe."

Then Jefferson turned to the rights of the people. "I am for freedom of religion . . . for freedom of the press, and against all violations of the Constitution to silence by force and not by reason the complaints or criticisms, just or unjust, of our citizens against the conduct of their agents." Jefferson said he was still a "well-wisher to the success of the French revolution," but he recognized "the atrocious depredations" French vessels had committed on American ships in international waters. Finally, Jefferson's credo encompassed his patriotism. "The first object of my heart is my own country. . . . I have not one farthing of interest, nor one fiber of attachment out of it, nor a single motive of preference of any one nation to another, but in proportion as they are more or less friendly to us.*

Ticked off one by one, Jefferson's political tenets furnished the basis for his drive for the presidency and became his party's program. A month earlier the Virginia and Kentucky resolutions had

*Thomas Jefferson to Elbridge Gerry, January 26, 1799.

come before the people, setting forth the limits of national power and protesting "the palpable and alarming infractions of the Constitution" in the Alien and Sedition acts. Taken together with the letters Jefferson wrote spelling out his ideas for a party program, these resolutions, Wilfred Binkley observed, "became the political bible of the Jeffersonians by 1800." Until the presidential election of 1840 the Republicans looked no further than these "undisputed articles of faith" when seeking a program with the broadest possible appeal to "the overwhelming majority of Americans."

Meanwhile, the pretense of nonpartisan government was dropped as Federalist prosecutors hauled more Republican printers into court. Federalists burned copies of the Boston *Independent Chronicle* at their Fourth of July picnic at Newburyport, hounded editor Thomas Adams until he was kicked out of the New Relief Fire Society, and finally indicted him for "sundry libellous and seditious publications . . . tending to defame the government of the United States." In the village made notorious by its witch-hunting, David Brown was arrested for distributing his criticism of the Adams administration among "the *Farmers, Mechanicks* and *Labourers*." Brown was convicted of "sowing sedition in the interior country" and sentenced to eighteen months in a federal prison. The prosecution of Vermont congressman Matthew Lyon was so trumped up, and the trial such a farce, that Senator Stevens Thomson Mason of Virginia turned the vindictive prosecution into a comic-opera incident by carrying $1,000 in gold to pay Lyon's fine. Jefferson, Madison, and other leaders contributed money, and at each stop on his way to Vermont, Mason was honored for his service to the Republican cause. From his jail cell, Lyon won reelection handily.

The cohesiveness of the Republicans amazed the Federalists, who had hoped that a few well-aimed prosecutions would end their troubles. Fisher Ames, one of the high priests of Federalism, put the matter bluntly. The discipline in Republican ranks was as severe as a Prussian drillmaster's, "and deserters are not spared." The lines were now drawn; the quest was for the presidency. Many Federalists, mightily disappointed that Adams had not declared war on France, importuned Washington to permit his name to go before the electors again. The retired president discouraged such talk but in the same breath denounced Republicans for their partisanship. "Let that party set up a broomstick and call it a true son of Liberty, a Democrat, or give it any other epithet that will suit their purpose," he grieved, "and it will command their votes in toto!"

The blueblood Federalists were disappointed because the Alien and Sedition acts had not brought a toning down of Republican plans to win elections and turn the country around. In Connecticut, no longer a Federalist sanctuary, Jefferson's aides circulated an address which declared that "there are two classes of people, the mechanics and farmers who produce goods for the community, and others living by cunning—merchants, speculators, priests, lawyers and government employees." This early potshot at the federal officeholders gave a capsule synopsis of the implicit Republican promise in the 1800 election—let the majority rule. A Briton who confessed he was no admirer of Jefferson deplored the flocks that gathered under the Virginian's standard. The tall vice-president "flattered the low passions of a mere newspaper-taught rabble." Unashamedly, Jefferson pleaded with his friends to work on behalf of a democratic victory in the presidential election. Unlike England, where only "a greediness for office" dominated party politics, Jefferson believed there was a substantial philosophical difference between the two contending groups in America. "I hold it as honorable to take a firm and decided part, and as immoral to pursue a middle line, as between the parties of honest men and rogues, into which every country is divided," he wrote.

While the Virginia Republicans were lining up friends, it was beyond doubt that the party now called Republican (or Democratic by its ill-wishers, who thought "democrats" were contempt-ible) was operating out of Jefferson's vice-presidential office. John Beckley, the former clerk of the House of Representatives, ran a Republican message center and kept Jefferson's friends informed of how the state elections were going. An early and hopeful sign was the victory managed by Pennsylvania Republicans in the fall of 1799. More fuel for the Republican fires came from the New York results in the spring of 1800, when Aaron Burr outmaneu-vered Hamilton in Manhattan and gave Republicans a majority of votes in the state legislature. Since the presidential electors would be picked by the state lawmakers, the New York victory stoked Burr's chances for a second place on the ticket. And after President Adams shook up his cabinet by ousting disloyal diehards, Hamil-ton's ill-tempered pamphlet attack on Adams was leaked to the public, further damaging the already battered Federalist cause. Amused Republicans read in the newspapers of a Winchester, Vir-ginia, farmer's wife who claimed she had found an egg in her hen-house on which "Thomas Jefferson shall be the SAVIOR of his Country" was visible. If this was a man-made miracle, so was the forthcoming collapse of the Federalists. As state after state swept Republicans into office, a Republican newspaper asked what had brought on the repudiation of Federalists. The unpopular excise tax, huge outlays for a 75,000-man army, a $12,800,000 annual budget, and the Alien and Sedition acts were high on the list of causes for the Federalists' downfall. "Democrats and their dema-gogues have had just complaint of the manner in which money is raised," Federalist Gouverneur Morris admitted, "and our ex-penditures are so far from economical that no applause is expect-ed on that score."

In Massachusetts and Connecticut the Federalists had fright-ened a band of Congregational ministers into exhorting their fol-lowers to work against the Jeffersonians. Jefferson's victory, the black-robed corps predicted, would lead to Bible burnings at the least, and wives and daughters being ravished by roving bands of Jacobins at the worst. "I do not believe that the Most High will permit a howling atheist to sit at the head of this nation," a Connecticut divine confided in his diary. The "confirmed infidel" was not bothered by the broadsides from Federalist newspapers, however, and journals in Jefferson's camp spread the word of a national program issued by a congressional caucus. Republican congressmen blasted away at the Alien and Sedition laws, decried monarchical tendencies in Adams' administration, called for a reduction in federal spending, and struck out at standing armies and a large navy. Drafted partly as an indictment of the Federalists, this caucus plan deserves to be thought of as a makeshift Republican party platform. Some of its sections probably came from Jefferson's pen.

Jefferson, Albert Gallatin, Madison, and the other Republicans knew their chances rode on the voting in three key states: New York, Pennsylvania, and Virginia. Their 32 electoral votes would decide the contest. Burr's dramatic triumph in New York foretold far more than the outcome of the 1800 election. In nearly all subsequent presidential contests, the Republicans would never feel assured of victory without the safety of the New York electoral votes. A brilliant and ambitious lawyer, northerner Burr was more palatable to many Federalists than Jefferson. When the election results started arriving in the half-finished capitol on the banks of the Potomac, the outcome was far from certain. New England went to the Federalists, all of the South except Maryland and North Carolina were for the Republicans, and despite a Republican majority of the Pennsylvania votes, seven electors (out of fifteen) were Federalists. In Virginia, one of five states where the presidential electors were chosen by voters directly, Jefferson scored a total victory.

There was only one hitch. Although the congressional caucus had nominated Jefferson and Burr, while the Federalists offered

Adams and Pinckney, the cumbersome constitutional machinery that was supposed to elect the foremost candidate for president broke down in practice and ground out a tie vote—seventy-three electors for both Burr and Jefferson. Thus the election was thrown into the House of Representatives, which the Federalists still controlled and where each state had a single vote. Burr, sensing that a miracle had happened, began pressing for the presidency and thereby alienated the friends of Jefferson. No matter, for Burr's old enemy finally had his revenge. Jefferson was a "contemptible hypocrite," Hamilton thought, but preferable to Burr. After a week of indecisive voting, Hamilton converted a key member of the Delaware delegation. A few more maneuvers were needed, but the outcome was the election of Jefferson, with Burr as his vice-president. Some scars showed, but the Republicans had avoided any parliamentary trick that might have given the Federalists the presidency in spite of the popular vote. The Jeffersonians also won control of Congress, thanks chiefly to victories in eighteen (out of nineteen) House contests in Virginia.

Now the Democrats, or Republicans, or whatever their enemies chose to call them, were on their way. Jefferson himself later viewed the outcome as the "Revolution of 1800," and in many ways he was right. Despite all the animosity and boardinghouse lobbying, the Federalists were prepared to turn over the administration of the national government to their opponents through a legal change of command. History recorded few such bloodless transitions, and the lesson was not lost on the patriots of '76, who thought that at long last the fruits of Concord and Yorktown could now be tasted. Jefferson hoped to tone down the party aspects of his victory by saying in his inaugural address, "We are all Republicans—we are all Federalists." The phrases in his message hammered home the Republican dogma: "The will of the majority was in all cases to prevail." Little more was needed to explain Jefferson's ideas of what constituted republicanism—"a wise and frugal government, which shall restrain men from injuring one another . . . and shall not take from the mouth of labor the bread it has earned." Until the Democratic party lost its identity in the tragic melee begun in 1854, its leaders tried to follow Jefferson's terse view of what was "the sum of good government."

Once he had settled into office, however, Jefferson made no pretense at being a nonpartisan president. In his personal habits and in his program to repair the Federalists' damage, he made an evident 180-degree turnaround from what had been going on in Washington. He stopped holding presidential levees, for they smacked too much of an aristocratic court. He offended the prissy braid-bedecked diplomatic corps by receiving ministers in his robe and slippers, and he sent out word that the nation's diplomatic corps abroad would be trimmed of all its fat under the watchful eye of his right-hand aide, James Madison. (Jefferson's selection of Madison as his secretary of state started an heir-apparentship for that office which lasted a generation.)

Then there was the matter of campaign promises. Jefferson kept them. He pardoned the political prisoners convicted under the detested Sedition laws, and Congress paid back their fines. The army was cut to a token force of less than three thousand officers and men. The navy's sails were trimmed, as all but thirteen ships were sold to private buyers. Just enough fighting vessels were kept to hound the Tripoli pirates. Excises, including the loathsome whiskey tax, were abolished. (Federalists claimed that the taxes on necessities such as tea and coffee should have been cut, instead of the levies on whiskey, which was a luxury; but farmers who made the whiskey and drank it regarded corn liquor as a necessity of sorts.) A determined drive to pay off the national debt was launched. As he later explained it, Jefferson's idea of republicanism implicitly was understandable to the average citizen.

Let the national government be entrusted with the defence of the nation, and its foreign and federal relations; the State governments with civil rights, laws, police, and [the] administration of what concerns the State generally; the counties with the local concerns of the counties, and each ward direct the interests within itself. It is by dividing and subdividing these republics from the great national one down through all its subordinations, until it ends in the administration of every man's farm by himself; by placing under every one what his own eye may superintend, that all will be done for the best.*

From this philosophy, taken with the grain of salt supplied by the Virginia and Kentucky resolutions, Jefferson's republicanism grew until an almost mystic faith developed around the yeoman farmer as the embodiment of the Good Citizen.

Jefferson's followers took his creed and built upon it during his first term, which was blessed with prosperity and a chance for breathing room while England and France stood toe-to-toe on the Continent. The pirates in Tripoli buckled in battle with American ships and marines, and the treasury began to show a sizable surplus. Shipyards resounded to the clatter of mallets and squeaks from winches. Farmers smiled as their corn, wheat, and tobacco went into the world market. "No sign appeared of check to the immense prosperity," Henry Adams wrote, "which diffused itself through every rivulet in the wilderness." As Jefferson's popularity rose, his rapport with Congress was unmatched. Federalist party regulars were hard put to find an excuse for their existence as partisans except that Jefferson had replaced a few of their faithful supporters with his friends. If the father of good Republican Abraham Bishop became the customs collector at New Haven, nobody minded too much, for most of the political plums were still held by Federalist appointees anyway.

Harmony seemed to reign in Washington. The Republicans in Congress acknowledged Jefferson's leadership, even when the president nipped plans for federal projects that would have created jobs. Although *jobs* is a key word in every politician's lexicon,

*Jefferson to Joseph C. Cabell, February 2, 1816.

Jefferson was the exception. Even Madison had almost slipped from grace by suggesting that some federal road-building projects might make sense. Not so, said Jefferson, and the "strict construction" view he took of the Constitution precluded what would in time become a major concern of the nation. He said that federal involvement in building post roads (carrying mails provided the excuse for helping states make highways) would create "a bottomless abyss for money . . . and the richest provision for jobs to favorites that has ever yet been proposed." Madison and his friends concealed their doubts and finally squelched them. Strict construction, indeed! The Constitution said Congress could establish post roads; it did not, in Jefferson's mind, also convey the right to maintain them forever at government expense. Told that some western post roads needed bridges, Jefferson had a ready answer: "Over all streams not bridged, a tree should be laid across, if their breadth does not exceed the extent of a single tree."

Nobody could budge Jefferson from his stand on simplicity in the conduct of the nation's business. Gallatin, his hardworking secretary of the treasury, wanted a weekly cabinet meeting. Jefferson thought this kind of regularity unseemly, and the widowed president preferred to have his cabinet members hold their business until dinner time, when, he promised, "You will always find a plate & a sincere welcome." Each of the five cabinet officers had a private secretary and a small staff. Jefferson expected his cabinet to practice democratic frugality and they did. Madison ran the far-flung State Department business with a handful of clerks. Gallatin ran the country in 1802 with a budget of less than $8 million and met the entire federal payroll of 9,237, which included the army and navy. Each year the national debt was whittled down, even though the Louisiana Purchase added $15 million (and worried Jefferson, too, because he was not sure that making the deal was strictly an implied presidential power).

Although a few disgruntled Federalists (and John Marshall's Supreme Court) kept the party embers glowing, the total command of Jefferson in Congress was evident. Describing the Massachusetts Republicans in the House, a bitter Federalist complained, "The Democratic delegation with one or two exceptions is close to the fag end of democracy." Increasingly, Jefferson's enemies tried to make *democrat* a term of derision. Yet the more the arch-Federalist *Columbian Centinel* shrieked "Democrat! Jacobin! Democrat!," the more Jefferson's republicanism expanded. "The *rabies canina* of Jacobinism has gradually spread . . . from the cities, where it was confined to the docks and mobs, to the country," a Federalist congressman lamented. Which was exactly the point, insofar as the Republicans were concerned. The Boston blue bloods were going to their graves voting the straight Federalist ticket. What the Republicans wanted, and obtained, was the broad-gauged support of the "city mechanicks" and the country farmers.

By the end of Jefferson's first term, the Republicans had gained voting strength and tied together an irregular belt that stretched from northern New England down to New York, moved inland to the farming areas of New Jersey and Pennsylvania, and then engulfed most of the South. The only Federalist pockets of resistance remained in the commercial strongholds in such port cities as Boston, Baltimore, and Charleston. Elsewhere, a few gentry sniffed and coughed when the republican breeze blew their way, but the evidence of total victory was impressive. In the new states, Republicans were lofted by the winds of change. In 1804, Jefferson lost only 364 votes out of Ohio's 2,957. Despite half-hearted Federalist warnings that virgins would not be safe in their beds if the infidel Jefferson stayed in the White House, he won all but 14 electoral votes. Meanwhile, in the statehouses Republican victories became monotonous, until Jeffersonians held the governor's post in every state, even in New England, but Connecticut.

All things must end, of course, and Jefferson's honeymoon lasted as long as any presidential love tryst ever has. Few were left to quarrel with the good prices paid to farmers, a treasury that was in danger of running a surplus, and a government so light-handed that most Americans had no connection with it outside the letters they mailed at a federal post office. "It may be doubted if any other President has ever employed party loyalty more effectively to procure legislation," Dumas Malone has noted; "but his party leadership was essentially personal, and from almost the beginning to almost the end it was undisputed." Nothing in America disturbed the calm of the political holiday. Then the clash of Napoleon's ambition with England's navy wrenched Americans from their comfortable ways, brought the impressment of American seamen, and finally threw the whole mess on America's doorstep when the frigate *Chesapeake* was seized just outside the Norfolk Roads by H.M.S. *Leopard*. Three broadsides from the *Leopard* brought the country to its feet, and Jefferson could easily have had a declaration of war against England had he desired it. Instead, he pulled off a feat of extraordinary presidential power by directing Republicans in Congress to pass his Embargo Act in a single day in the Senate, three more in the House. The business was finished by Tuesday—December 22, 1807. From that moment on, America was no longer a tiny semicolonial power resting easily in the New World. The United States would either bring England to heel, one way or another, or lose its independence.

At least, that is what Madison, the other cabinet officers, and the leading Republicans in Congress thought as they accepted the president's refusal to fight England over the *Leopard* incident; they hoped England would relent once she lost her bustling American market. The embargo proved a failure, for American ships were forbidden to carry American products abroad, and the British navy swept the French from the western Atlantic. To some degree the embargo breathed new life into the old Federalists, who made headway while more than 50,000 Yankee seamen and perhaps another 100,000 laborers and city-dwelling factory workers sought jobs. Rumblings among some of the Republicans in Congress became more evident amidst talk of rotted ships and spoiled hardtack. Determined not to seek a third term and convinced the nation's republicanism was more than skin deep, Jefferson began packing his bags for Monticello. Madison was his obvious choice for a successor, and the congressional caucus accepted that decision; but the embargo policy collapsed around Jefferson as he shuffled through the White House portico. He took his farewell by appealing to his countrymen to look beyond the troubled times and to cling to republican principles. "In their love of liberty, obedience to law, and support of the public authorities" he took solace and saw "a sure guaranty of the permanence of our republic." Jefferson believed that no more devoted democrat than James Madison ever lived, and he said that his successor "was the greatest man in the world." Assured that Madison would carry on as a loyal Republican committed to the ideals of '76, Jefferson predicted "that Heaven has in store for our beloved country long ages to come of prosperity and happiness."

A few reservations were needed to keep Jefferson's optimism within bounds. If stronger measures were required to preserve America's neutrality, some active party machinery would be needed to throttle dissenters such as Congressman John Randolph. United, the Democratic Republicans could easily overwhelm the Federalists, except in some isolated New England pockets. But with Jefferson in retirement and John Beckley dead, the party could revert to nothing more than a meeting of kindred minds. Beckley had died in April, 1807, and with him had died the party's wheelhorse, correspondent *extraordinaire*, and indefatigable counter of the few loaves and fishes parceled out to the party faithful.

Except for the congressional caucus, there was nothing at the national level resembling a Republican party. Apart from the Washington *National Intelligencer*, run by Samuel Harrison Smith, there was scant effort to inform the nation of an official party position. To some Jeffersonians he was "Silky-Milky" Smith (because he was too calm for the extremists), but to Madison he was a dependable friend. Madison embarked on the presidency after beating back weak efforts to elect James Monroe and George Clinton. The Monroe and Clinton boomlets, coming from splinter groups in New York and the South, collapsed so gently that there were few scars, and one man served as Madison's vice-president and the other would be his successor. In the House, the Jeffersonians held a 46-vote majority. All Madison had to do was keep peace with England and France, and among his fellow Democrats. The job was impossible.

TWO

An Era of Feelings—
Good and Bad

A Washington belle who attended Madison's inaugural ball noted that six-footer Jefferson had not stayed long but "seemed in high spirits and his countenance beamed with benevolent joy." By contrast, Madison (who stood about five feet, four inches), "seemed spiritless and exhausted." Indeed, if the fourth president began his eight-year tenure worn out, we have one explanation concerning his failure to use the Republican party in pursuit of the national interest. Jefferson had proved that a president had to be the chief of state and the head of his party. Madison, who had helped nurse the Democrats in their infancy, found himself perplexed by the teenager.

Madison and his charming wife Dolley had barely settled in the White House when the prospect of war with England seemed suddenly lessened by a diplomatic gesture from the British minister in Washington. For a time it appeared that England's tough blockade of Europe would be relaxed, and Madison was jubilant. The Republican's faith in economic coercion as a better weapon than a man-of-war in international crises seemed vindicated.

While awaiting confirmation of England's backing down, Madison was beset by petty problems. He knew from his own cabinet experience that he needed a trusted secretary of state; but a Senate faction within his own party kept the able Gallatin from the post, and it fell to a hack politician whose chief qualification was that "he can spell." Anxious to please everybody, Madison alienated various factions as he appointed inept men to post after post in an effort to keep one place open for Gallatin. The resulting cabinet had geographical balance, but with only a strong anchorman, there was hardly a semblance of teamwork. The discord was heightened by attacks from Congressman John Randolph, an extremist who wore his states' rights philosophy on his sleeve.

The president's joy over the prospect of a friendly gesture from England soon gave way to gloom, as the British minister's deal in Washington was repudiated. Madison had feared that war was inevitable, and yet he did little to unite his party behind a campaign of preparedness. Instead, little bands of ambitious congressmen and senators elbowed their way through the capitol corridors in search of special favors. Madison's idea of the supremacy of Congress over the other branches of government was good Republican doctrine but poor politics. The western and southern factions had one common ground—they wanted the country to expand into Mexico, into Cuba, anywhere there was land and room for slaves. This eagerness repelled New England Federalists, who liked the constitutional ban on slave imports after 1808 because it seemed to give them a chance to catch up with the southerners. Madison, unwilling to call for party unity and too worried about England to notice what was happening at the other end of Pennsylvania Avenue, was caught in the middle.

The fragmented Democrats in New York, Pennsylvania, and Virginia went their own way. New York Republicans had colorful leaders, with the Tammany Hall crowd, not yet a machine, tending to pull against the upstaters who flocked to Albany for patronage. Pennsylvania had no one like Beckley, who had once engineered fifty thousand *handwritten* ballots in an emergency; but Gallatin had a loyal following, as did Senator Michael Leib.

Leib, who was so much a Jeffersonian he had once proposed abolition of the navy, then turned on old friends in the Democratic Republican party holding the statehouse and started sniping at Madison and Gallatin.

If Leib was bad, Representative Randolph from Virginia was worse. Once the most ardent of Republicans, Randolph fought the administration during Jefferson's second term and proclaimed, "I love liberty, I hate equality." At the forefront of the Virginians who loathed slavery but defended the South's "peculiar institution," Randolph was a brilliant congressman whose talent was more for wrecking than building. He led the bolters, christened "Quids," who wanted no part of Madison and instead backed Monroe in 1808. Pushed by newspaper editor Thomas Ritchie, the regular Virginia Republicans beat back the dissenters and in time became a powerful party force known as the Richmond Junto.

As editor of the Richmond *Enquirer* Ritchie rose steadily in party circles, owing to his loyalty and his following throughout the South. With only local committees of correspondence left to keep party lines repaired, the newspapers assumed a vital role in the structure of the Federalist and Republican parties. The *National Intelligencer* was recognized as the official party organ, and it was believed that Madison's words went straight into the newspaper's columns to explain administration policy. Transportation was still by horse and ship, so that every locality had its own newspapers; the nonpartisan editor was a rarity. If he was a Federalist, chances were that he looked to the Boston *Columbian Centinel* for guidance, and with scissors and paste borrowed choice attacks on the Republicans. The editor with Jeffersonian leanings took his news items from the *Intelligencer*, but he also exchanged with brother Republicans who took their gospel from the Philadelphia *Aurora* or Ritchie's *Enquirer*.

Being an editor was one thing, being a printer another. Printing contracts went to loyal party supporters, and by Madison's time it was clearly established that contracts for federal and state statutes, proceedings, and other official matters went to the party faithful. Indeed, there were not that many plums available as rewards to loyal party workers, for (at least at the national level) Jefferson had tried not to upset the prevailing notion that federal appointees, unless they were terribly incompetent, should be retained. Although the incident that provoked the famous *Madison v. Marbury* case dealt with patronage, Jefferson blunted some of the efforts of his party's most contentious office seekers, and his successors tried to follow a similarly moderate course. Postmasterships and the collectors of customs in large ports were the real jewels of patronage, so desirable that men resigned from Congress to take what seemed to many a lifetime sinecure. Another democratic practice that Jefferson promoted (and Madison endorsed) was the low-key diplomatic establishment. Ministers were sent to Paris or London, not in return for favors, but only when a job was to be done, and their tenure was brief. Such a policy kept "our distant overseas agents . . . sensitive to American interests and policy," as Leonard White has noted.

Federalist editors made up for their lack of big contracts by appealing to partisans for fatter subscription lists; and in Boston, New York, Philadelphia, and other seaports, the commercial communities responded generously. Benjamin Russell, who had cut his eyeteeth while acting as a printer's devil, made the *Columbian Centinel* into the chief Federalist mouthpiece, which reached its most strident crescendo in Jefferson's heyday. When a disappointed and drunken Democrat (Federalists liked the alliteration) turned on Jefferson to expose a rumored liaison between Jefferson and a comely Monticello slave, Federalists gleefully hung the scandal before the nation. To the tune of "Yankee Doodle" the Federalist Boston *Gazette* set doggerel that included a verse.

You call her slave—and pray were slaves
Made only for the galley?
Try for yourselves, ye witless knaves—
Take each to bed your Sally.

Jefferson seethed privately but kept his peace publicly like a good democrat.

Not that Jefferson wore a rhinoceros' hide when he was the butt of these newspaper attacks, for he did believe an occasional prosecution of a libelous editor had its point. But, by and large, Jefferson had endured the barbs of editors from his cabinet days, and he believed that a genuine democrat had no other choice. For although Jefferson on occasion displayed the same pettiness as other men, as a party leader and president he saw himself as a pivotal character in an ongoing experiment—the republic of the United States. So when the editors tore him apart, Jefferson tried to be stoic, "conscious that . . . I have lent myself willingly as the subject of a great experiment, which was to prove that an administration, conducting itself with integrity and common understanding, cannot be battered down, even by the falsehoods of a licentious press.*

Between war scares in 1810 Madison had to not only fend off the Federalists' castigations but also witness an attack from the supposedly friendly Philadelphia *Aurora*. He would not recall the American minister in England, and he remained loyal to Gallatin when the treasurer's enemies closed in. Would he boot Gallatin and call a special session of Congress? "Nobody seems to know anything about these matters," a Republican editor moaned. "Mr. Madison possesses in a *pre-eminent degree* a faculty which very few men are endowed with, and that is, of *keeping his mind to himself*." The discredited British minister took comfort in Madison's plight. "At Washington they are in a state of the most ani-

---

*Thomas Jefferson to Thomas Seymour, February 11, 1807.

mated confusion," Francis Jackson reported, "the Cabinet divided and the democratic party going various ways."

Alas, Madison often seemed to please nobody but his beloved Dolley, and she could not vote. When Napoleon ordered his own blockade of England and Madison seemed in a quandary, the Baltimore *Federal Republican* unleashed a new attack: "Bonaparte knows as well how to manage James Madison as he does any of his vassal kings of Europe." Troubles grew apace as the Bank of the United States came up for recharter, an issue that would vex Democratic Republicans in the White House for another generation. The only bright spot was in Gallatin's department, where a budget surplus was used to further reduce the national debt. But a host of newspapers and congressmen in his own party attacked Madison, using as ammunition his own 1791 speech against the bank's unconstitutionality. The Clinton wing of the Republican party in New York hoped to make political hay out of Madison's embarrassment, and Vice-President George Clinton broke a 17–17 tie in the Senate to defeat charter renewal.

Madison was in trouble. Still, and the point needs to be underscored, an element of luck seemed to touch this democratic president, just as it had helped Jefferson (with the Louisiana Purchase) and would someday bless Jackson, Wilson, and Franklin D. Roosevelt. Madison got lucky when his bumbling, disloyal secretary of state had to be bounced; James Monroe let bygones be bygones to accept the cabinet post amidst rancor and mudslinging. "I accept the office in part," Monroe wrote Jefferson (who was still overseeing matters from a distant hill), with the "hope that some good effect will result from it, in promoting harmony at least in the republican party." Madison's spine stiffened; he refused to accept Gallatin's resignation and headed into the storms of an election year with most of his hatches battened down.

The president's precautions were but a step ahead of renewed assaults from within his own party. A leading Republican editor placed the headline, "Clear the Decks," on a series of attacks on Gallatin and (by implication) Madison. Democratic Governor Elbridge Gerry in Massachusetts revived the old bugaboo of an American king. Madison's old friend claimed there were Federalists who wished for "a secession of the northern states & the erection over them of an Hanoverian monarchy." From other quarters there were persistent rumors that the Federalists would throw their support to De Witt Clinton in an effort to replace Madison in the 1812 election. There were now Old Republicans, New Republicans, War Hawks, Clintonians, Smithites, and factions within factions of the national Democratic Republican party. A tired president made one last stab at patching up differences with England, then decided further negotiations were fruitless, and prepared the country to unleash "the dogs of war." The war drums were still muffled on April 21, 1812, when George Clinton died. Clinton's nephew was the heir apparent, but not if he listened to Madison's enemies, as the Albany *Register* advised. "Should New York remain silent? NO! . . . Her favorite son will yet receive the suffrages of his country. . . . It is time to have a change."

Congressmen in their caucus a month later thought otherwise. This device for choosing a presidential nominee had gained wide favor, and whatever opposition Madison had was silent, for the caucus voted 82 to 0 for his renomination. Elbridge Gerry was picked for vice-president. So far, so good. But then the New York legislature met and defiantly announced they would support De Witt Clinton, come hell or high water. Aided by young Martin Van Buren (who later admitted his error), Clinton made "the first active campaign for a presidential nomination" in history.

Within two weeks the country was at war with England. Madison's political hide, thin as it was, had been saved by a force of events that he seemed unable to control. In a rare show of harmony, the Republicans in Congress had backed Madison—almost to the man. Here was a president devoted to republican ideals, pledged to frugality and a small national budget, ready to launch the nation on an expensive war against the most powerful nation in the world. Thanks to economy-minded Republicans the army was pitifully small and the navy almost a floating joke. Yet the old Republican reliance upon militia as "the steely sinew of a free people," a shopworn slogan more than once disproved in battle, was taken up again.

While the nation moved to a war footing with painful slowness, the Republicans around Madison soon perceived that one section of the country was dragging its feet. New England bankers, angry over the revoked national bank charter, were not going to lend Gallatin the money he needed to pay the country's bills. (In 1812 all but two of the Boston banks were either founded or controlled by Federalists.) Republican frugality had cut the national debt to $45 million in 1812, but the high costs of war knocked all prospects of a balanced budget into a cocked hat and left the country with a $99 million debt at the war's end. What support the Republicans got for the war effort came from the South and the states beyond the Alleghenies.

Nobody pretended that sectional differences did not exist; they had existed since the days when a Virginia soldier at the seige of Boston in 1775 noticed that his Yankee comrades were "an exceeding dirty and nasty people."* A North-South cleavage was smoothed over at the Federal Convention in 1787 with the three-fifths compromise (slave states thus adding to their delegations in Congress). When the matter of permitting slavery to exist in Louisiana was debated in Congress, all pretenses were dropped. Northerners were unenthusiastic about the Purchase, and Connecticut Senator James Hillhouse taunted his southern colleagues for clinging to their "peculiar institution." Southerners in turn assured him that as a northerner he did not grasp the problem. "I

*The identity of the soldier—George Washington.

did not expect so soon to hear on this floor the distinction of *eastern* and *northern*, and *southern* men. Has it indeed come to this—are we to be designated by a geographical line?"

By Madison's time the slavery question kept bobbing up. Then the War of 1812 caused another split and the High Federalists in New England went so far in condemning "Mr. Madison's War" that they talked about seceding from the Union and setting up their own confederation. Northern Republicans had swung into line for the low taxes, reduced debt, and parsimonious federal administrations of Jefferson and Madison. The party was strongest in areas where the land values were lowest. But the voters were upset by the shock waves of the embargo, with its unemployment and falling profits. In New England pulpits a host of clergymen worried aloud on Sunday about the church-going habits of deists Jefferson and Madison. John Quincy Adams, first sent to the Senate as a Federalist, had become an apostate when he joined the Jeffersonians. His Boston friends never let him forget this political sin, and he, along with the Salem merchant, William Gray, who had also shifted parties, was snubbed by Federalists. "To lend himself to a party & *such a party!* " a Federalist snorted, when Gray's heresy became known. When one of Madison's supporters won an election, a dismayed Federalist wrote in the *Massachusetts Spy*: "The Democratic political pot has been boiling furiously for a year past; and we are sorry to find that an addition of scum has risen to the surface."

Madison's attitude toward New England during the war was, all things considered, magnanimous. He could have ordered some of the leading Federalists detained for their treasonable utterances, and the aims of the Hartford Convention (where the ranting delegates called for the nullification of unpopular laws) smacked of treason. But New England had supported DeWitt Clinton in the 1812 presidential race, and Madison the Virginian was reluctant to crack down on any part of the Union. Too, had he not

37

been the penman of the Bill of Rights, which promised citizens freedom of expression? Thus Madison gritted his teeth and took a pounding in every Federalist newspaper, none of which was more contemptuous of the president than the *Columbian Centinel.* "We are plunged into a war, without a sense of enmity, or a perception of sufficient provocation and obliged to fight the battles of a Cabal which, under the sickening affectation of Republican *equality*, aims at trampling into the dust the weight, influence, and power of Commerce and her dependencies." New England was being crucified by a president "in whose choice they had no part," with the consequence "either that the Southern States must *drag* the Northern States farther into the war, or we must *drag* them out of it; or the chain [of Union] will break."

Just when the Federalists were closing in on Madison, he proved that his political life was charmed. The Treaty of Ghent gave the country an honorable peace, and the news arrived in Washington at the moment when the Federalists expected to give the wiry little president an ultimatum. As the capital rocked from the fireworks celebrating news of the treaty, the Federalists skulked away and, for all practical purposes, their national party dissolved. The war also created a new personality who would make the party and the presidency everything that Madison had avoided—General Andrew Jackson, the hero of New Orleans.

Madison finished out his White House days basking in the glory of victory. The Second War of Independence had nudged the country from its second-class status into a new position of world power and expansion. The Indian tribes, for example, had made a bad move by their wartime link to England. Their removal from the old Southwest was resisted by Federalists in New England, partly in the name of humanity and partly because the northerners did not want more slave territory opened up in the cotton belt. Ironically, under a Democratic Republican president American shipping was bolstered by the war's outcome, and

38

still more paradoxically, Madison came out in the late stages of his second term for a rechartering of the Bank of the United States. A short interval of experience under state banks had convinced many Republicans that there could be worse things than a federally chartered bank. Younger men—notably Henry Clay, John C. Calhoun, Martin Van Buren, and William H. Crawford— were Democratic Republicans serving in the strong-willed Congress that was directing the nation's course. As long as the Union was safe, Madison did not mind at all.

The last of the Founding Fathers to give up his black knee breeches and silver shoebuckles, Madison was always hemmed in by a yearning for an informed citizenry that was beyond party. He realized that without a party organization the Jeffersonians could never have won power; but once that fight ended in their favor, Madison had no relish for cultivating party unity. In his eagerness to stand above partisan politics he fell below an acceptable standard of presidential leadership. Fortunately, Madison's luck held out when his party lines collapsed.

Whatever Madison's deficiencies as president, the Federalists by their vindictiveness and Anglophilism had made the "withered little applejohn" (as Washington Irving called him) look good. Their hatred of the well-meaning Virginian was almost without limit, as their resolution at the abortive Hartford Convention had proved. There they had called for a constitutional amendment that would prevent the election of a president "from the same state [for] two terms in succession." As Binkley noted, when the Federalists could not find an issue more important than this kind of personal vendetta against an honest (though sometimes inept) man, they were singing their swan song in the highest octave.

With the Federalists so routed that they only offered token opposition in the presidential race in 1816, the ascent of James Monroe from his secretary of state post to the White House was accomplished as expected, but by a rather close vote in the congressional caucus. For the third time in a row a Virginian slipped into the presidency, and while some Republicans were not too happy about that, the only alternative was another southerner, William H. Crawford, whom Monroe beat 65 to 54 in the caucus. And Crawford had been born in Virginia! The young adopted Georgian bided his time, however, and there was plenty of shuffling in the back rooms, as Clay, Calhoun, and other Republicans pushed for programs that would keep Congress in the saddle and vault them into national prominence.

America was still a nation of farmers; nine out of every ten working men and their families got up with the rooster and went to bed after feeding the cows. In higher circles, however, there was restless energy that could not be capped except in Congress, courtrooms, and state legislatures. The Federalists, forced out of presidential politics, still had one stronghold left—the Supreme Court. Chief Justice John Marshall dominated the court with his iron will, and even Democrats appointed by Jefferson and Madison had switched their philosophies once under Marshall's sway. While Jefferson was president, the court established its right to overturn the acts of Congress, and (under Madison) Marshall and his partners sanctified contracts, even crooked ones, in the legal monstrosity known as *Fletcher* v. *Peck*. During Monroe's first term the Democrats carried the state elections in New Hampshire and passed a law that in effect made private Dartmouth College into a state university. Argued before the court by alumnus Daniel Webster, the case went against the Democrats as the Federalist justices held that a corporate charter could not be upset by legislation. Coming at a time when some states were preparing to default on their indebtedness, the decision gave reassurance to investors, who soon poured millions into the budding railroad, insurance, and textile industries. Much of the ensuing prosperity, however, was directed north of the Mason-Dixon Line, while the panic of 1819 struck hardest at the southern farmers and planters, who saw prices drop on cotton (from 32 to 13 cents) and on wheat (from $1.45 to 72 cents a bushel). Monroe has not fared well in the history books. Except for the 1819 panic and the fight over statehood for Missouri, though, his administration fitted the mood of the country—a circumstance that political parties must sometimes accept even though it upsets the activists. Much like that of his predecessors, Monroe's republicanism sank to the marrow and was "more of an approach to government than a system. The democratic elements were united by a frame of mind, not by any kind of elaborate party mechanism."* Monroe's way was to exasperate such zealous partisans as Martin Van Buren, who loved the thrill of battle and chafed when the president gave a prized postmaster's job to an opponent. But that was Monroe's way; he made John Quincy Adams (the former Federalist and son of a Federalist president) his secretary of state and thus placed the New Englander in line for the presidency and gave his cabinet sectional balance.

Any tipping of the geographical scales was to be avoided in national politics at this moment when the southern slaveowners and northern businessmen were at a standoff. The southerners wanted plenty of room to expand and low tariffs, while the northerners favored a limit on slave territory and tariffs that would encourage infant American industries. In 1816 a slightly protectionist tariff had won in the House when 63 Republicans voted for it and only 31 against it (but nearly all the 31 were from the South). Four years later, with another tariff measure up, all but 8 of the 71-man southern delegation in Congress voted against it. Clearly, the Jeffersonian majority was now firmly opposed to tariffs for any other purpose than to pay the costs of government (at a time when the budget was nearly balanced and the national debt diminishing).

*Roy F. Nichols, *The Democratic Machine, 1850–1854* (New York: Columbia University Press, 1923), 258.

The tariff issue, it turned out, was just the tip of the iceberg. The balance of states was nearly even in 1819; there were twenty-two senators from the North and twenty senators from slave states, and the House was controlled by the Democrats, owing to the southern bloc.* Alabama and Maine were ready for admission, but so was Missouri (as a slave state), and that meant the South might become dominant in Congress through its greater population. The Louisiana Purchase had opened up a Pandora's box for the once-smug northerners who had long tried to hobble newly admitted states in efforts to preserve sectional equilibrium. Millions of acres in the trans-Mississippi country threatened the northerners' voting power in Congress as well as their peace of mind about such things as cold factory smokestacks, empty warehouses, and ships in dry dock. These interests could mount only feeble opposition to the Louisiana Purchase. But by 1819, whether they were called Federalist, Federalist-Republican, or even Democratic, their voice was to be heard over the Missouri statehood bill, for an obscure Democrat from upstate New York threw a time bomb into the whole machinery of the republic. Representative James Tallmadge, Jr., a lame duck congressman at that, introduced an amendment to the Missouri admission bill which provided that no more slaves could be imported into the fledgling state, and those already there were to be gradually emancipated.

Wily John Quincy Adams later said that the importance of the Tallmadge amendment was not understood "even by those who brought it forward." But, as Charles Sydnor has noted, the debate that followed "disclosed a secret; it revealed the basis for a new organization of parties." Party discipline, such as it was, could not be mustered in the face of the momentous question: How long

---

*Although still the nominal Republican party, the partisan group that stood on a Jeffersonian platform was splintering into factions. To avoid confusion, I have used the term Democrat for those public men who harbored Jeffersonian loyalties after 1818, most of whom became full-fledged supporters of Andrew Jackson in 1824.

could the Union continue, half-slave and half-free? Jefferson heard of the infighting at Washington and reacted with the wisdom of an elder statesman. The dreadful question thus raised "like a fire-bell in the night, awakened and filled me with terror. I considered it at once as the knell of the Union."* Every thoughtful American shared Jefferson's distress, and the compromise finally reached (Missouri came in as a slave state, but its southern border [36°30'] was to be the future limit-line for slavery) left everybody restless. The crisis passed, but the seeds sown during the disruptive controversy were full of tares. The Democrats and the nation would reap their bitter harvest in little more than a generation.

Once the Missouri pill was swallowed, the Democratic Republicans plunged into the business of president making. Crawford and his rival, Clay, had to take a back seat as the Federalists gave Monroe his second term by default. The congressional caucus ignored the election, so foregone was its conclusion. In Richmond, only 17 voters bothered to go to the polls; and in a state with a population of 938,000, the total Virginia vote was 4,321. In Mississippi, the entire turnout was 751, exactly 1 percent of the total population. Unquestionably, this was the nadir of party politics, and that was just fine with Monroe. The only electoral vote cast against him came from a New Hampshire senator with a sense of history—he wanted Washington to stand alone as an unopposed candidate.

Indeed, the lamb and lion seemed political bedfellows as the 1820 election results proved. Russell, the Boston newspaper editor whose federalism was of the deepest hue, calmed down so that when Monroe made a swing around the country and visited Beacon Street on his goodwill tour, Russell coined a timeless phrase. Monroe's benign influence in the White House, Russell said, had brought the nation "an Era of Good Feeling." Party labels were publicly eschewed, particularly by Monroe, and so downgraded in

* Jefferson to John Holmes, April 22, 1820.

the popular mind that a rising, hot-tempered Tennessee politician wrote the president that it was high time "to exterminate the monster called party spirit." Monroe no doubt agreed with Andrew Jackson. The only president ever reelected after a severe depression in his first term, Monroe was the last of the revolutionary generation that nursed an old-fashioned disdain of organized politics. Basically, these carry-over statesmen wanted to believe that informed voters, mainly farmers, were capable of exercising their judgment in the same way that conscientious independents in succeeding generations have professed to support *"the man, not the party."*

The founder of the Democratic party thought this notion was just so much hogwash. When Gallatin wrote Jefferson that the old parties seemed to have dissolved, the crusty former president replied: "Do not believe it. The same parties exist now as ever did." The old crowd favoring a monarch had put on a new coat of "consolidation" to gather all power into a federal orbit. Never a states' righter to the degree of the South Carolina firebrands, Jefferson nevertheless foresaw a shrinking of the powers left in local hands and lamented the signs pointing to a costly, business-dominated national administration: "Although it is not yet avowed (as that of monarchy, you know, never was), it exists decidedly, and is the true key to the debates in Congress."*

John Taylor of Caroline, an apostate Republican who hardly ever agreed with Jefferson in his later years, thought the aged statesman's assessment was about right. Federalism, Taylor said in 1823, had dropped its old name but had "hidden itself amongst us." Monroe showed some of the old Republican spunk when he vetoed the Cumberland Road bill, justifying his act on the strict construction grounds dear to southerners. But at times it seemed that the president was more interested in his wife's decorating of the White House than in seeing good Democrats appointed as federal marshals and customs collectors.

Perhaps Monroe reflected the nation's desire for a breathing

*Jefferson to Albert Gallatin, October 29, 1822.

space from politics. At any rate, the country embarked on a binge of canal building and cotton growing to such an extent that politics was of declining interest, except in the capitol corridors and around courthouse stoves. There were some rumblings of party loyalty, however, in the face of Jackson's advice to Monroe to appoint "characters most conspicuous for their probity, virtue, capacity and firmness, without regard to party." The selection of a former Federalist for the Albany postmaster's job disgusted newly chosen Senator Van Buren from New York and caused such an imbroglio that Monroe had to settle the business at a cabinet meeting. House Speaker John Taylor angered some of his New York supporters when he helped the Clinton faction in a Democratic by-election, and paid for his indiscretion by losing the speakership in 1821 to Virginian Philip Barbour.

New York was setting the tone in politics on several fronts, for a strong movement there to give all white males over twenty-one a vote was gaining momentum. This spurt to enlarge the electorate gave a fright to old-timer James Kent, a Federalist judge who thought the growth of population in New York City was "enough to startle and awaken those who are pursuing the *ignis fatuus* of universal suffrage." Kent decried the immigration that was threatening his town "with the burdensome pauperism of an European metropolis." But the Tammany Democrats saw things another way, and they joined with the Bucktails to push through liberalizing election laws that dropped old property qualifications and thus added a mighty host of recently arrived Irish and other immigrants to the voting rolls.*

The tide favoring a broader suffrage continued to surge in all

*This is as good a time as any to say that New York factions were a host unto themselves. Among the Democrats there were at times Clintonians, Bucktails (who were against Clintonians), Locofocos, Hunkers, Barnburners, Free-Soilers, and the Albany Regency. Most of the distinctions were among Democrats who were either tied to principles or who gave their allegiance to a leader (and his appointive power). A. M. Schlesinger, Jr., *The Age of Jackson* (Boston: Little, Brown, 1948), is one of the best treatments of the maze of intraparty intrigue in New York.

sections of the country until only South Carolina clung to the old system of choosing presidential electors in its state legislature. Elsewhere, the Democratic party gained converts by its ready acceptance of the expanded voting rolls. In Back Bay Boston, Democrats picked up strength as the fading Federalists sniffed at the immigrant population as unworthy of the franchise. Well-financed and highly organized political machines did not develop until after the Civil War, but from 1820 onward (as cheap trans-Atlantic fares permitted thousands of Europeans to come to American ports in steerage holds) these new arrivals found a friend in the Democratic wards of Boston, New York, Philadelphia, or Baltimore. The tenement districts built by wealthy Americans became the natural clustering places for opportunistic Democratic office seekers, who learned that a friendly handshake and a stack of firewood for a sick family spread many ripples of loyalty.

Meanwhile, the fires of partisan politics, banked by Monroe's "fusion policy," were beginning to burn more brightly as 1824 approached. Van Buren held no animosity toward Monroe simply because he had "been born and reared on the red clay grounds of the Old Dominion," but the busy New York senator decried Monroe's indifference to the "disjointed state of parties." Richard Hofstadter observed that Monroe bore some responsibility, not only for the factionalism within his own party, but also for the shaping battle over his successor. By naming John Quincy Adams as secretary of state, he had given this presidential stepping-stone to a man who "was never a good Federalist, and after his conversion he never became a good Republican." Van Buren begged the old Republicans to regroup: "This [is] the proper moment to commence the work of a *general resuscitation* of the *old democratic party*."*

*Richard Hofstadter, *The Idea of a Party System: The Rise of Legitimate Opposition in the United States* (Berkeley: University of California Press, 1969), 228–29.

Were the two parties dead or only moribund? The word from Monticello gave heart to those who wanted to work unashamedly for a Democrat. All men are "naturally divided into two parties," Jefferson counseled. First there are those "who fear and distrust the people," and they are opposed by men "who identify themselves with the people, have confidence in them, cherish and consider them as the most honest and safe, although not the most wise depository of the public interests." By whatever name they traveled, Jefferson said, the two groups—Federalist and Republican, or "Aristocrats and Democrats"—"are the same parties still, and pursue the same object. The last appellation of Aristocrats and Democrats is the true one expressing the essence of all."*

These were warming words to a few Republicans, who started calling themselves Democrats and worried about electing a president who would take a party stand on the fermenting issues of a tariff policy, the national debt, and territorial expansion. In keeping with the trend toward a more open system of electing a president, some Republicans began talking about a nominating convention instead of a congressional caucus. The old Republicans hoped for a New York-Pennsylvania-Virginia alliance that could insure victory. Van Buren preferred the old caucus nomination, but Ritchie (who, like Van Buren, favored William H. Crawford) began drumming for a convention in the summer of 1822. The Richmond *Enquirer* reported that the race was shaping up as a contest between Crawford and Adams, but the old-fashioned way of picking a candidate was questioned. "We can see no objection, in any man or set of men, proposing a scheme to collect the sense of the people. . . . Would not that mode be better than a congressional caucus?" Six months later, a respectable turnout gathered for the caucus, but some delegates, including Pennsylvania's, stayed

---

* Jefferson to Henry Lee, August 10, 1824.

away. "King Caucus" was not quite dead, but the message was clear.

For once the New England factions dropped their old hatreds long enough to back Adams. The *Columbian Centinel*, once the voice of the Federalist party, and a persistent enemy of John Quincy Adams, changed horses now that there was no longer a political midstream. Adams, the *Centinel* said, was preferable to "any northern man." Balanced against Monroe's reaching for a nonpartisan election were the reports from his two predecessors. "No free Country has ever been without parties, which are a natural offspring of Freedom," Madison wrote. "An obvious and permanent division of every people is into the owners of the Soil, and the other inhabitants." These words had the glowing approval of Jefferson, whose personal fortune had disappeared. Yet as he suffered hard times, Jefferson counseled friends, "In every political society, parties are unavoidable."

The weak bonds holding the Adams Republicans together were about to break under the scornful attack of Van Buren, even after his candidate became paralyzed in the summer of 1823. Crawford had come down with a skin inflammation, but after an inept physician had treated him, the Georgian was left paralyzed, blind, and unable to utter a sound. When Crawford's sight was partially restored and he began to speak, the news of what was termed a stroke was leaked to the newspapers. With an air of uncertainty the congressional caucus gave Crawford the nod. On the surface the Democrats appeared to have unity, but soon the spell was broken when the recalcitrant Pennsylvanians held a state convention at Harrisburg and placed Andrew Jackson at the head of their ticket. The Pennsylvania convention repudiated Crawford's nomination, saying that it was "in total disregard and contempt of the voice of the people." "This convention cannot consider that caucus as held with a view to promote the harmony of the party . . . but with the single view to promote the interest and success of William H. Crawford . . . in the vain hope that the American people might be thus deceived into a belief that he was the regular democratic candidate."*

Crawford was unable to campaign, Adams was too stuffy to work hard for the office he dearly coveted, and Clay strained every nerve to send the election into the House, where his great strength lay. Calhoun was also eager to serve. The campaign generated great excitement, much of the enthusiasm appearing in the ground swell for Jackson despite the fact that the professional politicians were dead set against Old Hickory. Van Buren, who later worshiped Jackson, at this time feared that the general had made a deal with his archenemy, DeWitt Clinton, and so he went down with a Crawford banner nailed to his sinking craft. It was a time of trial for the New York Regency Republicans, who were caught in a petty squabble. They had ousted Clinton from a canal board, and the voters protested this spiteful action by rejecting Van Buren and his friends. Temporarily unsaddled by an underling's miscalculation (Judge Roger Skinner had reported Clinton was politically dead, and then the storm broke), Van Buren rebuked his henchman with the classic statement: "Judge, there is such a thing in politics as *killing a man too dead!*"

Strange as it seemed, Jackson, the man who had called on Monroe to kill once and for all "the monster called party spirit," became the great beneficiary of the partisan feelings that surfaced in 1824. The monster had refused to die, though Monroe did all he could do to kill the old Republicans by his disregard of parties in his federal appointments. Eight years had worked more than wonders. Samuel Bowles started his Springfield *Republican* in Massachusetts to combat the diehard Federalists. Every crossroads seemed to have a campaign newspaper. More people could vote, and drum-beating party newspapers explained to voters that

Niles' Weekly Register, March 13, 1824.

they had a perfect right to decide who the next president ought to be, and no congressman should be making up their minds for them. Yet that was how the election of 1824 came out. Jackson had a majority of the popular vote but lacked a clear majority in the electoral college. The House fiddled and fumed and finally turned down Jackson and Clay in favor of Adams.

Clay, who, with 37 electoral votes, had been the last runner in the four-man race (Jackson had 99), was instrumental in Adams' selection. The Philadelphia *Observer* immediately published a charge that Clay had made a secret deal with Adams and was to be named the heir-apparent secretary of state for his support. Clay challenged the anonymous writer to a duel but wound up looking ridiculous when no shooting took place and he was named secretary of state. A foreigner who happened to be in America was shocked that the fuss, which led to Clay's being hung in effigy and Adams' castigation by the pro-Jackson press, soon blew over. More than one European who observed presidential campaigns as they began to heat up anew after 1822 was amazed at the manner in which all the vituperation and scandalmongering before the elections gave way to sullen silence, but no violence, once the results were known. What Americans began to take for granted—the tacit acceptance of majority rule— was part and parcel of the direction the country took from 1800 onward.

Politics had become a dirty business, there was no doubt of that. When Jackson's name first was bandied about in the presidential shuffling, ugly old stories were revived of his "adulterous" relation with his wife (she had not been legally free to marry, it turned out, after their nuptials). The tall Tennessean had already killed one man and was ready to do battle again, but he had to learn that in a political contest Americans took scandals with a grain of salt. A candidate's personal life was one thing, but his record and his promises were something different.

Southerners were touchy, of course. The odor of Clay's deal with Adams clung to the new secretary of state, and when John Randolph said that the Kentuckian was "so brilliant and yet so corrupt that like a rotten mackerel by moonlight [he] shines and stinks, and stinks and shines," a duel was soon fought. Shots were fired, but only egos were harmed. However, the loyalties of both men to the old Republican party had long since died.

Some hatchets were buried along the way. Van Buren realized he had no chance with Crawford and began cultivating men in other states who had been last-ditchers for the disabled Georgian. Jackson's friends brought in a St. Louis lawyer, Duff Green, to edit a newspaper founded with the avowed goal of electing Old Hickory president. Green, who had met Jackson on an Ohio River keelboat, was similar to the general in that he was not above beating a rival over the head with a cane. His Washington-based *United States Telegraph* columns were eagerly copied by Jackson's followers in every state. In Clay's back yard, Amos Kendall, a Dartmouth graduate who edited the *Argus of Western America* at Frankfort, quarreled with his old patron and switched to Jackson's camp in 1826. Short-lived campaign newspapers committed to Jackson blossomed like dandelions. On a broad front, party morale was sustained by this American phenomenon, and the Indian fighter's friends even invaded the heartland of conservatism with the birth of the Boston *Jackson Republican*.

There was no stopping the military hero of New Orleans. His charisma enabled Jackson to win single converts, while his newspaper friends persuaded droves of lukewarm Republicans to climb aboard the bandwagon. Jackson's campaign picked up steam enough to overcome the mistakes of his well-intentioned managers. For all Van Buren's skill he had a devious streak that his enemies denounced as personal aggrandizement, and indeed it surfaced at a crucial moment to seriously impair the Democratic party's national strength. He helped fashion a tariff bill that was meant to fail, but in so doing, it would embarrass a faction within the party hostile to Jackson. As expected, the bill angered New England protectionists and southern planters, but a strange coalition of Democrats both for and against Jackson mustered enough votes to pass it. Then, in the Senate Van Buren himself was maneuvered into a corner and had to vote for the offensive bill, which is known in history as the Tariff of Abominations. The sectional schism of the party, fostered by the Missouri Compromise, widened. Almost to a man the southerners voted against the measure. In South Carolina, offended planters fell to the work of erecting defenses against what they considered a usurpation of the Constitution and plotted strategies for an ultimate test of national unity.

Thus, by outsmarting himself and the other anti-Clay men in Congress, Van Buren helped insure the election of Jackson in 1828, but the price was higher than they had dreamed. When the hateful issues of high tariffs and slavery came to dominate the political spectrum, Jackson stood firm on the preservation of the Union, while militant southerners spoke of reassessing "the value of our union." Calhoun's brilliant but unpalatable talk about preserving the rights of a "concurrent minority" only revealed the South's awareness that its once-dominant position in the nation's political life was in jeopardy.

The Jackson steamroller could not be denied. The Virginia dynasty was unofficially declared at an end when the Richmond *Enquirer* swung behind Jackson. Adams' support in New England ebbed, and his four years in the White House turned into one long campaign for Old Hickory. Van Buren liked to look back on the Virginia Resolutions of 1798 and say, "Madison's report was the flag under which the Republicans conquered." However, the truth was that for the third time in American history a personality overpowered all other claimants for the presidency. The names of Washington, Jefferson, and Jackson evoked an emotional response; the majority trusted them first and asked questions later.

On the other hand, Madison, Monroe, and the two Adamses had been pushed into place by party loyalty or through unusual circumstances; the people had not pulled them into power. The times were changing so fast, and the names were changing, too. Adams' friends made one last effort as Republicans, and the Jacksonians went into battle with a name they found perfectly respectable: the Democrats. Henceforth, Jacksonians dropped the old Republican tag as they shouted Old Hickory's praises and extolled "the Democracy" as their party label. The people, pulling the Democratic party, were on the move.

THREE

The Jacksonian Revival

By the 1830s religious ardor
struck deep into the American psyche in upstate New York, sped
along the old frontier line west of the Alleghenies, and then finally
reached the Mississippi. Akin to this spiritual uplift was a following that adored Andrew Jackson and would not rest until their
aging hero was in the White House. The old Republican party was
abandoned by the Adams crowd, so that by 1826 the only ones
still talking about "the principles of '98" were part of the New
York-Virginia axis that Van Buren and Ritchie promoted. Nobody cared that Jackson had gone to the Senate in 1823 and voted
for a protective tariff and internal improvements. Nor was there
concern because Jackson's managers in New York tried to suffo-
cate a bill providing for universal male suffrage, which at least
on the surface sounded like good Jeffersonian doctrine. Only one
thing mattered—the hero of New Orleans was available. Jackson
men held conventions in state after state to endorse Old Hickory,
never asking where the Tennessean stood on the tariff, on the bank
charter, or any other burning issue.

Candidates with such unquestioned credentials are rare. There
have been a handful in American history; Washington, Jefferson, Jackson, Ulysses S. Grant, Warren G. Harding, Franklin D.
Roosevelt, and Dwight D. Eisenhower are probably the only
ones who would qualify. In short, the best and the worst of our

presidents went into the White House with such mass appeal that the races against them were lost causes from the outset. Jackson, once he started hankering for the presidency, had the good fortune to attract Van Buren, Ritchie, and Calhoun into his camp. Calhoun, looking out for himself as a potential successor, had his ambitions first sidetracked, then derailed. Van Buren, with help from friends in Philadelphia and Richmond, revived the old Republican party, gave it a new name, "restored party rivalries," and forged "a national organization of monumental durability."* If America was about to slide into the slough of nonpartisanship, Jackson was the man whom the old party war-horses gambled would be their savior.

The fact is that the men who flocked to Jackson's banner were a conglomerate that included a few old Federalists, a few Clintonians, and more than a few opportunists who merely wanted to serve a winner. But the barricades in 1828 were manned by the old-line Republicans who professed to believe that "the Democracy" stood for the same principles that Jefferson had brought forward more than a generation earlier. When a group of Lynchburg, Virginia, citizens began soliciting funds for a pro-Jackson newspaper early in 1828, they chose the name *Jeffersonian Republican* and announced that their paper would be " 'conducted with a strict regard to Republican principles . . . which were advocated in the memorable period of 1798–9' . . . on which Mr. Jefferson was elevated to power." Their program was to " 'maintain the constitution in its original purity, by confining the administration of the government to a strict construction,' and to defend the reserved rights of the States and of the people," the Richmond *Enquirer* reported.

Thus Jackson Democrats voted for the general without the vaguest idea of where he stood, for example, on rechartering the

*Hofstadter, *The Idea of a Party System*, 238.

United States Bank. They figured that he was a Jeffersonian, and that was all they needed to know, because this implied that Jackson was for low taxes, for a quick retirement of the national debt, and for less rather than more concentration of federal authority. Voters were sure he would pull the British lion's tail whenever he got a chance. The stories about Jackson's being slashed by a British officer's sword for his courage as a tad back during the Revolution, true or not, were probably worth several thousand votes, since Anglophobia was a strong vote getter among Jeffersonian Republicans.

Jackson did not win by a landslide, but he won handily enough (a plurality of about 150,000 votes, and 178 electoral votes to Adams' 83). The trail leading to Pennsylvania Avenue was smoothed over by experienced men who first recognized the political realities. The caucus system would not help them, so they went out of their way to make sure it was discredited. Early in 1827 Van Buren pleaded with Ritchie to start booming for a national convention that would cinch Jackson's nomination. Such a device, Van Buren argued, would solidify the old Republicans, while Adams and his friends would refuse "to become parties to it, [and] would draw anew the old Party lines & the subsequent contest would reestablish them." Not only would a convention nomination of Jackson help revive the Republicans "by substituting *party principles* for *personal preferences*," but Jackson's candidacy as a Democrat (and his election on their ballot) would contribute to "the revival of old party distinctions. We must always have party distinctions and the old ones are the best which the nature of the case admits."

This was plain talk. Even though a national convention did not gain widespread support, Van Buren's points were well taken. Through state conventions and legislatures Jackson's name went on the ticket (with Calhoun as his running mate), and he was elected by voters who were anti-British, anti-Adams, antimonopoly, and pro-Jackson.

No serious candidate for the White House up to that time had ever rolled up his sleeves or hitched a team of mules. Now Jackson found he had friends whom he had never met but who were rabidly committed to his candidacy. They were not interested in where he stood so much as what he stood for—a chance to curb the big bankers, to whittle the Boston crowd down to size, and to prove that a man of humble origin could aim for the nation's biggest job. To the old-time Jeffersonian Democrats, Jackson sent assurances that he was of the soil and for the men who tilled it. Slaveowners liked his southern background, and northern workers found his rise from poverty appealing. Being born in a log cabin was a distinct political asset.

Untiringly Van Buren helped fit together the pieces of a crazy quilt into some semblance of an organization that would blend southern planters "and the plain Republicans of the North" into a winning campaign. The events of March 4, 1829, had their beginning at the January 8, 1828, anniversary of the Battle of New Orleans. Citizens committed to Jackson's election scheduled banquets and fund-raising events to coincide with the famous date establishing their hero's glory. Of talk about tariffs, canals, and banks there was little, but much praise for the lanky Tennessean who "had licked the British" as they had never been beaten before.

Our forebears had great appetites and were not ashamed of them. When the Yankee farmers of Cheshire, Massachusetts, wished to honor President Jefferson, they sent him a cheese weighing 1,235 pounds. This enormous Cheshire cheese, their spokesman said, was sent to Jefferson, as a mere "peppercorn" of the people's esteem for their president. When Jackson was inaugurated, hundreds of his devoted followers swarmed into the White House, broke the presidential china, ground mud into the carpets, and gave their host a 1,400-pound cheese, which they hacked at with cleavers and knives until only a small hunk was left for the tired president.

In turn, Jackson gave the people some food for thought. He pledged to check the power of "a monied aristocracy of the few" in favor of "the Democracy of numbers," to prevent the laboring men from becoming "hewers of wood and drawers of water to the monied aristocracy of the country through the credit and paper system." As one witness at Jackson's inaugural said, the day's festivities proved "it was the People's day, the People's President and the People would rule."

Jackson's friends in the newspaper business made sure that their chieftain's words had a wide audience. After Jackson broke with Duff Green, he turned to Francis P. Blair, who had succeeded Amos Kendall (now a Treasury official) on the Frankfort (Kentucky) *Argus.* Together with a third Kentuckian, John C. Rives, these newspapermen became Jackson's closest advisers and were called his Kitchen Cabinet, after the president's official cabinet had displeased him. In 1830 they established the Washington *Globe*, and, blessed with $50,000 a year in government printing contracts, the Kentucky triumvirate saw that other newspaper editors who backed Jackson had their share of patronage, too. One of Jackson's allies, William Marcy, is supposed to have said, "To the victors belong the spoils." Indeed, the end of nonpartisan appointments was in sight. Jackson replaced nearly one thousand federal officeholders, as complacent postmasters, customs collectors, and marshals found that someone in Washington was paying attention to how people voted. When the *National Intelligencer* (no longer a favored Democratic organ) printed a list of fifty-seven newspapermen who had been appointed to federal jobs, Jackson probably regretted there had not been more. Curiously, although Jackson's name is forever linked to the spoils system, the truth is that he appointed more old Federalists to jobs than all his Republican predecessors had. What mattered was that the men close to Jackson approved the way he handled federal patronage, mainly because it helped keep aright the party keel that desperately needed caulking.

Until Jackson's advent, the old-fashioned idea was that a gentleman might desire an office, but oftentimes he hurt his chances if he worked hard for it. (Thus the sleight-of-hand caucus method for picking a candidate.) Among Jeffersonians this pretense had its supporters, and even Madison tried to seem available, but not eager, by claiming he wished to avoid "the appearance of a spirit of electioneering, which I despise." After 1828 the emerging Democratic leaders were often men of little formal education who were anxious to get ahead. They idolized self-made Andrew Jackson. Some were lawyers who had earned their shingles by a short reading of the laws, "often without enough practice to keep their minds and energies fully occupied," as Hofstatder observed. Along with small-scale merchants, bankers, and newspaper editors, they constituted the hardworking core of the revitalized Democratic party. Men of this stamp saw no point in being coy about running for office. Under Jackson's banner they merged their interests with those of the small farmers, who made up over 80 percent of the voters, and marched into the fray.

The time had come to drop the old trappings. When a renegade Federalist such as Daniel Webster and a bitter anti-Jackson man like Calhoun could call themselves Republicans, the carry-over term from Jefferson's day had outlived its usefulness. Clay's backers helped hasten the change when they took the name "National Republican" for their splinter party, hoping to force Jackson out of the White House in 1832. (Jackson had played into their hands briefly, in 1829, by calling for a constitutional amendment to limit presidents to one term.) A kind of draft was needed to make certain that the sixty-five-year-old president would run a second time, and this was engineered by Van Buren and the Kitchen Cabinet through a nominating convention held in Baltimore in May, 1832. Here delegates from every state but Missouri placed "King Caucus" in a coffin and proclaimed themselves honest-to-God Democrats. Somewhat stuffily, Van Buren later said that the change was dictated by the anti-Jackson crowd's use of the honorable old Republican label, which forced the drawing of "the line of demarcation between them as broad and as well defined as possible." Closer to the truth was the fact that the people themselves liked the name and wished to be identified with "the Democracy." As the National Republicans grudgingly admitted, "there seemed to be a magic" in the word Democrat.*

Before the final deed was done, Jackson hit the opposition in the solar plexis with a veto message the likes of which the country has not seen before or since. The Bank of the United States charter was not scheduled to expire until 1836, but for a variety of reasons the managers decided to seek a new charter on the eve of the 1832 presidential campaign. Every story needs a villain, and in Jackson's melodrama the bad guy was the bank president, Nicholas Biddle. A Philadelphia aristocrat of great abilities, Biddle had sprinkled about loans to newspaper editors favorable to the bank in a covert but obvious effort to muster public opinion behind the recharter. Although the bank was well managed, Biddle had made enemies among many local politicians, whose feathers had been ruffled by the bank's tough loan and currency policies. Added to these difficulties was the long-standing distrust of the farmers and planters for the men who held their mortgages.

While it was still far from certain that Jackson would run in 1832 (he was getting on and exceedingly depressed by his wife's death), the Democrats' inner-circle strategy was known in the summer of 1830. Clay warned Biddle that "a strong party headed by Mr. Van Buren, some Virginia politicians, and the Richmond Enquirer, intend, if practicable, to make the Bank question the basis of the next Presidential election." Chestnut Street in Philadelphia was then what Wall Street was in 1932, a stalking horse for all the resentment against the bank, based on real or imagined abuses of its considerable powers. It was easy for Van Buren to

*James S. Chase, *Emergence of the Presidential Nominating Convention,* 1789–1832 (Urbana: University of Illinois Press, 1973), 252.

rig resolutions in the New York legislature demanding an end to the bank, but this animosity was too broad-based to have been a mere political manipulation. Nor is Bray Hammond's statement, "It goes without saying that Andrew Jackson himself did not understand what was happening," totally fair. Whether Jackson reasoned the bank's business through or not, he was a Jeffersonian and thus listened to advisers who explained that the bank's currency control allowed "the steady transfer of wealth from the farmer and laborer to the business community."*

That was about all Jackson needed to know. The president went along with the plans of Van Buren, Roger Taney, and Kendall to do the bank in, neatly and finally. The National Republicans, hoping to embarrass Jackson by making him either sign the recharter or veto it, recklessly pursued their legislation for recharter. Once again, the smugness of a political group passing legislation to force an opponent into an uncomfortable position was about to boomerang. Clay and Biddle, moreover, had underestimated Jackson's popularity and the sagacity of his informal cabinet.

In the meantime, Van Buren, the logical successor to Jackson, pulled wires at the Baltimore convention to make Jackson's nomination certain. In a sense Jackson was drafted, for he would have been happy to step down. Time was needed, however, to entrench the newly shaped Democratic party, and Van Buren (just approaching fifty) could wait, while also making the ousting of Vice-President Calhoun certain. The cabinet was reshuffled, the anti-Jackson forces were frozen out, and the Baltimore convention climaxed the political purging needed to make the Democratic party more than a one-man show. Endorsements from state legislatures and conventions would have been enough to place Jackson's name on every presidential ballot. But the convention device created a

*Schlesinger, *Age of Jackson*, 125.

ticket, established some procedures for future nominations, and broadened the rank-and-file participation in the electoral process. Nowhere else in the world were national leaders picked by the people, but now even the preliminary steps were left up to men far removed from the seats of power. The Baltimore convention also endorsed majority rule with a vengeance. Two-thirds of the 320 delegates had to approve the party nominee for vice-president, and the states would vote by the unit rule (a majority within the delegation would make the choice for all the state's votes). The two-thirds rule, "which was to bedevil the Democratic party for over a century," was aimed to silence critics who had charged that a minority could force their vice-presidential candidate on the party. The unit rule was adopted to prevent "endless fragmentation of the votes by suppressing the minority members."*

The acceptance of Jackson as the party nominee was so manifest that the delegates hurriedly went on to the business of picking the vice-president. Van Buren was not eager for the job, but again the vindictiveness of his opponents proved the power of a political backfire. Van Buren had resigned as secretary of state to become minister to England, but Clay thought that a Senate rejection of his nomination would humiliate Van Buren and "kill him dead." Van Buren had already learned his lesson, but Clay had not. The Senate rejected Van Buren and thus vaulted him into party prominence as a maligned hero second only to Jackson in the eyes of the party faithful. So the grass-roots elements united at Baltimore; the Jackson-Van Buren ticket provided geographical balance to set the stage for act two of the 1832 campaign—the death of the bank bill.

Congress passed a sticky tariff bill and then sent to the White House the bank charter renewal for the president's signature. For three days Jackson's inner circle drafted his message. Then on July

*Ibid., 266.

10, 1832, the bomb was dropped. Written mainly by Kendall, and toned down by Taney, the long message let several clear ideas stand out: the bank was not only constitutionally shaky, it was wrong on principle, for it made rich men "richer by act of Congress." Not only would wealthy men benefit, but *foreign* rich men. "It appears that more than a fourth part of the stock is held by foreigners," the veto message read, and it was easy to identify in the public mind who those rich foreigners were: Englishmen. There was a lot more, but the slaps at "monopoly and all exclusive privilege . . . at the expense of the public" were enough to stir up all the hornets' nests from Charleston to Charlestown. No veto message has ever been circulated so widely. Biddle's newspaper friends wailed in vain, for there were not enough votes to upset the veto; and the bank issue was so visceral that to any perceptive citizen it was clear that Jackson and his rejuvenated party would easily capture the presidency in November. "The Country," said one ardent Jacksonian editor, "owes a new debt of gratitude to its venerable Head for bringing this subject to its notice this early, thus fearlessly and directly. It has called down upon him the vindictive hatred of a MONIED OLIGARCHY; but the people will sustain him."* The Boston *Post* printed the bank's epitaph: "Biddled, Diddled, and Undone."

Voters understood certain messages more clearly than some of their leaders imagined. A few years earlier, the anti-Jackson men in Massachusetts had passed a law prohibiting the sale of "ardent spirits" in lots of less than fifteen gallons, so that the laboring man was forced to buy in a licensed tavern and to pay more for his gill of rum. Then the "Democracy arose in all its wrath to end such discrimination against the poor man," defeated the bill's sponsors, and hustled through its repeal. Bankruptcy laws were making headway, and despite some factional bickering among Democrats,

* Quoted in Bray Hammond, *Banks and Politics in America: From the Revolution to the Civil War* (Princeton, N.J.: Princeton University Press, 1957), 409.

imprisonment for debt was assailed in Congress and in state legislatures until this vestige of medieval credit control disappeared wherever Democrats had control.

Often the target of much legislation promoted by the Democrats was the creditor, the note holder, or the town banker, who invariably lived in a two-story brick house on the hill. Their interests conflicted with the large numbers of voters moving into the Democratic party, and as the Frenchman Alexis de Tocqueville noted in 1835, "when the Democratic party got the upper hand, it took exclusive possession of the conduct of affairs, and from that time, the laws and the customs of society have been adapted to its caprices." De Tocqueville thought that wealth in Jackson's America, "far from conferring a right, is rather a cause of unpopularity." The Frenchman also perceived that the "two chief weapons which parties use in order to obtain success are the *newspapers* and the public *associations*." Newspapermen Blair, Kendall, and Rives set the party line in Washington, but independent journalists came into Jackson's camp for a variety of motives, including *pro patria*. William Cullen Bryant, once a Federalist, numbered among the latter group as he reasoned himself away from the conservatives and carried the influential New York *Evening Post* into the Democratic column. America was becoming a country of joiners, and it seemed that every crossroads village had a temperance society, Bible association, volunteer fire company, Masonic order, or veterans' assembly. One way or another, local political figures found ways to turn these groups into adjuncts of their party at voting time. Few Democrats ever wandered into the temperance meetings, however; and in New England the Washington Temperance Society was simply an offshoot of the Federalist party dedicated to curbing the twin evils of rum and the Democracy. As one wag put it, sometimes the only discernible difference separating the two parties was between the hangers-on and the hung-over.

In the South, the Democrats were torn internally by Jackson's hard-line stand on the limits to a state's rights. As a Jeffersonian, the president conceded local control over such matters as the courts, police, and education; but the talk about nullification was scary. Madison, still alive and distressed that his 1798 writings provided ammunition for the southern "Nullies," denounced any implication that a state could veto an unpopular federal law. Virginia Governor John Floyd, unable to share Madison's views, grew to despise Jackson. After Old Hickory's reelection, Floyd wrote in his diary: "Should he still pursue his ignorant and violent cause . . . we will never see another President of the United States elected."

If Jackson's tenure in the White House had brought on an era of bad feeling, it was only because the trend during his presidency was a harking back to Jeffersonian Democracy. As Charles A. Beard noted, "Jeffersonian Democracy simply meant the possession of the federal government by the agrarian masses led by an aristocracy of slave-owning planters, and the theoretical repudiation of the right to use the Government for the benefit of any capitalistic groups, fiscal, banking, or manufacturing."* Substitute for the slave-owning aristocratic planters the self-made professional men who had their fingers on the farmer's pulse and you have Jacksonian Democracy defined. Jackson's *facto factotum*, Amos Kendall, said it more succinctly: "The world is governed too much." Dozens of Jacksonian newspapers repeated this key phrase in their editorial columns, perhaps unaware that they were paraphrasing Jefferson. The 1832 Democratic convention had not bothered to write a platform, but if it had, Kendall's terse slogan pretty well fitted the party's mood and would have sufficed.

Thus the old strains of Jeffersonian republicanism were blended into the Democratic party philosophy that Jackson accepted as a legacy. Monopolies and corporations—legal privileges created by

---

*Charles A. Beard, *Economic Origins of Jeffersonian Democracy* (New York: Macmillan, 1915), 467.

the few and for the few—were symbolized by the Bank of the United States, and with its fall all such financial boons were jeopardized. Not that the Jackson men were above dealing themselves in on profitable directorships on state bank boards, but at least these were controlled by the states and were not gifts from a federal Congress or president sworn to serve the total public interest.

The old guard of privilege, John Marshall, had been Jackson's nemesis. The Marshall court had pinned Jackson's ears back by affirming the rights of the Cherokee Indians, who were about to be hustled out of Georgia and removed to the Indian Territory. Jackson, with the full approval of his following, thumbed his nose at the court and sent the Indians westward, making more room for southern settlers and opening rich bottomlands for the planting of cotton. Upon Marshall's death in 1835 Jackson left his imprint on the future with the appointment of Roger Taney as chief justice. The Democratic court found its opportunity to stamp Democratic ideas on property rights in 1837, when the Charles River Bridge case came before the Supreme Court. The issue involved a toll bridge which was a splendid money-maker until a second bridge (that eventually was to be toll-free) was built, provoking the first bridge's owners to sue for redress. The toll bridge proprietors lost their case, because the Taney court said that while property rights were sacred, "we must not forget that the community also have rights and that the happiness and well being of every citizen depends on their faithful preservation."

Jackson disliked—not necessarily in this order—Indians, the public debt, and paper money. The Indians were taken care of, so next the public debt had to be paid off. With prospects of a bulging Treasury, the distribution of surplus money to the states was arranged. Then he leveled his sights on paper money, which was "shinplaster" currency in a variety of forms and values. The Treasury Department was instructed to accept only hard money (gold or silver) for the sale of public lands at $1.25 an acre (over fourteen million acres were sold the year before). The purpose was to help bona fide settlers and to curb land speculators, which was good Jeffersonian reasoning, except that the ultimate effect was nearly the reverse of what Jackson had intended. At the time, however, Democrats applauded Jackson and agreed that Jefferson himself could not have done better.

Amid the peace and prosperity of 1836 the Democrats again held a Baltimore convention. To no one's surprise, Vice-President Van Buren was hailed as the people's choice. Richard Mentor Johnson of Kentucky was Jackson's choice for the ticket balancer, and the president cared little for whispers about Johnson's common-law mulatto wife. Unkind Democrats from Virginia were said to have hissed when Johnson was nominated, but even with the two-thirds rule in effect, the word from the White House was out, and Johnson was in. For the moment, the two-thirds rule was forgotten in the unanimity of the day.

The nomination of Van Buren gave him "favorite son" status in New York, which now had forty-four electoral votes, and thus afforded him a tremendous head start in the campaign. Being a Democrat had its drawbacks, however, for during 1836 there were a few disturbing signals of trouble over slavery. The business had not been settled in 1820 as the old-time Democrats had fervently prayed. A deluge of petitions to Congress from the newly formed abolitionist societies were automatically tabled under the "gag rule" demanded by southerners. The obstreperous *Liberator*, a radical antislavery newspaper printed in Boston, infuriated so many southerners that they demanded, and finally obtained, a post-office order keeping it hidden in mail sacks below the Mason-Dixon Line. A political innocent, James G. Birney, freed his slaves in Kentucky and started a journal dedicated to abolition through political action.

Van Buren gave the antislavery advocates scant attention as he rode Jackson's coattails into the presidency. Van Buren was also unaware of the financial woes fermenting during a time of rampant speculation and reckless borrowing. The Democrats had been true to form in passing a modified tariff in 1833 that had calmed down those angry southerners whose mutterings about nullification and secession had made Jackson's blood boil. Meanwhile, the National Republicans plunged into a war on a broad front against Jackson's program. Their newspapers campaigned against the Tennessee autocrat (as they termed him), whom they began to call "King Andrew I." Allied with the Anti-Masonic party from New York and Pennsylvania, they took a new name, Whigs, because Whigs traditionally opposed the king, and in their view Jackson was acting like an Americanized version of George III.* The Whig party soon attracted an odd assortment of politicians mainly held together by either their intense dislike of Jackson or grievances piled up from being out of office for a decade. Thus southern planters and northern factory owners joined forces in an effort to thwart Democrats, but in the presidential campaign Van Buren was able to use all the devices made popular during Old Hickory's campaign—torchlight parades, campaign hats and vests, slogans, songs, and symbols. (Such devices made it easier for semiliterates to pick a candidate on the ballot; Whigs took a raccoon for their pet, and Democrats placed a crowing rooster at the head of their tickets.) Although the Democrats won, they lost one-time Jacksonian strongholds in Georgia and Tennessee. Encouraged Whigs aimed toward 1840.

The election of Van Buren gave the country its first practical politician in the White House. He had worked his way up the ladder, serving as judge, state senator, New York attorney general, governor, United States senator, and then (reluctantly, at first) as vice-president. He loved the Democratic party, and his views on

*The Anti-Masonic party was a patchwork organization formed to hound from office so-called grand kings of Freemasonry, who allegedly used their secret order as a political base.

party philosophy were simplistic—low taxes, no national debt, states' rights, and a strict construction of the Constitution. In short, his roots went deep into the same soil where Jefferson's republicanism had flourished. In physique he was everything Jackson was not—short, bald, pot-bellied, and easily lost in a crowd. Still he was the embodiment of the public man whose time had come, for he liked the hurly-burly of smoky meeting rooms, the back-patting, and the remembering of names. His qualities for leadership, Hofstadter noted, came from "his liking for people, and his sportsmanlike ability to experience political conflict without taking it as ground for personal rancor." Indeed, when his old adversary De Witt Clinton died, Van Buren had delivered a convincing and magnanimous eulogy.

Jackson, who valued loyalty above all things in his friends, looked to the most loyal man around him when he fixed his gaze on Van Buren, the tavern keeper's son who had scratched his way to the top of the heap just as Jackson had done. The nation was prospering as ribbons of steel were laid up and down the seaboard, and the boom in railroad building kept pace with the rise of real estate prices. After a disastrous fire swept part of Manhattan, lots in the burned area were snapped up "at most enormous prices, greater than they would have brought before the fire, when covered with valuable buildings."* The first boat fired with anthracite coal in its engines steamed up to Van Buren's old stomping ground at Albany. Gaslights for homes and convention halls were the latest sign of national well-being.

Then came the crash of 1837. All the sins of wildcat banking, land speculation, hard-money collections, and an overexpanded economy running on lots of credit and little cash came home to roost on the White House balcony. Democrats affectionately called Van Buren "the Little Magician," but there was no magic that

* Josef and Dorothy Berger (eds.), *Diary of America* (New York: Simon and Schuster, 1957), 204 (Philip Hone diary).

would prop up failing banks and falling commodity prices. Moreover, Van Buren saw nothing in the Democratic party philosophy that obliged him to bring the federal government into action as a means of stemming the spreading depression. There were bread riots in New York, respected banks in New Orleans and Philadelphia collapsed, and cotton prices tumbled so fast that heavily mortgaged planters were forced into bankruptcy. The Democrats responded by pushing for an independent central Treasury that would curb the state banks and by promising to return to specie payments for all federal payments or receipts. This was Van Buren's antidote to the paper-money craze, and it helped bring back some old friends who had strayed into the Whig camp. Nor was the laboring man forgotten. An executive order required a 10-hour work day, as Eugene Rosebloom reminds us, for navy yards and other public works. The time-honored Democratic pledge of "tariffs for revenue only" and opposition to federal subsidies for roads and canals kept taxes low. Squatters on public lands also got a break when Congress decided to given them the first right to buy their preempted farms on fairly easy terms.

Land in the West was not dirt cheap, but it was close to it. Thousands of settlers moved West and there found Democrats entrenched in lean-to courthouses and river town post offices, as the frontier leaped across the Mississippi and pushed into the Minnesota and Iowa territories. The Democratic policy of cash payments for public lands held down speculation, a fact stressed at voting time to settlers along the upper Mississippi. Van Buren appointed the first governors of these western outposts, and the Democratic appointees in turn surrounded themselves with loyal partisans in judgeships, in the territorial legislature, and even in the humble offices of the justices of the peace.

A typical Democrat who profited from the westward course of history was William Williams Chapman, a congressional delegate from Iowa from 1838 to 1840. Chapman was born in Virginia and started practicing law there, then moved to Burlington, Iowa, when it was still part of the Wisconsin Territory, and was elected a delegate to Congress when the Iowa Territory was created. After serving in the Iowa constitutional convention, he headed for Oregon, served in the state legislature there, and helped found the Portland *Oregonian*. Then he was appointed state surveyor general in 1858. Chapman died at eighty-four, having served the Democratic party and having been served in turn for over forty years by the honors and jobs it could bestow.

Similar stories of patronage could be told in Wisconsin and Minnesota, where Democratic appointees laid the groundwork for statehood, which would bring loyal Democrats into Congress within the next decade. Meanwhile, in the settled areas, party workers scrambled for offices and power within the gift of state governments. Pennsylvania, glorying in her claim to be "the keystone in the democratic arch," had a variety of Democrats vying for influence, led by Simon Cameron and James Buchanan (their Scots-Irish ancestry was no drawback). Cameron was a sometime newspaper publisher (*Bucks County Democrat*, Pennsylvania *Intelligencer*, Harrisburg *Republican*) with banking and business interests. He helped Buchanan go to the Senate in 1833, a favor that was repaid when Cameron was made an Indian claims commissioner. Buchanan, a former Federalist, became a Jackson Democrat in 1828 and steadily rose in the party. He won the support of southerners who liked his stand on slavery: it was wrong, but it was legal. From the House of Representatives he was appointed to the ministry in Russia, then came home to be a senator. Van Buren offered him a cabinet post, but Buchanan stayed in the Senate, with one eye set on the White House. Men could be extremely patient in those days.

New York and Virginia were the other key spokes in the Democratic wheel. Van Buren's tight hold on his home territory meant that his friends Silas Wright, Azariah C. Flagg, and William

Marcy would have much to say about statewide patronage while Tammany could go its own separate way in Manhattan. As in Pennsylvania, the Democracy looked benignly on reforms that broadened the suffrage and protected the debtor, and it applauded talk from Washington concerning strict constructionism on constitutional matters. New York, after all, had built the Erie Canal with her own resources. So why should tax dollars from her self-generated prosperity be used to build roads and canals in Alabama or Kentucky? The old Albany Regency was in control.

No such claim could be made for the Richmond Junto. William C. Rives was eager for the presidential nomination, but he was against the administration's independent Treasury bill; his dissent helped split the Democrats into state bank and loyalist factions. Travelers going farther than fifty miles might need a half-dozen state and railroad bank notes to pay for their trip. Commercial banking in the West was in the disaster stage, but the old despisers of the United States Bank turned their spleen on Van Buren's hard-money program. Ritchie, dismayed by the turn of events, reluctantly abandoned his friends who liked "pet" state banks and supported Van Buren. The Whigs won the congressional elections in 1838, installed a Virginian as Speaker of the House, and vowed to shake the Old Dominion from its party moorings a year hence. In alarm Ritchie appealed to the people of Virginia: "Are you prepared to put down 'the Northern President with Southern principles?' Are you prepared to disgust the whole Northern Democracy, the best friends, as a party, which we have there, by discarding our staunchest friends in all the North?" To make matters worse, the Whigs were openly talking about nominating Virginian John Tyler as their vice-presidential candidate in 1840.

Perhaps Van Buren was overconfident. Not only had bread riots occurred in New York, but in New Orleans the wharf was crowded with bales of eight-cent cotton nobody would bid on. Undaunted, the president fell back on his Democratic principles and said the federal government "could not help the people make a living." "The less government interferes with private pursuits, the better the general prosperity," he insisted. The independent Treasury bill finally squeaked by Congress while dozens of banks, mainly in the South and West, closed their doors.* The Republic of Texas had friends in Congress who wanted the former Mexican province admitted into the Union as a slave state, but with cotton prices at an all-time low and so many northerners ready to erupt if the matter came before the Senate, it seemed judicious to leave the issue smoldering for a bit longer.

Then a most peculiar thing happened. As Lee Benson noted, "The Whigs went out of character and infringed on the Democratic patent." The Whigs fooled a lot of their followers and most of the Democrats by nominating General William Henry Harrison as their standard-bearer. Harrison was another Jackson, an Indian fighter and a westerner of immense popularity; and nobody knew where he stood on any public issue. Van Buren found it hard to take Harrison or the ensuing "hard-cider" campaign seriously.

In May, 1840, twenty-one states sent delegates to the smug national Democratic convention in Baltimore, to go through the ritual of renominating Van Buren and, for the first time, to write a party platform. Mercifully brief, the nine resolutions were an echo of Jefferson republicanism infused with the spirit of Jackson. The platform struck at internal improvements, a national bank, and monopolies; praised the concept of the Constitution "strictly

*The battle of the Independent Treasury Act is further proof that the two parties have historic positions. The purpose of the act was to give the federal Treasury exclusive control over government funds and thus prevent the favoritism that led to deposits of enormous sums in a chartered national bank or in the so-called pet state banks. Overturned by the Whigs in 1841, the act was revived in 1846 by the Democrats and provided the nation's fiscal system until 1913, when another Democrat signed the Federal Reserve Act and made the independent Treasury an anachronism.

construed"; and asserted "that every citizen and every section of the country, has a right to demand and insist upon an equality of rights and privileges." For slaveowners, it was a platform from the "northern man with southern principles," because it reaffirmed Van Buren's position that Congress had "no power, under the Constitution, to interfere with or control" slavery. "All efforts by abolitionists," it read, "are calculated to lead to the most alarming consequences." And finally, it took a swipe at the flag-waving, home-grown citizens who were trying to make it harder to become a naturalized citizen. Jefferson's "liberal principles embodied in the Declaration of Independence, which makes ours the land of liberty, and the asylum of the oppressed of every nation, have ever been cardinal principles in the democratic faith, and every attempt to abridge the present privilege of becoming citizens ... ought to be resisted with the same spirit which swept the alien and sedition laws from our statute-book." Van Buren took that plank so seriously he had the Virginia and Kentucky resolutions distributed as campaign literature.

The Democrats went into the 1840 race with abundant optimism. Van Buren thought the blustering Whig tactics were a farce. The president and his backers had not figured, however, on the Whig strategists who were tired of losing campaigns pitched on issues. Led by Horace Greeley's campaign newspaper, the *Log Cabin*, the Whigs made Harrison appear to be another flesh-and-blood Jackson and depicted Van Buren as a champagne-swilling aristocrat.

> Let Van from his coolers of silver drink wine,
> And lounge on his cushioned settee.
> Our man on his buckeye bench can recline,
> Content with hard cider is he!

Whereas Democrats from Jefferson's time onward had organized voters by appealing to their interests, the Whigs, hoping to ignore the issues, used both old and new campaign techniques to popularize Harrison. Harrison was smoked out on slavery and said he was not an abolitionist. But he was not encouraged to take stands. Instead of discussing their record on the bank or road building, the Whigs lit bonfires, held torchlight parades with log cabins mounted on wagon beds, and waved banners for "Tippecanoe and Tyler, Too!" to woo voters away from their Democratic loyalties.

This presidential campaign was the first to employ such frankly demagogic terms, and some of the ideas used by Whigs have been refurbished in virtually every campaign since 1840. Even so, Van Buren might still have won except for a few slight miscalculations. Thurlow Weed, the Anti-Masonic party boss who longed to be a power in national politics, taught the New York Democrats a few lessons in organizing an election. That the Democrats were mystified by the demagoguery of the Whigs was manifest. Van Buren sensed that something was going wrong and he hurled instructions to this friends to watch out for frauds at the ballots and other chicanery. The outcome was full of puzzles. Illinois, which should have gone for Harrison, went for Van Buren by a whisker, and New York, which Van Buren assumed would go his way, barely slipped into the Whig column. Pennsylvania was lost by 239 votes. Of the key states, only Virginia stayed in the Democratic column.

Van Buren was stunned. He found it hard to believe that voters had been lulled into the Whig fold by promises; indeed, Harrison had promised nothing. "Time will unravel the means by which these results have been produced," he reckoned, "& the people will then do justice to all."* Van Buren retired from Washington, convinced in his heart that a few years would work a miracle. He

---

*Quoted in James Curtis, *The Fox at Bay* (Lexington: University of Kentucky Press, 1970), 206.

was merely going on a four-year leave of absence and would be back on March 4, 1845, to undo the mess that the Whigs were sure to make of the nation's affairs.

No Whig, especially a New England Whig, had made much mention during the campaign of the fact that both Harrison and his running mate were born in Virginia. In fact, both had also been Republicans at one time, and when Harrison became ill and died a month after his inauguration, fate thrust the presidency upon a man who was an old Crawford Democrat, a lukewarm Jackson Democrat, and a seasoned opponent of the bank —John Tyler. Tyler, by his frugality and his regard for states' rights, managed to anger as many Whigs as he pleased Democrats, which ruined him in his party's councils. Furthermore, the Texas issue would not die and Tyler *was* from the South. The South was changing, of course, but not much. The old tidewater aristocrats reluctantly gave up the name Republican but rejected "the name of democrat which had obtained in the North, and it was never until the election of 1840, that decent persons could willingly stomach the name" in the parlors of Charleston, Mobile, and Richmond.* Meanwhile, as the southerners laced their tea with brandy and wondered aloud if black slaves were really humans, Yankee abolitionists asked in their newspapers if slaveowners could be human; and New York businessmen wished they would both shut up and let them handle their accounts in peace. All three groups had probably voted Whig in 1840.

During Tyler's tenure the hottest political issue was Texas' annexation. Calhoun mounted the whirligig again with a plan to bring another southern state into the Union and thereby boost his final chance for the White House. As secretary of state, Calhoun negotiated an annexation treaty that failed in the Senate, mainly owing to the northern opposition. The Texan republic permitted

Southern Quarterly Review, October, 1847, quoted in Binkley, *American Political Parties*, 128.

slavery but restricted the importation of slaves "from all parts of the world except the United States." That was the rub, for many northern men thought Calhoun was angling for a way to offer a ready market for the surplus slave population in the older South and thus perpetuate slavery.

Van Buren might have stood above the controversy and slipped into the 1844 nomination without great difficulty, except that he was asked by a convention delegate to give his opinion of Texas annexation. Van Buren then did a dangerous thing. He came straight out in a public letter and declared his opposition to annexation (not on the slavery issue, but on the ground that annexation would provoke a war with Mexico). This bold stroke from a man of principle charred Van Buren's chances for the nomination, though his supporters whistled in the dark when British-baiting Lewis Cass (Jackson's secretary of war), Senator Buchanan, and Levi Woodbury (another alumnus from Jackson's cabinet, known as "the Rock of New England Democracy") began making presidential noises.

A Baltimore convention was now part of the Democratic ritual. President Tyler, repudiated by the Whigs, sent his friends there to argue that he should be nominated by the 266 optimistic delegates. The two-thirds rule, dropped in 1840, was brought back to distress Van Buren's friends, who thought the reasons given for its revival "so palpably absurd that it would be offensive if urged by any man of common sense to an intelligent audience."* The roll was called in alphabetical order, and the issue was not settled until the last delegation, Virginia, voted for the rule. This nailed the coffin on Van Buren, for he led on the first ballot by a wide margin, but not by the magic two-thirds majority. Lewis Cass's strength rose as Van Buren's fell, but nobody had the necessary majority through eight ballots.

*Jabez D. Hammond, *Political History of the State of New York* (Syracuse, 1852), 451.

Then the first dark horse in American politics—so dark his name had not been mentioned until the eighth ballot—left the delegates gasping at their own temerity. James Polk (who had earnestly solicited the vice-presidential nomination) had forty-four votes on the eighth ballot. Then when New Hampshire swung his way on the ninth, the stampede bore down all opposition in a few minutes. As delegates hurried to switch their votes, the Polk bandwagon was off at a gallop.

"Who is James K. Polk?" the Whigs laughed. The first telegraph line in the nation flashed the news to Washington. Clay must have been elated, for it seemed that at last his chance to live in the president's house was at hand. Polk's friendship for his fellow Tennessean Andrew Jackson, his service as Speaker of the House, and his experience as governor of Tennessee were indications to Whigs that the wiry southerner was a has-been. "I knew they would nominate a nobody," Polk himself was quoted as saying, when he was informed of the convention's choice. Eighty-four years later, a Democratic soothsayer (praying for Al Smith's election) talked like a good Whig and said, "No President has been so quickly and completely forgotten as Polk after he finished his single term." But in truth Polk was not a nobody in 1844, and in 1979 no careful historian would rate Polk at the bottom of his class.

He was a hard worker. John Quincy Adams, who knew something about the job, admitted that Polk "worked like a galley slave" during his White House tenure. More recently, Bernard DeVoto said of Polk, "His integrity was absolute. . . . He was to be the only 'strong' President between Jackson and Lincoln."

In the spring of 1844, the Whigs had a different perspective. They hoped to turn the northern tide against the Democrats by hammering the Texas issue to death. As it happened, the mood of the country was for some spread-eagle diplomacy. Even Adams thought it was only a matter of time before Cuba would be annexed. And the British were talking tough about Oregon. Presidential candidate Polk made it plain that he was for a move into Texas and for a hard line of talk with England. No candidate had ever hurt himself by shaking his fist at Britannia, and Polk knew that "54–40 or fight!" was going to win a lot more votes than it lost. The Democratic platform was the 1840 program with a few additions, notably a claim to the whole Oregon territory and a firm pledge to "reannex" Texas. The Whigs countered with hosannas for a regulated national currency (a national bank, in other words), a tariff for revenue with some protective features, and a reform of the presidential veto power. Whig Henry Clay swallowed the whole pill and was nominated in triumphant expectation that the lightning, at long last, was about to strike.

Instead, Polk the unknown became the president–elect. Waving the Union Jack to frighten the Anglophobes, Democrats shouted that it was Polk "or *delenda est Britannia*." Southerners who wanted more room for slavery expansion marched to the beat of the Democrats' drums, and northerners who feared the ghost of the United States Bank and favored the Jeffersonian economics preached from the editorial columns of Polk's newspaper supporters turned their backs on Clay. Factions in New York, Pennsylvania, and Virginia buried the hatchet and screamed slogans about Texas and Oregon until they were hoarse. All three states went for Polk, and with their votes went Clay's last hopes.

"Polk! Great God, what a nomination!" Thus the governor of Kentucky reacted when he learned that Polk was the party's standard-bearer. Other fainthearted Democrats learned to soft-pedal their doubts after the voting came in with what had been incredible speed (the new telegraph lines were spreading). The bombastic Democratic editor who had urged Polk's election to fulfill the "Manifest Destiny" of the young nation had been far better attuned to the spirit of his times than most men then realized. Henry Thoreau, no lover of the Democratic party, was honest enough to say: "My needle is slow to settle—varies a few degrees and does not always point due southwest . . . but it always settles between west and south-southwest. The future lies that way for me." So it also lay for the country, Americans decided, as they voted that fateful fall of 1844. The antislavery Liberty party candidate drained away 15,000 votes from Clay in New York—that helped. Tennessee was lost by 113 votes. But somebody had to get down to cases with England about Oregon, and Texas was as American as bourbon and beefsteak already. After Polk's narrow victory, Congress reacted by passing a joint resolution of annexation. Texas was officially in the Union (unless somebody wanted to raise a nasty constitutional objection).*

All this took place a few days before Polk's inauguration. Democrats converged on Washington, their sabers rattling, while Horace Greeley fumed at the three Whigs who had voted with the unanimous Senate Locofocos (all Democrats were Locofocos to Greeley) to pass the Texas bill, 27–25. "By our proceedings in getting possession of Texas, we have declared ourselves the enemies of the civilized world. . . . People of the United States! What shall yet be done to turn aside this storm of unjust war from our borders?" Greeley had more ammunition in his editorial box to fire away at Polk; in fact, he was simply warming up.

Polk shrugged off the Whig outcries and did his homework. Van Buren had been crushed by the 1840 election, seared by the uncomfortable thought that the wisdom of the majority was not an infallible test. Polk, barely chosen to head the party and the nation, had no doubts whatever. The Whigs had won in 1840 with their "coonskin fooleries" and slogans, but the Democrats had learned a few tricks. They came back with their catch phrases full of English devils and Mexican generals. Ten months earlier Polk had been the defeated former governor of Tennessee. Now he

*In fact Polk was a "minority president," for he lacked about 25,000 votes of having a clear majority. The final count was Polk 1,339,368, Clay 1,300,687, and James Birney, the Liberty (antislavery) party candidate, 62,197.

was president of the United States, even though his nomination and victory had defied all traditions. He was no longer a political accident. Polk believed in himself and he sensed what the country wanted and needed. He was ready to take charge of his party and his country.

FOUR

~~~

Democracy or Slavocracy?

After the triumphant Polk years
the Democratic party embarked on a suicidal course that came
within an inch of killing the party altogether. In one sense, Polk
was only bringing to a close the westward course of the empire
Jefferson had started, but over all the questions hung the pall of
enslaved blacks in a world that was outlawing human bondage.
Men moved in and out of the party as they changed their minds
about the bank, about the tariff, even about slavery; but the commitment to keep moving West was engrained into the party leadership somewhat and into the Democratic rank and file completely. When Van Buren misread that sign, he lost the nomination
and sulked for four years.

Polk, ready to capitalize on the luck that had thrust him into
the seat of power, had vowed in his acceptance of the nomination
that he would serve only one term. He impressed everybody with
his drive and soon had the Oregon question settled. Over a year
passed, however, before a combination of Mexican bluster and
Yankee jingoism erupted into war. The Whigs yapped at Polk's
heels over Texas, as Greeley ripped into him for "a most unconstitutional appliance of Presidential power"; but Polk's message
to Congress charged Mexicans with shedding "American blood
upon American soil!" The western counties in Iowa and Wisconsin sent their boys into battle and then named counties Polk,

Taylor, and Cerro Gordo to remind them of their glory. Even so, the loudest and most-listened-to voices in Democratic counsels had a Dixie drawl, for many expansionists became converted to the southern idea that slavery would survive as long as new territory was added to the Union. It seems fairly clear that most Americans were willing to accept slavery as a fact, albeit an unpleasant one, so long as the slaveowners stayed below the thirty-sixth parallel. A growing number of southern Democrats, however, were unable to discuss the matter quietly. They snorted epithets aimed at the northern abolitionists who provoked public displays of outrage when fugitive slaves were manacled and sent home. An unhealthy partisanship forced Polk to think about the party background of his generals even when their military fitness was a more pressing concern.

This jockeying for power led to speculation on whether General Zachary Taylor was a Democrat or Whig. Taylor's virtue was singular, for he was a professional soldier with no political background whatever. But he also had drawbacks. He was a slaveholder and a native of Virginia. After his victory at Buena Vista, Taylor's name was blazed across the country, first on telegraph wires and then in the newspapers. Envious Whigs, recalling the popularity of Harrison a few years earlier, kept their eyes on Taylor. His position on the issues was unimportant. Was he a Whig, and would he run for president?

The answer to both questions was yes, but there was more trouble brewing for the Democrats in their once-comfortable New York bastion. The New York Democrats swallowed the forty-ninth parallel for the Oregon boundary (not the well-advertised 54–40) without difficulty and commended Polk for supporting the independent treasury law and the lowered tariff. They skirted the Mexican war issue by adopting a resolution in their convention urging "a speedy and honorable peace" and then proceeded to nominate Silas Wright for governor. Wright should have won

easily, but the conservative Hunkers, Anti-Renters, and other factions tore each other apart, and the Whig candidate was elected.*
A similar tale of woe came from Pennsylvania, except the stunned Democrats there blamed their loss on the lowered Democrat tariffs. All this news was bad enough, but there was more. In the congressional elections that fall, the Whigs gained a majority of eight votes in the House. As far as the president was concerned, he failed to see any difference. "With a large nominal majority in both houses," Polk had complained earlier, "I am practically in a minority."

Polk looked at his lame-duck Congress and decided that "several cliques and sections of the Democratic party are manifestly more engaged in managing for their respective favourites in the next Presidential election, than they are in supporting the government in prosecuting the war." A Pennsylvania Democrat had added to Polk's woes by seeking a ban on slavery in any territory that might be acquired from Mexico; then Congressman Preston King, another Democrat, piled fagots on the fire by resurrecting David Wilmot's proviso on slavery—all of which came at a time when Polk was more worried about winning the war than what would come later. Polk called King's resolution a "fire-brand . . . which can result in no good," but he threw the matter before his cabinet. They endorsed "the line of the Missouri Compromise . . . west to the Pacific." This, Polk believed, was the cold water needed to douse firebrands. Repeatedly, the Democratic president winced when northern members of his own party harped on laws to proscribe slavery above the 1820 compromise line. Polk made it clear that he thought the slavery issue in the West was an absurdity, since "slavery would probably never exist" there anyway.

Only 100 congressmen in the 228-member House that met in

*Spiritual descendants of the Shays's rioters, the Anti-Renters were angry farmers fed up with the oppressive perpetual lease system. Wright, though sympathetic, had prosecuted the rioting ringleaders.

March, 1847, were holdovers from the days when the chamber rang with exultant cries for a triumphant march into Mexico. The Whig majority (including freshman Abraham Lincoln from Illinois, the only Whig in his state's delegation) turned the tables by passing a resolution condemning a war that had been "unnecessarily and unconstitutionally begun by the President." Undaunted, Polk saw the war carried into the streets of Mexico City, and when a peace treaty was tortuously but finally negotiated, he told blustering southern Democrats that he wanted California admitted as a free state, without any slavery strings attached. He honestly thought that once California was admitted, "the whole difficulty would be settled, and . . . the Free-Soil agitators or Abolitionists of the North would be prostrate and powerless . . . the country quieted, and the Union preserved." Polk thought and acted in the Democratic tradition, basing his actions on a conviction that the majority ought to rule, plus a sound hunch that the arid western soil and climate would never grow a stick of cotton.

The fuss over the Wilmot and King resolutions, even though the antislavery men were outmaneuvered, had been a close call. Polk's friends scurried in search of an alternative that would take the onus of slavery off Congress. The president wanted the Democrats to offer the country a solution that would appeal to all sections, and he thought he had found it in the announced intention of stretching the thirty-sixth parallel to the California coast. Then ambitious Senator Lewis Cass of Michigan wrote a much-publicized letter in December, 1847, suggesting that the slavery question in all territories should be settled not by Congress but by the territorial legislatures. Moderate Democrats breathed easier, for this seemed a fair application of "squatter sovereignty" to the party's discouraged middle-of-the roaders.

During Polk's last year in office he brought together most of the pledges made in the 1844 party platform. Oregon was a territory, Texas had been "re-annexed," the Bank of the United States had been thwarted, tariffs had been lowered, and the president had practiced "the most rigid economy in conducting our public affairs" by vetoing a pork barrel handout known as the harbors and rivers act. "To call the mouth of a creek a harbor does not confer authority to expend public money on its improvement," the Jeffersonian president said. Perhaps no president in the nation's history was more conscientiously committed to implementing the planks in his party's platform—or so successful in carrying them into action—than Polk. All the while he remained a complete politician and even practiced shaking hands so that he could handle the inevitable two thousand guests at White House levees. In his last annual message, Polk managed to hold up the mantle of Jefferson and Jackson. "The president represents," he said, "the whole people of the United States."

Polk's popularity had waned, however. The Whigs had made inroads into the Democrats' majorities, there was no doubt of that, particularly where smart managers like Thurlow Weed of New York held sway. Silas Wright's defeat in New York proved Weed and his friends could overwhelm the alliance of Tammany and the Albany crowd; but there was much talk of nominating Wright at the 1848 convention, before the farmer-politician died of apoplexy.

Democrats came and went—so did Whigs—but below the statehouse levels it is likely that there was little concern over a man's political affiliations. That is, unless he was an abolitionist. Jabez Hammond, who knew New York politics like the back of his hand, admitted that "the abolition party . . . contains more wealth and talent . . . than any other political party in the state. . . . It was further admitted, that there was not a single county in the state that could by [any] possibility elect an abolitionist *as* an *abolitionist*." In other words, the voters were still fairly conservative and not ready for political extremism. Soldier-explorer John C. Fremont's exciting western travel accounts, which were best sellers for that time, fitted the nation's mood. Certainly the New York businessman agreed with his Mobile counterpart in condemning the antics of William Lloyd Garrison, the fiery editor of the *Liberator*, who denounced slavery as "the most inexcusable of crimes."

No practical politician was ready to call a slaveowner a criminal in 1848, but former president Van Buren came close to it, thus throwing a wrench into the Democrats' machinery. In one sense the Democrats had matured as a party; they created a regular national committee, held a convention (in Baltimore, of course), and ruled that a state delegation would have the same voting strength it had in the electoral college. The two-thirds rule was reenacted, while a proslavery resolution from the fire-eater William Lowndes Yancey was squelched. Instead, the convention stuck by its plank from the 1844 convention and merely reaffirmed that "Congress has no power under the Constitution to interfere with or control the domestic institutions of the several States." Yancey, almost eager to break up the nation, took defeat with no sportsmanship whatever. The time-honored resolution promising adherence to "the liberal principles embodied by Jefferson in the Declaration of Independence" was dusted off, and the revolutions erupting in Europe, "prostrating thrones and erecting republics on the ruins of despotisms in the Old World," were hailed.

Beneath the rhetoric there lay trouble, however, for two sets of New York delegates had pushed their way into the convention hall. One faction, calling themselves "Progressive Democrats" (Barnburners to their enemies), trooped off to a separate meeting in upstate New York that had all the earmarks of a disaster. Van Buren was their hero, and though Lewis Cass won the Baltimore nomination handily, the bitterness of the former president's crowd was disquieting. A Democrat was supposed to bury his troubles at the convention, not carry them home in a bag.

Cass's nomination was a distinct move toward middle ground by the Democratic leadership. The Liberty (antislavery) party had picked two lesser-known politicians and was groping for support when a conglomerate of dissidents converged on Buffalo to organize the Free-Soil party. Resolved to "maintain the rights of Free Labor against the aggressions of the Slave Power, and to secure Free Soil for a Free People," the delegates embraced Van Buren as their standard-bearer. A group of disillusioned Democrats shrieked with enthusiasm as their platform spit out a challenge to the regular Democrats. "We accept the issue which the Slave Power has forced upon us, and to their demand for more Slave States and more Slave Territory, our calm but final answer is: No more Slave States and no more Slave Territory." For the gauntlet thus thrown down, Van Buren got a total of nine votes in the entire state of Virginia.

Furious regular Democrats, angry at Van Buren for accepting the Free-Soil nomination, missed the message. Perhaps they had been misled by the way the 1844 ticket had been fashioned and carried to victory. Then, Robert J. Walker, a gifted northern-born Mississippian who knew how to unite sectional hopes and balance them against fears, had easily moved a political unknown into the White House. "The easy success of Walker's dynamic formula . . . fascinated the slavocrats and gave them a fatuous obsession as to their own invincibility," a modern scholar has observed.* Van Buren's third hat in the ring should have warned party leaders that the ground swell behind the old president's candidacy was far more than a mere popularity contest. The excitement caused by the Wilmot and King resolutions had touched off one of the deepest emotional reactions in American history. When an old party war-horse such as William Cullen Bryant pulled out of the regular lineup and switched the support of his influential New York *Evening Post* to the Free-Soil candidate, there was no surer sign that the old base of Democratic strength in a key state had eroded. The

*Binkley, *American Political Parties*, 149.

older splinter parties had been nativist oriented or (like the Work-ingmen's party) had too narrow a base, but the antislavery plat-form magnetized and pulled together old Know-Nothings, new Whigs, and ancient northern Democrats.

Van Buren turned out to be the Democratic spoiler. "Cass had declared himself against the prohibition of slavery in the territo-ries," the *Evening Post* noted; "Taylor had said nothing on the subject." So a mute candidate won New York, but Cass and Van Buren together had outpolled Taylor by 16,000 votes. Pennsylva-nia also turned on the Democrats, so that Cass lost by an electoral count of 163 to 127. Taylor won because the Democracy could not lose in New York and Pennsylvania and gain the lost 62 votes elsewhere. The Free-Soilers had made the difference, for in eleven states they picked up sizable blocs in the legislatures, and in Con-gress they captured thirteen seats. Cass carried Ohio, but in the statehouse a Free-Soiler-and-Democrat coalition sent Salmon P. Chase to the Senate.

The Whig party had no platform at all. Instead they whipped up resolutions that were, in effect, a panegyric for Taylor without any practical program. Voters ignored this oversight, and the fact that Taylor carried more slave states than free ones (eight to seven) was proof that sectionalism was still not a key factor in presiden-tial politics. Although it may have been true, as Van Buren said during the campaign, that "the minds of nearly all mankind have been penetrated by a conviction of the evils of slavery," the real break in party alignments over the slavery question was postponed by adroit politicians who exploited the voters' lethargy.

Cass turned over in his mind the narrowness of his loss and thought ahead to 1852. Meanwhile, the nation was confronted with the problem posed by California statehood. The gold rush, with all its lures, had brought thousands into the northern section of California and made admission a hot topic in Sacramento and Washington. Taylor took the same position as Polk—to let California come in on its own terms, slave or free. The difficulty was that the United States were now evenly balanced, with fifteen free and fifteen slave states. Southerners realized that California was certain to be free, as a constitutional convention soon indicated. That meant two more free-state senators, and this gnawed at the vitals of the slave-state politicians, who looked at the map and saw all that northern territory (some organized, some not) and then glanced at the relatively small area below the thirty-sixth parallel that was potential slave country.

Henry Clay, not a Democrat since his youth, came up with a solution that postponed the day of reckoning for the diehard slavery men. What became the Compromise of 1850 permitted California to enter the Union as a free state, abolished the slave trade in the District of Columbia (but not slavery), unhitched the New Mexico Territory from any free-state movement, and gave the South a tougher fugitive slave law. Taylor opposed the plan but the Democrats bullied enough senators into line in the hope that a sectional schism could be avoided. Senate Democrats Cass, Douglas, and Jefferson Davis twisted elbows, and New York merchants sent Congress a petition, bearing 25,000 signatures, supporting the compromise. Out of sixty senators, only four voted for the entire package, but after Taylor's death (following a hot Fourth of July, when he drank too many iced potations), the piecemeal compromise was patched together.

Greeley despised the Fugitive Slave Act and was unreconciled. "Is there any use in throwing up rockets to warn the wilfully blind?" he chided the Democratic "doughfaces." But in the South, *De Bow's Review* was equally unhappy. "The final act is not yet, but soon. There is a precedent in the British [emancipation]. . . . *They will use the precedent.* We know the rest." The motion to admit California as a free state had the support of seventeen Democrats and fifteen Whigs. The margins had become razor thin, but they were still margins. (Once in the Union, California went Democratic to the hilt, electing a Democratic governor, congressmen, and senators.)

Although moderates hailed the compromise, neither party wanted to take full credit for all its features. In Georgia, the angry governor called for a state convention once the California statehood bill had passed. Talk of secession was in the air, but Georgia Unionists scurried about, fused the Union Democrats with their Whig counterparts, and won control of the convention. Instead of blaring forth with a call for secession, the delegates approved a moderate "Georgia Platform," which praised the compromise but warned northerners that any tipping of the delicate balance would disrupt the Union. Aging Thomas Ritchie, who became the party's spokesman when he started the Washington *Union* at Polk's request, was upbraided by southern extremists for supporting the compromise. Ritchie's memory stretched back almost fifty years, so that he knew the value of party allies in northern states; but a caucus of forty-four disgusted southern congressmen called for a new party newspaper to support the Dixie interest. Ritchie bowed to the pressure but fired a last warning from his "political deathbed." To the North he cautioned that "the South is in earnest" and urged Democrats to deny the presidential nomination to any man who truckled to the demands of "fanatics" from either section.

The "fanatics" were crowding into the limelight, however, with much talk of "principles over party," a distinction that has wrecked the Democrats more than once. Ritchie's slogan, "The rights of the states and the union of the states," offended the growing band of political activists who were dissatisfied with the regular parties—the Democrats because they did too much, the Whigs because they did too little. A major crisis in the nation's body politic was at hand.

The decade following the Compromise of 1850 was in many ways one of the most exciting, and certainly the most tense, in American political history. What kept the lid from blowing off? A lingering loyalty to the Democratic party must be part of the answer. The venerable men, most of whom had started their political careers as Democrats of one sort or another, passed from the scene in rapid order. First Clay, then Calhoun, Webster, and Ritchie went to their graves. Younger men—Buchanan, Stephen A. Douglas, William H. Seward, Weed—eagerly moved in to fill the vacuum with a sense of opportunism that did not adapt well to the changing conditions of the 1850s. The bread-and-butter issues, such as a national bank or a lower tariff, were submerged in the din created by fears concerning the expansion of slavery.

The nation's sanity was preserved, in part, by the greatest of all panaceas for political fevers: prosperity. A railroad-building boom gave a push to the infant iron and boiler industries, while a nation still predominantly of farmers and planters sent cotton, tobacco, corn, and wheat to global markets in prodigious quantities. In 1850, cotton and tobacco accounted for 62 percent of the country's exports ($134 million); wheat and corn came up far behind with 20 percent. Citizens reaping fortunes in intersectional banking, real estate, and commerce held no brief for either Whig or Democratic radicals who blithely spoke of disunion as a blessing, provided slavery was abolished. Men of means in Boston and Charleston lined up with the conservative Democrats, so that without anybody's conniving, the party of Jefferson and the little man was clearly becoming dominated by an oligarchy struggling to keep King Cotton on top in the South and Prince Dollar enthroned in the North. In short, had the Jeffersonian Democracy turned into a dollar-grubbing slavocracy? Critics thought they had the answer.

After Taylor's death the new president, Millard Fillmore, veered toward middle ground, and the Whigs, as usual, drifted into the political shoals. In state after state the Democrats proved resilient, reviving hopes that the slavery issue would lie dormant. Thus Democratic prospects for the 1852 presidential race ranged from mild to unbounded optimism. The main problem was picking the right candidate. Cass was too old, Douglas was too young, and in between lay a political graveyard. Sam Houston's candidacy, after a brief flurry, was stillborn. Levi Woodbury, the New England favorite, died just as his campaign was attracting attention. Southerners were touting "Young Hickory," William Butler of Kentucky, until he stubbed his toe with some plain talk on slavery that scared the northern wing of the party. Buchanan, as always, was eager for the nomination. The old timetables had been discarded and it was no longer necessary to hold caucuses and conventions for almost a year in advance of the November balloting. The change had come through the magic of the telegraph key, which permitted the faithful in St. Louis and Chicago to know what occurred in Baltimore on the same day it happened.

The idea of a balanced ticket appealed to all factions of the party, but the southerners insisted that the nominee must be friendly toward the Compromise of 1850, and they were particularly insistent on enforcement of the Fugitive Slave Law. Douglas talked wildly about annexing Cuba, an idea that was acceptable since it would put more slave territory under the Stars and Stripes. As time went by, however, the gossip churned attention for the man who told his closest friends he would not run. Indeed, said Franklin Pierce of New Hampshire, even placing his name before the convention "would be utterly repugnant to [my] taste and wishes."

The worst Pierce's enemies could say about him was that he had resigned from the Senate in 1842, owing partly to his wife's dislike of Washington and partly to his fondness for bourbon and branch water. He had returned to New Hampshire, practiced law, turned down a chance to be Polk's attorney general, and served in the Mexican War as a militia brigadier. Nonetheless, his name was not placed before the Baltimore convention when the balloting began. The hopes of Cass, Buchanan, Douglas, Marcy, and a raft of favorite sons rose and fell. Cowered by the two-thirds rule, the Douglas men gave ground but fought back on the twenty-ninth ballot. Anti-Douglas men turned to Cass on the thirty-second ballot when they had 123 votes—71 short of the nomination but enough to give the old war-horse's friends hope. They called for an adjournment to line up the needed delegates during endless arm-twisting sessions in Baltimore saloons and hotel rooms. Bespattered spitoons and busy bartenders were proof that the Cass men were earnest in their quest.

The thirty-third ballot might have gone to Cass except that the southerners were wary of this man from Michigan. Cass was for squatter sovereignty, but the full implication of that stand disturbed the ringleaders from below the Mason-Dixon Line. A firm commitment to the Missouri Compromise boundary was what the key southerners wanted from their candidate. Cass's total reached 131, then he began to slide. Not until the thirty-fifth ballot was Pierce's name brought before the convention, when Virginia went for Pierce after assurances that the New Englander was solidly in favor of the 1820 compromise line. The New England states took the bait, but Pierce then had a mere 29 votes. Ten more ballots followed, with only this faithful handful sticking to Pierce. The dark horse seemed a bit too dark until Kentucky switched to Pierce on the forty-sixth ballot. There was more shuffling and some desperate last-minute maneuvering, but North Carolina started the stampede on the forty-ninth ballot when an obscure delegate made an electrifying speech for Pierce and cast all the Tarheel votes for the lawyer from Concord. The name of Pierce's home town augured well, for the party needed a candidate "safe on all dangerous questions."

Predictably, the Cass men forgot their animosity. After all, they had stopped Buchanan. And Douglas' friends were happy, for they had derailed Cass's ambitions. A serious breach in the party's national stance had been avoided. Indeed, nearly everybody was pleased except the candidate's family. Pierce's son heard of his father's nomination and wrote his mother: "I hope he won't be elected, for I should not like to live in Washington and I know you would not either." Meanwhile, the Whigs met Pierce's candidacy with a sneer. Forgetting the boomerang they shaped in 1844, they asked: "Who is Franklin Pierce?"

Democrats answered with a flood of campaign pamphlets and broadsides. The Virginia and Kentucky resolutions, still the basic party bible, were reprinted as proof of the historic continuity of the Democracy. Nathaniel Hawthorne wrote a biography of his friend that would not become a bookseller's bonanza until a century later. William Cullen Bryant's New York *Evening Post* was back in the fold extolling Pierce's talents, and Martin Van Buren, proving that bygones were bygones, wrote a letter from retirement in praise of his party's standard-bearer. Such weapons shored up the Democratic effort, but the Whigs were undaunted as they discerned a variety of chinks in Pierce's armor. They pounced on Pierce as an anti-Catholic drunk with a cowardly military record. Pierce's fondness for the bottle became a campaign issue, while he denied any complicity in a New Hampshire vote that prevented Catholics from holding state office. His neighbors in Concord testified to Pierce's sobriety, and his old comrades-in-arms gave evidence that he had left a sickbed to fight valorously.

The Whig candidate was also vulnerable. Pompous old General Winfield Scott was derided as "Old Fuss and Feathers" and, horror of horrors, was a supporter of a national bank. Scott was an inept campaigner, but the election hinged more on a salving of wounds within the Democratic party than on a voter's rejection of Pierce. Southern renegades tried to embarrass Pierce with a call for him to make a public statement on his stand on slavery. Pierce never answered their letter. The Free-Soilers in New York and New England made noises but ultimately, because they could not swallow Scott, stood pat with Pierce. Pierce and his running mate,William R. King of Alabama, easily swamped Scott, losing only four states despite a slender majority of the 3 million votes cast.

Pierce's landslide election meant that at forty-eight he would be the youngest occupant of the White House ever. But the Democrats sorely needed some youth to counterbalance the tight squeeze they had been pushed into by the old-fogy leadership, which anxiously sought to avoid internecine battles over slavery. Almost overlooked during the presidential campaign had been the release in book form of Harriet Beecher Stowe's serial, *Uncle Tom's Cabin*, which had first appeared in a Washington newspaper. In the North the book sold by the thousands and was hailed by abolitionists as a new weapon in the arsenal against slavery. Southern apologists for slavery attacked the book as a wretched misrepresentation of their institution. Mrs. Stowe's best seller, the lackadaisical enforcement of the Fugitive Slave Act and the obstreperous pleas of the *Liberator* for immediate emancipation soon revived the suspicions of southerners in both the Whig and Democratic parties.

The northern Democrats wanted to keep the lid on the slavery issue. There were problems in the country beyond the slavery question that the party needed to tackle—a railroad linking the two coasts, a homestead bill that would favor settlers over speculators, and a fair tariff policy—but it was hard to talk about these matters when the extremists were screeching vindictive proslavery slogans to counter abolitionist demands. Prosperity provided the leavening agent as cotton reached forty-one cents a pound in 1853 (up from nineteen cents in 1848) and sea-island cotton exports jumped from 8.3 million pounds in 1851 to over 12 million pounds the next year. Voters patted their thick pocketbooks and by 1853 the Democrats had a congressional majority, most of the state legislatures, and the governorships in all but a handful of the thirty-one states. Not until the 1930s would Democrats again have such a dominating position.

"If only Pierce in 1854 had been as wise as Polk in 1848," party historian Henry Minor once observed. What he meant was that Pierce let his hand slip from the tiller of the ship of state, that is, the Missouri Compromise line which Polk had insisted upon holding, and all hell broke loose in 1854. For the next eighty years Democrats tried to explain to each other what had happened. There were lots of reasons, but they all came down to the Kansas-Nebraska bill, one of the greatest political blunders of all time, committed by a Democrat who only thought he was gaining a toe hold on the presidency. Senator Douglas jammed the bill through Congress before the country was fully aware of what was taking place. Its main purpose was to organize the Nebraska Territory, but Douglas held out a carrot for the southerners by dividing the unorganized region into two territories, specifically declaring the Missouri Compromise "inoperative and void," and permitting slavery above 36°30' if the actual settlers voted for it—a stipulation he called "popular sovereignty."

When the full impact of the Kansas-Nebraska Act hit the North, a tidal wave of reaction swept southward, gaining force until it reached Washington. There, perceptive men voiced their dismay. Senator Sam Houston predicted that if the Missouri Compromise were repealed, "I will have seen the commencement of the agitation, but the youngest child now born, will not live to witness its termination." Thirteen northern Democrats from the nation's breadbasket—Ohio, Illinois, Indiana, Iowa, and Pennsylvania—joined their southern brethren to pass the bill. Editor Bryant, back in the Democratic party, begged Pierce to veto the obnoxious bill. "To persist in the foolish scheme of Senator Douglas can only result in whittling away the Democratic party into shavings," he warned.

Pierce, loyal to his cabinet and too much inclined to listen to them (he was the only president ever to have the same cabinet through his entire term), signed the Kansas-Nebraska Act.* Jubilant proslavery Democrats danced a jig, but what they were listening to turned into a funeral dirge by the fall. The Democrats lost their places in all but two northern states; New York fell, and in Pennsylvania anti-Nebraska voters sent twenty-one men to Congress. As the *Evening Post* noted, "Men who have acted together in the same party their whole lives long find themselves dissociated . . . men who never acted together on political questions before rush into each others arms."

Droves of old-line Democrats deserted the party in New England, Ohio, Illinois, and Iowa. Only some wavering by professional politicians, ever fearful of an early commitment, restrained wholesale defections to the coalition of former Whigs, Free-Soilers, and antislavery Democrats who had met in July, 1854, at Jackson, Michigan, to establish a new party. Claiming to be true Jeffersonians, these upstarts finally called themselves Republicans and thus captured by default the standard of the Democratic party's founder. The Springfield (Massachusetts) *Republican*, preserving its honored name from Jeffersonian days, picked up the tempo and along with the New York *Tribune* gave the new party powerful weapons in the shaping war of words.

Reports of the Democratic party's death proved premature, for the combination of prosperity and a half-century of patronage kept the panic caused by the Kansas-Nebraska schism from becoming a complete rout. In fact, Pierce vetoed another internal improvements bill, and federally appointed holdovers in California made the alarms of 1850 over the free-state constitution seem unwarranted. Undeniably, the North was gaining the upper hand

*In 1928 Henry A. Minor wrote of the Kansas-Nebraska Act: "This was a measure proposed by a Democratic leader, passed by a Democratic Congress and signed by a Democratic President, and the Democratic party has not yet recovered from its effects." (*The Story of the Democratic Party* [New York: Macmillan, 1928], 242).

in population (20 million people out of 31.5 million in 1850), which naturally led to some resentment of the slavocracy that held onto the Senate as its bastion. But in 1855 the Democrats regained some of the ground lost during the heat of the previous year, to the extent that Douglas wrote a southern friend, "The tide is now completely turned. The torrent of fanaticism has been rolled back almost everywhere." Moreover, the Irish and German immigrants were still Democrats, and the New York *Staats Zeitung* reflected a common fear when it recoiled from the threats implicit in the nativists' chants in the Know-Nothing party ranks.

Despite everything the southern Democrats could do, Kansas was still trying to gain admission as a state with an honest constitution.* Senator Charles Sumner of Massachusetts unleashed an attack on the Democrats in his "Crime against Kansas" speech, which included a personal attack on a veteran South Carolina colleague. A kinsman of the South Carolinian, Democratic Representative Preston Brooks, strode onto the floor of the Senate and beat Sumner with a cane until the Yankee was unconscious. The incident revealed the bitterness that was taking hold of a nation that had once worshiped at the shrine of majority rule. "In the main," said the Richmond *Enquirer*, "the press of the South applaud the conduct of Mr. Brooks. . . . We consider the act good in conception, better in execution, and best of all in consequence." The "vulgar abolitionists in the Senate . . . have been suffered to run too long without collars. They must be lashed into submission." This was no way to bind up wounds or promote national harmony, but the southern oligarchy had a friend in the White House, so they faced the 1856 presidential contest with almost arrogant optimism.

In a break with tradition, the Democrats trooped to Cincinnati for their 1856 convention, passed a platform that still hailed

---

*A stacked convention at Lecompton had produced a constitution allowing slavery, which Kansas voters rejected—1,926 for and 11,812 against.

"the liberal principles" of founder Jefferson, but went on to endorse the Kansas-Nebraska Act "as embodying the only sound and safe solution of the 'slavery question.'" "We recognize the right of the people of all the Territories . . . acting through the legally and fairly expressed will of a majority of actual residents . . . to form a Constitution, with or without domestic slavery." With the Irish and German immigrants (most of them Catholic) already a sizable voting bloc, the platform welcomed more with a swipe at the xenophobic Know-Nothings in which it condemned "a political crusade . . . against Catholic and foreign-born" contrary to "the spirit of toleration and enlarged freedom which peculiarly distinguishes the American system of popular government."

A few fist fights between the Missouri "free" Democrats and their proslavery rivals enlivened the convention, but Buchanan led on the first ballot and finally reached a two-thirds majority on the seventeenth tally. Douglas' candidacy fizzled because he was tainted with his "popular sovereignty" leanings, but Buchanan had been safely packed off to England as the American minister and thus had missed the Kansas-Nebraska imbroglio.

Meanwhile the Know-Nothings, after a fast start, began losing their backers. The old Whigs defaulted, and the new Republicans looked for a winner in the fabled military hero and former Democrat, John C. Fremont. "The Republican party has taken the place occupied by the Democratic party, while modern Democracy has fallen far behind ancient Federalism," Greeley told thousands of New York *Tribune* readers. The new party's slogan—"Free Soil, Free Speech, Fremont"—was almost too clever. The Republican chieftains, who soon realized that Fremont's name would not appear on southern ballots, directed their whole effort at the North, particularly populous New York and Pennsylvania. The old New York-Pennsylvania-Virginia axis, which had held together from Jefferson to Pierce, had to be broken if Fremont was to win.

Pierce then made one of his best moves. He appointed a prominent Pennsylvania Democrat as territorial governor of Kansas, and John White Geary decisively cleaned up the mess made by pro-slavery appointees in "Bleeding Kansas." Geary's fair-mindedness was widely advertised in the Democratic newspapers as proof that the Democrats still meant business when they spoke of majority rule "of actual residents" in the territories. "Business is reviving," the St. Louis *Republican* reported, "confidence is restored; men talk more kindly of each other; the axe, the saw, and the anvil are heard in their different vocations." New York and every state north of the Hudson went for Fremont, but a determined effort by free-soil Democrats and Whigs fell short in Pennsylvania, which was Buchanan's native state. That victory, along with majorities in Illinois and Indiana, gave Buchanan the fifty-one votes needed to counterbalance Fremont's New England sweep (not until 1932 would New England again vote Democratic). Also, all the South, except Maryland, plus California fell into the Democratic column. The Republicans cut into the Democrats' majorities in Congress, however, and two old party wheelhorses, Lewis Cass and Henry Dodge, were defeated.

The bunting for Buchanan's inaugural probably was still in place when the new president was handed a crisis almost as monumental as the Kansas-Nebraska time bomb. On March 6, 1857, the Supreme Court issued its opinion in *Scott* v. *Sanford*—the famous Dred Scott case—which held that the Missouri Compromise had indeed been unconstitutional, that Congress could not interfere with slavery in the territories without violating the Fifth Amendment. As if to rub salt in the wound, the court said that a black slave had "no rights which the white man was bound to respect." For the North the worst part was the court's declaration that even the territorial legislatures could not prevent slavery. Until a state was admitted into the Union, the existence of slavery was guaranteed by the Constitution.

Here was another hornet's nest for the bachelor president and his party. In their wildest dreams the slavery men had not planned to push slavery into Oregon and Minnesota, but now the highest tribunal in the land said they could. And since a majority of the justices were southerners, including Chief Justice Taney, it seemed to thousands of northerners that "the South was engaged in an aggressive attempt to extend the peculiar institution so far that it could no longer be considered peculiar."*

Admittedly, it would have taken a superman to have handled the newest flare-up with dignity and magnanimity. But Buchanan was neither saint nor superman. He was a politician, and so he looked for a safe way out. A Unionist of Jackson's stamp would probably have ignored the Dred Scott decision, but Buchanan cut the ground from under an able territorial governor in Kansas (Robert J. Walker, the Pennsylvanian-turned-Mississippian) who had succeeded Geary. Ignoring the governor's advice to disregard a proslavery constitution from Kansas as a trumped-up job, Buchanan sent the spurious document on to Congress and asked that Kansas be admitted as a slave state.

Even party loyalist Douglas could not stomach this blunder. The outrage of newspaper editors, Union Democrats, and most of the northern Democrats in Congress was proof that this presidential error could not go unchallenged. Douglas carried his five-foot-four-inch frame into the White House and tried to persuade Buchanan to back down. Well aware that he owed his election to the loyal slave-state Democrats, Buchanan tried to chastise Douglas by blocking the Illinois senator's patronage and firing his friends. Then in a fair vote the Kansas settlers rejected the proslavery constitution, and when Buchanan still tried to force it upon Congress, the Kansans voted it down again. A last effort to make Kansans approve the so-called Lecompton constitution or bide their time until the territory had ninety thousand residents was blackmail of the worst sort. So Kansas remained a territory, and Buchanan was

* John A. Garraty, *The American Nation* (New York: Harper & Row, 1966). 390.

still president; but the stench created by all the maneuvering wafted northward. Each whiff made converts to the Republican party and weakened the Democrats. Buchanan, convinced he was only doing the right thing, was storing all the dynamite next to the furnace.

Unable to perceive the winds of change that were blowing against political props for slavery, Buchanan and his cabinet were then hit by something they could understand—a collapse of the nation's vaunted prosperity. Touched off by the bankruptcy of an Ohio insurance company, the panic of 1857 had the usual aftereffects of ruined speculators, bank closings, and longer breadlines in the cities. A winter visitor to Iowa City noticed that "almost every one here who isn't getting drunk is getting rich, or thinks he is." The crash came that spring and with it sobering second thoughts about the railroad boom, the cotton boom, the western lands boom. The New York Democrats, who had fallen back into their old habit of feuding among themselves, joined forces to thrash the new Republicans in the state elections. As long as slavery was not the issue, Democrats did well in the North.

When the shuffling for Senate seats began, however, the Republicans knew their quips about slavery would damage Democrats in every northern hamlet. Douglas came up for reelection in 1858, with Buchanan eager to see the Little Giant get his comeuppance. To keep his presidential hopes alive, Douglas had to win in Illinois. Pitted against Abraham Lincoln, Douglas finally gained enough votes in the state legislature to keep his seat. But Lincoln earned a moral victory and his trenchant debate had forced Douglas into a renewal of his "popular sovereignty" pledge, which, since the Dred Scott decision, was now old hat to some Democrats and positively enraging to the southern extremists. Elsewhere the Buchanan Democrats were on the defensive, as twenty-five antiadministration congressmen won in Pennsylvania, New York, and New Jersey.

The Democrats' archenemy, Horace Greeley, gloated when

Douglas was reelected, for the Republican editor knew that the southern wing of the party could not stand Douglas and would not support him in 1860. "Mr. Douglas would be the strongest candidate that the Democratic party could present for President," Greeley predicted when the returns came in, "but they will *not* present him. The old leaders won't endure it. As he is doomed to be slaughtered at Charleston it is good policy to fatten him meantime." Simple arithmetic was on Greeley's side. If Fremont could carry the North by 100,000 votes in 1856, a Republican candidate in 1860 might conceivably win the presidency by sweeping the free states and leaving to the South their short end of the electoral college stick. Certainly Buchanan was doing his best to alienate the North and West. He vetoed another homestead bill and then (like a good Democrat) boldly announced he would do the same to all river and harbor bills that came to his desk. The southern Democrats were also unenthusiastic about the proposed legislation to link eastern railroads to California and Oregon. A Minnesota Democrat, dismayed by the rejection of the homestead bill, pointed a finger at the southern wing of his party. "I . . . have been attached to the Democratic party from my boyhood," Representative James Cavanaugh said. Yet the southern Democrats, "to a man almost, vote against the free, independent labor of the North and West."

Meanwhile, a "stop Douglas" move was generating steam in the South. Circumstances played into the anti-Douglas faction's hands. At the 1856 convention the delegates had casually picked Charleston for their next gathering. The intervening alarm over the Dred Scott case, the Kansas troubles, John Brown's raid, and anger over "popular sovereignty" now made a convention in the heartland of southern extremism perfect—for the Republicans. The fire-eating Democrats figured on either having things their own way in Charleston or bolting the party and splitting votes exactly as the Know-Nothings had done in 1856 to assure Buchanan's victory. But this time, the split would bring a Republican into office and hasten the breakup of the Union which Yancey and his extremist friends thought inevitable and (for the South) beneficial.

Deceived by the wild cheering of the Charleston galleries, the fire-eaters tried to push through a platform plank that would have made the Dred Scott decision a permanent fixture, while the northern Democrats wanted to soften the harsh dictum by saying that the party would "abide by and faithfully carry out" decisions on slavery handed down by the Supreme Court. The difference seems small now, but it was big enough then to send the convention into a turmoil. Buchanan's supporters, eager to embarrass Douglas, blocked the nominating process until after the platform had been adopted—a move that hurt the Illinois senator and helped widen the breach between the two most vocal wings of the party. The battle wore on, with both sides switching votes on the slavery plank as they tried to gain every advantage. Pleas for party harmony were useless. "We are for principles," a Mississippian shouted. "Damn the party! "

Adoption of the two-thirds rule meant Douglas' chances were slender, but when fifty-nine southern delegates stormed out of the hall, it was obvious no candidate could be selected. After ten days of bitter squabbling, the convention adjourned, scheduled to re-convene in Baltimore in June. When the New York delegates threw their support behind Douglas at Baltimore, the toned-down plank on slavery was passed, and Douglas was nominated on the second ballot. Acrimony was prevented by the withdrawal of several southern delegations, starting with the march of Virginians from the hall. The southern dissenters trooped to Richmond and, with "doughface" Caleb Cushing of Massachusetts in the speaker's chair, went through the motions by adopting their rejected plank on the immutability of slavery in the territories. Buchanan's men were calling the shots, and to no one's alarm Vice-President

John C. Breckinridge of Kentucky was nominated handily. Not content to leave matters there, Buchanan publicly declared that the party had not, in fact, made a regular nomination. In short, to keep Douglas out of the White House, Buchanan did all he could to hand the presidency to the opposition.

Buchanan's efforts to deny Douglas the presidency were one of the few successes he had achieved as president. His party was rent with faction, his cabinet was dominated by men who expected secession and perhaps welcomed it, and Old Buck sat in his chair staring out at the unfinished Washington Monument full of bitterness.

Meanwhile the Republicans, perfectly willing to surrender all rights to be on ballots south of the Mason-Dixon Line, had gleefully smashed the dreams of William H. Seward and nominated Abraham Lincoln. Douglas made what was regarded as an unseemly gesture; he campaigned hard and made speech after speech supporting his ideas on slavery in the territories. Breckinridge did not campaign; but he did not need to, since only he and the Constitutional Union candidate were on all the southern ballots and Lincoln was on none.* As the jubilant Republican strategists had figured, every free state except New Jersey went whole hog for Lincoln, leaving the Democratic party in a shambles. The railsplitter had 1.8 million votes to Douglas' 1.3 million, but the shorter candidate from Illinois garnered only three electoral votes from New Jersey and nine from Missouri.

Smug fire-eaters thought they had finally made their point. Lincoln was moving toward Washington and they were moving out of the Union. The party of Thomas Jefferson had come to this impasse, a fact not lost on Lincoln when he had declined a speaking engagement at a Republican rally in Boston, held to honor

---

*The Constitutional Union party was also known derisively as the Do-Nothing party, for it had no platform and no program except to preserve the Union and uphold the Constitution.

Jefferson. Lincoln observed how curious it was "that those supposed to descend politically from the party opposed to Jefferson should now be celebrating his birthday . . . while those claiming political descent from him have ceased to breathe his name everywhere." Then Lincoln launched a fitting anecdote: "I remember once being amused at seeing two partially intoxicated men engage in a fight with their greatcoats on, which fight, after a long and rather harmless contest, ended in each having fought himself out of his own coat, and *into* that of the other. If the two leading parties of the day are really identical with the two in the days of Jefferson and Adams, they have performed the same feat as the two drunken men." * And so it must have seemed to those 1,837,000 Americans who voted for Lincoln in 1860.

For fifty-six years in a six-decade span, nominal Democrats or real ones had been in the White House. The party's appeal to this nation of farmers and planters had been awesome. Then the party's leadership misinterpreted the underlying causes of Pierce's landslide victory in 1852, and Democrats were buried under an avalanche set in motion by their leaders' blunders, stubbornness, and self-delusion. Only two Democrats would reach the White House during the next seventy-two years. The party would soon be fighting for its very life. Under Buchanan, the slavocracy had captured the Democracy and almost destroyed it.

---

*Quoted in Merrill Peterson, *The Jefferson Image in the American Mind* (New York: Oxford University Press, 1960), 163.

FIVE

Waving the Bloody Shirt

Generations of Americans grew up listening to newspaper editors and professors who had neatly broken American history into two periods. From 1800 to 1860 was the Democratic era, and from 1860 to 1932 was the Republican period. This was all too neat. Some pundits said the first era permitted the exploitation of the black man and the second allowed the exploitation of our vast natural resources. To some extent the nineteenth century was the Age of Exploitation, but it was also the century of vastly changing political manners and morals. The Democrats, after almost committing hari-kiri, managed to survive. But the wonder is that the Republicans lost a single presidential election between 1860 and 1912; only by a fluke could a Democrat win in much of the North. A financial panic, an election campaign slur against the Irish voters, or a split in the Republican ranks was needed to keep the Democrats from sliding into oblivion.

The election of Lincoln had left the Democratic party in a shambles. Greeley had correctly predicted how the Republicans might win: "An Anti-Slavery man per se cannot be elected but a Tariff, River-and-Harbor, Pacific Railroad, Free-Homestead man *may* succeed." On these matters alone the Democrats were whipped, for the party and its leaders were either hostile or indifferent to issues that drew to the polling places thousands who were not concerned about slavery. Republicans denied that theirs was a sectional party and instead "stressed the current 'degeneracy' of the Democratic party," but in the border states many voters who had not been Democrats dropped their old Whig ties and defended the floundering party against northern attacks.* The New York business community was in a state of shock after Lincoln won. August Belmont and William B. Astor, men of considerable wealth, had appealed to rich businessmen to prevent Lincoln's election on the ground that a Democratic defeat would jeopardize nearly $200 million owed to northerners by southern customers. A million dollars was said to have passed through the party coffers and the Tammany Hall tills in a vain effort to elect Douglas.

Meanwhile, Buchanan fretted out his term in Washington, while an exhausted Douglas took to his sickbed and died in June, 1861. The seven seceding states walked out of Congress and left the Republicans in charge. Reasonable efforts to reassure the fire-eating secessionists that they had nothing to fear from Lincoln make strange reading now, for the southern extremists who were in control itched for a fight. Eager to prove he was not a blind partisan, Lincoln chose Gideon Welles as his secretary of the navy. "I need a man of Democratic antecedents from New England," he reasoned. It was too late to be rational, but Lincoln tried.

Once the war started, optimists thought the shooting would end by late July; the pessimists figured it might take until Christmas. Essentially leaderless, the northern Democrats in Congress gave Lincoln what he sought and vowed that their patriotic duty was clear. As the state militia units were filled for federal duty, Democrats pushed into the recruiting halls and harangued governors for commissions. In Illinois it was said that forty out of sev-

*Hofstadter, *The Idea of a Party System*, 268.

enty regiments had Democrats as commanding officers. Lincoln himself did not ask a man's party background when he signed commissions; he appointed six major generals in the early days of the war, five of whom were Democrats. Of the 110 brigadier generals appointed that first year, 80 were Democrats.

Then came the shock of Bull Run, the panic retreat back to Washington, and a shifting away from bipartisanship in Congress towards a relentless effort to entrench the Republicans as the only "win-the-war" party. They had enough fuel to build a warm fire under the Democrats, for in the breadbasket of the nation, so-called Peace Democrats were saying that the war ought to be called off. Congressman Clement Vallandigham of Ohio was their spokesman, and their motto became: The Union as it was, the Constitution as it is. In New York City, Democratic Mayor Fernando Wood had won election despite opposition from Tammany Hall, and he seriously proposed that the nation's largest city declare itself neutral.

There were early signs that a concerted effort to discredit the Democrats was afoot. George W. Jones, a former United States senator from Iowa, had written a friendly letter to his old friend Jefferson Davis while still serving as the American minister at Bogota, New Granada. He returned home in December, 1861, and was thrown into jail. The fact that Jones had written to Davis before the war started was ignored. After a few months in the Fort Lafayette federal prison, Jones was quietly released, having never been charged or brought to trial.

What happened to Jones soon became standard medicine for old-line northern Democrats who would not keep quiet. In Dubuque, Iowa, scores of Irish and German immigrants in the river town had flocked to the banners of the Democracy during the Know-Nothing scare of 1856. In 1862 they rallied around Dennis Mahony, editor of the Dubuque *Herald* and Democratic candidate for Congress. Warned that public opinion would not tolerate criticism of the war effort, Mahony shot back a scorching reply. "It is not those who criticize the flagitious acts of the Administration . . . who give aid or comfort to the enemy, but those who approve of and applaud the acts of despotism which have brought the Federal Government into disparaging contrast with the despotisms of the Old World."

Federal marshals, armed with an executive order "Relating to Political Prisoners," needed little urging to see treason in such remarks. Mahony was arrested in the middle of the night and shuttled from jail to jail until he wound up in Washington's Old Capitol prison. Other Peace Democrats in Illinois (including a recently elected congressman), Iowa, and Ohio—most of them newspaper editors and lawyers—were rounded up in similar fashion and sent to eastern jails to cool off. John W. Kees, editor of the Circleville (Ohio) *Watchman*, earned his bread and water diet by blasting the local postmaster (who allegedly urged Kees's arrest) as "a traitor, a thief, to the extent of his very limited brains, and if he has any of that article, they are the brains of a slimy viper!"* Most of these Democrats were released after the congressional elections. But the word *Copperhead* was creeping into the political language of the day, as a term synonymous (in Republican circles) with Democrat.

The war drums rolled until the toll was sickening. "Little Mac"—General George B. McClellan—had taken over command of the Union army and was going to outflank Richmond for a clean stroke and end the war. But nothing worked out as McClellan planned, and since he was known to be a Democrat, the whole Peninsular campaign looked suspicious to his critics in Congress. Lincoln backed McClellan, suffered through the general's "bad case of the slows," and finally gave up. Anguishing over slavery, Lincoln drafted his Emancipation Proclamation. All the issues of the war were suddenly merged into one moral judgment.

*Wood Gray, *The Hidden Civil War* (New York: Viking, 1942), 88.

Lincoln went one way and Congress went another after the war settled into a bloodbath pitting inept Union generals against Lee and his lieutenants. Long casualty lists in northern newspapers scared Republicans who were uneasy about Lincoln's commitment to party principles. The lanky commander in chief was more interested in winning the war than elections, which struck some professional politicians as a bad sign. Then the northern Democrats, some of them for peace, some for a tough war policy, but all dead set against emancipation of slaves as a declared national policy, made substantial gains in the 1862 congressional races. The North wanted to end slavery in the South, but exactly what was wanted elsewhere was still not clear.

Local elections had been disturbingly close for Radical Republicans, who suspected all Democrats. Fusion tickets that blended Republican candidates with War Democrats took most of New England, but in Rhode Island, Democrat William Sprague won without opposition. In Maine, Republicans won but their plurality was cut and a Democrat unseated the Republican incumbent in Congress. In Oregon, a War Democrat ran for Congress and a Peace Democrat tried for the statehouse, but both lost to the Union party ticket headed by a former Democrat. Regular Democrats won in Ohio, Indiana, and Pennsylvania. Horatio Seymour and the New York Democrats marched to victory, supported by a state convention platform that denounced the arbitrary arrests of civilians, nearly all of whom seemed to be of the Democratic persuasion. The New York delegation in Congress, which had been overwhelmingly Republican, was replaced by eighteen Democrats and twelve Republicans. Regular Democrats running for Congress in Illinois beat five War Democrats and captured the state legislature, then promptly chose a Peace Democrat for the Senate. War Democrats won elections in Missouri, Wisconsin, Delaware, and New Jersey. Out-and-out Republican wins were rare. In Kansas a War Democrat lost to a former Douglas Democrat who had switched to the Republicans. But the Ohio "dove," Vallandigham, was soundly defeated to the consternation of the Mount Vernon *Banner*, which held that the Peace Democrat's loss was "greatly lamented by all good Union-loving Democrats."*

Lincoln went about his business in search of a winning general, but the Radical Republicans had other ideas. The House set up a Joint Committee on the Conduct of the War, which soon launched its witch hunts and laid down a propaganda barrage that ripped holes in the Democratic ranks in every northern state save one—New York. Elsewhere, the zealous Radicals made Democratic generals into scapegoats, demanded that all citizens support the war without a whimper of criticism, and insisted that a slur against the Lincoln administration was as treasonous as a Confederate sniper's bullet. Public pressure mounted after the enormous Union casualties at Chancellorsville and Fredericksburg sent waves of depression across the North. Then, when conscription laws were passed and fell hardest on the Democratic wards in New York, the ensuing draft riots were laid at the doorstep of Peace Democrats. Manton Marble, the outspoken Democratic editor of the New York *World*, called such charges trumped-up Republican buncombe, but then a false report of a draft call in the *World* made Marble squirm.

The northern casualty lists were dreary reading and made the draft inevitable but unpopular. "What the conscript bill means," the Democratic Iowa City *State Press* declared, is "your money or your life." Many Democratic newspapers hinted that a vote for the Democracy in 1863 would prevent enforcement of the draft law, but the ambush of two federal marshals in Iowa who were searching for draft dodgers quickly took on political overtones. The murders were blamed on a subversive militia group, the "Democrat Rangers," allegedly formed to prevent operation of the draft law.

*Quoted in Christopher Dell, *Lincoln and the War Democrats* (Cranbury, N.J.: Fairleigh Dickinson University Press, 1975), 174.

Republicans also claimed that a conspiracy was afoot in the North, working through a secret society known as the Knights of the Golden Circle. Incidents varying from a train wreck to a spoiled barrel of army pork were blamed on the knights, whose existence took on life mainly in Republican newspaper columns. Nonetheless, the knights must have seemed real to midwesterners such as the one who recalled that most of the knights "were the ignorant scum of the democratic party, misled into wrong doing."

The Democrats no longer rated a capital *D* in such circles, which widened as the dead, wounded, and missing lists reached into the hundreds of thousands. By 1864 there was speculation as to whether the Democrats should even hold a convention, but on July 4, August Belmont called the delegates to order in Chicago. No serious opposition to General McClellan developed (he was the party's only war hero, if indeed it had one), and he was chosen on the first ballot. A Peace Democrat was picked for the second spot, and the brief platform called for a speedy restoration "of all the States to their rights in the Union" with an amnesty for errant southerners. Immediate efforts to end hostilities were recommended, so that "peace may be restored on the basis of the Federal Union of the States." This clause, drafted by the Vallandigham coterie, was at once branded the "war-failure plank." Backed into a corner by his war record, McClellan repudiated the plank in his letter of acceptance.

The outcome of the 1864 contest was not as foreordained as hindsight makes it seem. Lincoln was too busy to campaign, and the radicals in his own party were disgusted with the moderate president's lack of party loyalty. When victory dispatches from Atlanta and Mobile Bay told voters the tide was at last turning, they responded by giving Lincoln and his new running mate (and former Democrat) Andrew Johnson a landslide-sized triumph. Lincoln and Johnson ran on the Union party ticket, the word Republican being dropped as a sleight-of-hand device that allowed former Democrats to backslide painlessly. McClellan, who carried New Jersey, Delaware, and Kentucky, won 12 electoral votes; Lincoln had all the rest—212 electoral votes. If there were any surprises, they came from New York, where Lincoln won by less than 7,000 votes, and Pennsylvania, where the Union Republican ticket led by only 20,000 ballots. Absentee ballots from soldiers were overwhelmingly Republican, a fact not lost on Republican party leaders who looked beyond the day when Lee would finally surrender. Benjamin Wade, Thaddeus Stevens, and Charles Sumner were not going along with Lincoln's mild Reconstruction plans, and they certainly did not want the eleven seceded states, bound to be Democratic, hustled back into the Union with full voting rights in time for the 1868 elections.

Lincoln's assassination made the Radical Republicans' ascendancy certain. Andrew Johnson soon fell from favor when he tried to tone down the vindictive plans of the Radicals, and to the Republican high priests his decline was further proof that the president fitted their stereotyped image of a Democrat. For Johnson was not only a former Democrat, he was also a drunk. The only item missing was the "bloody shirt," which was soon waved with fervor. "All Democrats were not rebels, but all the rebels were Democrats," the Republican press and the Radicals in Congress sang in unison. Spoken to a crowd where the lives of listeners had been touched by the carnage at Cold Harbor or Petersburg, the message was all too clear. Johnson was discredited, Democrats were jeered when they spoke kindly of the beleaguered president, and northern voters in a wide swath from Maine through the midlands and on to Oregon forsook their old party ties. In the Midwest, opportunists tied the bell of treason on the Democratic cat and then raged in public statements. "The Democratic party may be described," Indiana's governor bellowed, "as a common sewer and loathesome receptacle, into which is emptied every element of treason North and South, and every element of inhumanity and barbarism which has dishonored the age."

There was some backlash, of course. John Quincy Adams II, whose New England credentials as a Boston Brahmin were unquestioned, was "so repelled by the policies of the Black [Radical] Republicans who took over national leadership after Lincoln's death . . . he switched to the Democratic party." This descendant of two presidents "ran five times for governor on the Democratic ticket in Massachusetts and lost every time, because . . . running as a Democrat in New England in the years following the Civil War was equivalent to running on the Communist ticket" after World War II.*

Social pressure was intense. A student at the University of Iowa, wearing a copper penny badge to show his Peace Democrat sympathies, was expelled amid protests from the Democratic newspapers. The election results told a dramatic tale of reversed loyalties. The Maine-to-California triumph trilled by orators at victory banquets had a solid basis in fact. In Maine, once a Democratic stronghold and then a nip-and-tuck state up to 1860, the Republicans captured 68 percent of the vote. And in California, overwhelmingly Democratic from 1850 to 1860, the Republicans won 56 percent of the vote. In some states, like Vermont, where Democrats had never fared too well, the party shrank until the local wags jested that a lone vote against Republican candidates was cast by the town drunk. After a half-century of Democratic-appointed officials in the territories, the Republicans now had their chance to flex the power of patronage in the West. Meanwhile, West Virginia and Nevada were dragooned into becoming states during the Civil War, thus adding to Republican majorities in Congress that had already been swelled by the admission of Kan-

*L. H. Butterfield, "A Family Tells Its Own Story," *North Carolina Historical Review*, XLIV (1972), 175.

sas in 1861. Nebraska and Colorado completed one phase of the western expansion, with Republicans elected to replace territorial Republican appointees. Political opportunism always attracts droves of lawyers, and those attorneys who wished to fare well in the new states and territories acknowledged that their future lay with the Republican party. They borrowed allusions from their eastern brethren to condemn Copperheads, former rebels, and Democrats—all in the same breath. Such loyalty would be rewarded with federal jobs in New Mexico, Arizona, and the Dakotas.

The efforts of fanatical Republicans to overwhelm and perhaps destroy the Democrats had a comic side, however, in the writings of David Ross Locke. Locke wrote dime tracts under the pseudonym of Petroleum V. Nasby, "Postmaster at Confedrit X Roads, Stait of Kentucky," in a dialect that made thousands chuckle— maybe even some Democrats. When the 1868 presidential elections loomed, Locke wrote *The Impendin Crisis uv the Dimocracy* to poke fun at the coats of many colors worn by contending Democrats. The Democracy had so many positions that "In it every sole may find rest. . . . Would he pay the debt, but pay it in greenbax? Look at Pendleton. Wood he pay it in gold? Reed Seemore's Cooper Institoot Speech. Is he a war Dimokrat? Blare is our candidate. Is he a secessionist? Wade Hampton and Booregard [both Confederate generals] run the Convenshun. Ther is an assortment uv prinsiple—let evry one choose for hisself."

Poking fun at the Democrats was great sport, but the party could not be killed by ridicule. Nor was it so dead as the Radical Republicans who had tried to hold its funeral desired. The Republican party was without a reed of support among whites in the South, a fact Ben Wade and his friends could live with since there were an overwhelming number of northern states (twenty-two, with more on the way); but the quick passage of two constitutional amendments was part of the Reconstruction package solely aimed at giving the recently freed slaves their civil rights, including the right to vote. While the Radicals held the whip, the defeated southern states painfully crawled back into the Union on the Republicans' terms. The region was divided into five military districts, with commandants empowered to protect the blacks' civil rights. Carpetbaggers held sway in most of the Old Confederacy until 1877, but the resulting bitterness only made the region into a one-party section that would exalt white supremacy long after the opposition had stopped waving the "bloody shirt."

While the South lay prostrate, the only hope for Democrats was in a holding operation, for even such Republican stalwarts as Greeley suffered pangs of conscience as the Radicals' vindictiveness seemed limitless. Greeley endeared himself to thousands of southerners when he posted bail for Jefferson Davis. And a few moderate Republicans balked at efforts directed from Washington to make the very word *Democrat* anathema whenever a monument to Union veterans was dedicated at northern courthouse lawns and cemeteries. Few Democrats were ever invited to join the Grand Army of the Republic, a Union veterans' group that practically functioned as a wing of the Republican party. Over 400,000 veterans held annual GAR encampments, took stands supporting the radicals, and went out of their way to intimidate Democrats either in Congress or trying to go there. The Fortieth Congress (March, 1867, to March, 1869) had 55 Republicans and 8 Democrats in the Senate, with none from Georgia, Mississippi, Texas, or Virginia admitted. In the House there were 174 Republicans who easily intimidated 49 Democrats and Independents. The only important issues besides Reconstruction problems concerned the tariffs and greenbacks—currency that was discounted when a contract called for gold payments. Predictably, tariffs went higher and the hard-money crowd prevailed.

King Cotton had moved over for King Corn, and the midwestern farmers who filled America's granary had also fulfilled Murat Halstead's prediction of 1860. Newsman Halstead had perceived that the midwestern Democrats were dead set against the extension of slavery: "A good many of them will eventually become the most intolerant Republican partisans." These voters were frightened by the Copperhead bogeyman and willing to listen to harangues against "rebel Democrats" until their newfound faith in the Republicans could not be shaken. The Republican party, they believed, had been responsible for preserving the Union; thus they marched in lockstep behind the banners of Republicans for most of the next three generations. Even when high tariffs hurt them, when hard money made it more difficult to pay mortgages, and when overcapitalized railroads gouged them unmercifully, the midwestern farmers stayed in the Republican party. Democratic appeals for "the same currency for the bondholder and the ploughholder" went over their heads, which they shook as stories of the Ku Klux Klan came out of the South. The pre-Civil War dream of a South-and-West alliance of farmers was a chimera.

The one man in the nation whose remarks echoed Jeffersonian principles was in the White House, but scarcely anybody was listening to President Johnson (except a few, such as the twelve Democratic senators who voted against his conviction at the impeachment trial). "Mr. Jefferson never said a truer thing than when he declared that large cities are eye sores in the body-politic," Johnson said. "Our true policy is to build up your villages, build up your rural districts, and you will have men who rely upon their own . . . and let the power of the Government remain with the middle class! "

Johnson was barely saved, but instead of a bandwagon his procession resembled a funeral as the national convention moved into its modern stage in 1868. In its New York headquarters, Tammany Hall played host to delegations from all the states. Democratic partisans upheld one of the cardinal canons of a convention—exuberant optimism. George Pendleton from Ohio pushed for a platform plank promising to pay off the war bonds in greenbacks instead of gold. Salmon P. Chase, the old Democrat who had served in Lincoln's cabinet, was now chief justice and anxious to seek the presidency. President Johnson had a few delegates, mostly southerners, who quickly gave up when their cause seemed hopeless. Former New York governor Horatio Seymour, who went to the convention to work for Chase, emerged as a dark horse after twenty-one fruitless ballots. On the twenty-second ballot Ohio switched to Seymour and the rush was on, despite the New Yorker's protest from the floor that he would not run. A genuine draft then took place while Seymour was in an anteroom. "No other American has ever received the nomination of a major party against his will," Seymour's biographer noted in 1938. (That statement was still true until 1952, when Adlai Stevenson was drafted.)

Grant was picked by the Republicans on their first ballot. If Grant had been anything before the war, he was a Democrat. There had even been talk early in 1868 that Grant might be drafted by the Democrats, but the Old Guard in charge of the Republican convention had all the machinery well oiled, and Grant the Butcher (when a Democrat) was now Grant the Savior of the Union. Republican newspapers featured reports of race problems in the South and ripped into a letter written by Seymour's running mate, Francis P. Blair, Jr., to hint that a Seymour-Blair victory would reopen all the war wounds then healing. Blair's preconvention letter had condemned the Radicals' Reconstruction program and urged that whoever won the presidency should "declare these acts null and void, compel the army to undo its usurpations at the South, disperse the carpetbag State governments, allow the white people to reorganize their own governments and elect Senators and Representatives."

Seymour, following the traditional conduct of presidential candidates, scarcely campaigned. This suited Republicans, for they picked apart the Democratic party platform which the southerners had helped write. It demanded abolition of the Freedmen's Bureau that was propping up carpetbag regimes in the South. Blair's letter was the target of Horace Greeley, who set the tone for the Republican press. "Americans!" Greeley warned, "if you want another civil war vote the Blair ticket." When Seymour was mentioned, the allusions included a charge from the in-and-out Democrat, editor William Cullen Bryant of the *Evening Post.* Bryant backed Grant and suggested that Seymour had a background of mental problems. Built on the facts of Seymour's father's suicide and his mother's senility, the story was magnified in the Republican press until it seemed that Seymour's genes would certainly lead him straight to an insane asylum.

How many voters believed such nonsense will never be known. Enough favored Grant to insure his election, but Seymour still polled 47 percent of the popular vote—and this without a single vote in his column from the unreconstructed states: Mississippi, Texas, and Virginia. Democratic victories in New York and Oregon were a hopeful sign, but Republican gains in the Carolinas, Alabama, and Florida meant that they knew how to utilize the newfound black voting strength. Democrats kept Kentucky and Georgia in line. But thousands of white southerners avoided Democratic ties after the war, and the old Whigs were particularly reluctant to help rejuvenate their former opponents. In Tennessee and Alabama old-time Whigs were said to hold the Democracy responsible for the disastrous collapse of the South. Mississississippi elected James L. Alcorn its first Republican governor. A former Whig, Alcorn was committed to working with the new black voters—only for as long as he could dominate them.

The failure of Seymour's candidacy in the Midwest was owing to skillful Republican propaganda, but there were Democrats in the midlands who thought they were paying a high price for their loyalty to the Grand Old Party. A Milwaukee newspaper complained that Wisconsin "has now consented to labor for the benefit of New England; to pay New England prices for everything we wear; take what New England will give us for our produce . . . and help enrich the moneyed aristocracy of the East."* Such discontent was not channeled into effective political action; the Democrats argued among themselves over Negro suffrage, hard-money currency, and tariff reforms. They agreed, however, that Grant's postmasters were a set of knaves. The Syracuse (New York) *Courier* editor was one of many Democratic newsmen who insisted Republican postmasters notoriously delayed delivery of the *Courier* and other Democratic newspapers. The Baldwinville postmaster was accused of occasionally throwing Democratic newspapers in the trash bin, "but when a package of loyal [Republican] newspapers reached him, the alacrity with which he flew around and put them in boxes was beautiful to behold."

The Chicago *Tribune* developed as the organ of midwestern Republicans and kept the lid on restless Republicans who fretted about high railroad rates and forty-five-cent corn. The farmers whose votes revived the Democratic party in local and state elections throughout the corn belt were interested in high commodity prices and low tariffs; but these goals ran counter to the desires of the so-called Bourbon wing of the party, which was essentially business dominated and supported by conservative Democrats. The party's purse strings were controlled by Bourbons (inventor Cyrus McCormick was a top contributor in the Midwest) who had little sympathy for reduced tariffs or civil service reforms. Thus the farm voter was left a choice between the Radicals, who at least had a program, and the poorly led Democrats, who often were unsure of what they wanted or how they would get it.

Even fate intervened to leave the Democrats in more confusion than the most spiteful Republicans could have wished. As the 1872 elections loomed, Vallandigham, trying for a comeback, whipped

---

*Quoted in Horace S. Merrill, *Bourbon Democracy of the Middle West, 1865–1896* (Seattle: University of Washington Press, 1967), 31.

up a program he labeled the New Departure. The energetic former congressman called for a civil service based on merit, graduated income taxes, and an end to public land grants to corporations. The Ohioan made fun of President Grant's wild dreams of annexing Santo Domingo, decried the Whiskey Ring scandals, and caused a host of Democratic newspaper editors to hail his ideas as the shot in the arm desperately needed by the party. Cheered at the Ohio Democratic convention, where his platform was endorsed with enthusiasm, Vallandigham returned home to defend an accused murderer. While making a point in the courtroom, the controversial Democrat placed a pistol he thought unloaded to his head, pulled the trigger, and sent a bullet into his brain. The New Departure platform died less dramatically, as yet another bizarre event took shape.

The 1872 presidential election had all the ingredients of a comic opera, except that the outcome had tragic consequences. Fed up with Grant's administration, a group calling themselves Liberal Republicans, led by Carl Schurz and Horace Greeley, held their own convention in hopes that a ticket featuring an honest man might capture the nation's fancy. Charles Francis Adams, a Boston Adams and descendant of two presidents, probably could have had their nomination but for his Brahmin mannerisms. Somewhat in despair the Liberal Republicans compromised on Greeley. Then, incredibly, the Democratic convention chose Greeley by default; they had nothing better to offer. The irony of the shaping contest moved General William Tecumseh Sherman to remark to his Republican brother: "Grant who never was a Republican is your candidate and Greeley who never was a Democrat . . . is the Democratic candidate." Indeed, Greeley had been pummeling Democrats since 1840, and Republicans could reach in the dark for campaign ammunition chosen from Greeley's own arsenal. "I never said all Democrats were saloonkeepers," he had said in 1860. "What I said was that all saloonkeepers were Democrats."

Recalling these barbs made many a befuddled Democrat wince. Democrats admitted that Greeley gave Grant a run for his money, but the unlikely nomination was clearly a marriage of convenience rather than a love match. Greeley's seriousness and hard campaigning against overwhelming odds glossed over the essential fact that the ticket was a farce. Too many Democrats could not forgive Greeley for the spiteful attacks on the Democracy in his New York *Tribune* columns for over thirty years, while Irish and German Democrats feared Greeley's zeal on behalf of prohibition laws. The Crédit Mobilier scandals touched the vice-president along with a host of senators and congressmen (including James A. Garfield) when the graft-ridden scheme became public during the campaign, but voters easily overlooked the corruption in Washington to give Grant a landslide victory—286 electoral votes to Greeley's 62. Crushed by the loss, Greeley retired to his farm, and within a few weeks he was dead. The party of Jefferson and Jackson was again at low ebb.

Despite Grant's glamour, more waving of bloody shirts, and the power of the GAR phalanx, voters took a second look when hard times hit the country. The impact of the 1873 panic, touched off by the failure of Jay Gould's efforts to curb the gold market (which, to his credit, Grant helped prevent), upset Republican control of the House. Dozens of safe GOP seats fell during the 1874 elections. Unemployment and the scarcity of cash became pocketbook issues that gave Democrats a 60–vote edge, although the Senate remained Republican dominated. The upsurge, along with victories in key gubernatorial elections, gave the Democrats reason to believe that after twenty years the party had real prospects of capturing the White House. Breadlines and higher interest rates whiplashed the jobless city dweller along with the debt-ridden farmer. "Hard times," the GOP governor in Ohio admitted, "is our deadliest foe."

Even one hundred years later, the events of 1876–1877 seem odd. First, the majority of the voters favored Samuel J. Tilden, the Democratic nominee. Nobody disputed that point. Second, the outcome was at first announced as a clear Tilden victory. Rutherford B. Hayes went to bed thinking he had lost. Four months later he was the president-elect, and Tilden's supporters denounced the maneuvering that gave Hayes the victory.

Between Tilden's nomination and Hayes's inauguration, the nation came as close as it ever had to upsetting the principle that has been the guiding genius of American politics—the peaceful transition of power to an elected leader of the opposition. After the votes had been counted but the outcome was still in doubt, Henry Watterson called for the converging on Washington of 100,000 vigilant Democrats, including "ten thousand unarmed Kentuckians," to see that Tilden got a fair count. Former general Wade Hampton's rifle clubs in South Carolina, outlawed by Grant's order, were reorganized as Hampton-Tilden musical clubs "with twelve four-pound flutes" supposedly ready for battle. The electoral contest hinged on disputed ballots in Florida, Oregon, South Carolina, and Louisiana. The tension was mounting as March 4 loomed and it seemed likely there would be no president to inaugurate. Then a congressionally devised commission made up of eight Republicans and seven Democrats took the controversial ballots under study and by a strict party vote decided in Hayes's favor in every case. Tilden was stuck with his 184 votes and Hayes finally had 185. How?

In all likelihood the wealthy Democrats in the North were willing to sacrifice Tilden for a standpatter like Hayes. "The Democratic business men of the country are more anxious for quiet than for Tilden," Congressman James A. Garfield believed, "and the leading southern Democrats in Congress . . . are saying they have seen war enough." The southerners had no great love for Hayes, but they wanted the federal troops out of the three states where the disputed ballots came from the only remaining carpetbag administrations.

Often a lot of little things creep into the decision-making process, too. Hayes had told a southern newspaperman he thought that carpetbag rule in the South had been a failure. A Republican could say that and get away with it, but perhaps Tilden would have been too afraid of being called a Copperhead to have said what did not sound seditious when uttered by Hayes. As late as February 26, 1877, the powers-that-be gathered in a Washington hotel and the deal was carried to the handshaking point. Hayes would be the president and the Democrats would call off a threatened filibuster (which would have prolonged the anxiety by withholding the final electoral count). In return, Hayes would withdraw the federal occupation troops, appoint a southerner to his cabinet, and support a southern railroad route to the Pacific.

All the circumstances point to the Wormley Hotel compromise, for Hayes had not been in office two months when the three carpetbag administrations collapsed. A southern man was appointed postmaster general, and a bill for a southern railroad to the Pacific was dropped into a congressional hopper. So Hayes was president, by one vote, and the deal was signed, sealed, and delivered within the next few months.*

The 1876 election turned out to be a great lesson for the country. Tilden could have been surly or worse, but he showed a kind of sportsmanship that is rarely seen in political campaigns. Nor did Hayes gloat over his narrow victory; he went about his business of living up to the promises his managers made. All this despite the probability, as historian C. Vann Woodward has said, that if

---

*A brilliant account of the "bargain of 1877" is found in C. Vann Woodward, *Reunion and Reaction* (Boston: Little, Brown, 1966), wherein the Wormley Hotel deal is regarded as a too-simple explanation of a complex series of compromises.

the votes had been fairly counted, Tilden would have won "by a vote of 188 to 181."

Soon the implications of the compromise became apparent. The Republicans gave up their hopes of making inroads in the South and resigned themselves to the perpetual loss of the former Confederacy to a newly formed coalition of old Whigs, Bourbon Democrats, and the last remnants of the Jefferson-Jackson branch of the Democracy. The upstart third parties (the Grangers and the Greenbackers were already making noises) would remain a distinct minority, and Congress would be Republican dominated. No Democrat had been elected president for twenty years. Big businessmen who contributed to the coffers of both parties apparently were satisfied with the way things had been going, except for the few Grant scandals and the Boss Tweed mess in New York, for the Republicans had planted an important seed between the cracks in the Wall Street pavement: the Grand Old Party was the upholder of prosperity. Until deep into the twentieth century, that message was woven into the campaign banners of every presidential election by the men who met the payrolls, owned the bonds, and held the mortgages from Beacon Hill to Knob Hill. Thus the Democrats became the party of the "outs," able to win congressional seats only when a depression shook the voters' confidence.

Never before and perhaps never again will the wealthy in America have a field day comparable to the last twenty-five years of the nineteenth century. Senators were still chosen by the state legislators, and rich men usually won. The wartime income tax was gone, trusts were legal devices for testing consumers' ability to "pay all the traffic will bear," and interest on the national debt was paid to investors in gold. The robber barons of the age were, for the most part, exercising their tremendous power to make money while they stayed within the law.

Most Americans were law-abiding, God-fearing folk and four

out of five still lived on a farm. Farmers in the prairie states and Old South read of New York parties aglow with diamond stickpins and tubs of champagne, but their fare was plain and becoming plainer. Squeezed by the deflationary tendencies of Republican hard-money policies, midwestern farmers held back from an alliance with the struggling southern planters because of prejudice and lack of leadership. White tenant farmers fell to the bottom rung of the ladder and were politically ineffective. Meanwhile, wages plunged so that a factory hand's pay envelope in 1877 shrank by 60 percent from 1873 levels. NO HELP WANTED signs were posted to dishearten breadwinners, some three million of whom were looking for work a year after Tilden's defeat. Labor was still unorganized but angry, and the word *strike* began to dot big-city newspaper columns.

The growing disparity between the nation's haves and have-nots provided the issues that laid to rest all the prewar problems save one—the tariff. Indeed, Democrats and Republicans managed to argue the tariff rates with angry shouts until the 1930s. But the older issues were passé. The Treasury was now part of the federal government (as the Jacksonians' legacy), and slavery was a dead issue (with civil rights for Negroes still a moot point). The South had paid its price for secession and was down at the heel, stumbling through a maze of local problems. Farmers in all sections saw their low-priced commodities bring good prices in city markets and believed it was up to the Federal government to keep them from foreclosures in a land that seemed brimming with plenty.

The little men finally found their champions in a Democratic congressman from Missouri and a Republican senator from Iowa. Richard Bland and William B. Allison drafted legislation to repeal the Resumption Act (much loved by the holders of gold bonds) and begin the minting of at least two million silver dollars a month. However tame this bill now sounds, it was attacked as a harebrained scheme to ruin creditors by financiers who implored Hayes to veto the dangerous interference with the free market forces of supply and demand. Hayes, true to his calling, vetoed the law. Aroused farmers in the Midwest threatened and cajoled until the corn belt Republicans joined the cotton Democrats to override the veto, and they stopped the forced destruction of greenbacks carried on under the Resumption Act. The political doctors had agreed with the farmers' diagnosis of the country's illness—deflation—and Congress swallowed hard but passed bills to throw more millions into the nation's vaults, pockets, and purses.

While the rest of the world moved at its own Victorian pace, the politically active Americans spent most of the next generation preoccupied with the questions of currency control, silver coinage, and tariff policy. Without great enthusiasm, the Democrats edged toward a moderate position on currency, owing in part to the nudging they received from the Greenback party stalwarts who came into the Democratic fold. On the silver question, the demand for unlimited coinage of the huge surplus of silver bullion piling up in the West finally split the Democrats into two camps, with the Gold Democrats providing a sour-faced denouement. In fact, the Greenback party might not have come into being in 1878 if the Democrats had welcomed the disgusted midwesterners with clear-cut programs for repeal of the Republican-created hard-money policy. Iowan James B. Weaver walked out of the Republican party but had no place to go except a third-party coalition of farmers and laborers. Bolting from the Grand Old Party, Weaver said he could not join the Democratic party because it was a band of me-tooers who "camped every four years exactly where the Republican party camped four years before."

Not all Democrats were timid, but it was a time when they had to be circumspect. The southern wing was coalescing behind white codes that were blessed by the Supreme Court in the Slaughter House Cases (a Republican court had set the stage for a series of decisions that eventually made the "separate but equal" clause part of the supreme law of the land), which put blacks in the back of the trains and in shanty schools for the next seventy-five years. Thus the Republican jurists gave the Bourbon Democrats all they wanted in the way of justification for one-party rule, and the state legislatures used the opportunity to make voting a white man's privilege below the old Missouri Compromise line. Although northern Democrats only shook their fingers at their southern friends, there was plenty of trouble in the big cities, where both parties vied for fat streetcar and paving contracts, patronage plums, and other bountiful rewards for municipal and county election victors. New York City was a panorama of political plunder, ranging from Jay Gould's manipulations in railroads to the courthouses and the customhouses. After the New York *Times* exposed the Tweed scandals, Democrats apologized for Tammany Hall's corruption but in turn pointed to scores of city halls in other cities where Republicans had nephews and cousins on padded payrolls. Faint cries for civil service reform were heard, but when fanned by newspaper exposés of arrogant machine bosses who controlled Philadelphia, Boston, Buffalo, Cleveland, Chicago, St. Louis, and lesser cities, the tide began to run with the reformers. Hayes was finished.

Grant's friends tried to dust off their hero but found the pressure too strong and had to abandon their third-term hope, settling for a dark horse in James Garfield. His running mate, the former customs collector of New York, was handpicked by the Old Guard, who could not stomach a simon-pure ticket. The Democrats' convention in Cincinnati turned into a bland affair; Tilden was ill and no other northern leader of great stature was anxious to do battle except General Winfield Scott Hancock of Pennsylvania. One of the party's untarnished war heroes, Hancock won on the second ballot and took an Indiana congressman for his running mate. The platform writers could not overlook "the great fraud of 1876–77, by which, upon a false count of the electoral votes . . . the candidate defeated at the polls was declared to be President. . . . The Democratic party, to preserve the country from the horrors of a civil war, submitted for the time in firm and patriotic faith that the people would punish this crime in 1880." To woo the western vote there was a crack at the Orientals. "No more Chinese immigration, except for travel, education, and foreign commerce, and that even carefully guarded." Then there was the act-of-faith plank, calling for "honest money, consisting of gold and silver, and paper convertible into coin on demand . . . and a tariff for revenue only."

Nobody could prevent the Greenback party from running a ticket, but a return of good times placed both the Democrats and the agrarian-backed group on a treadmill. Hayes's honesty, the treatment of blacks in the South, and old roots of Republican loyalty in New England swung the balance despite an early fall scare when a Democrat won the Maine governorship in a shocking upset. After that tremor the old pattern emerged; Hancock won only in New Jersey, Nevada, California, and the South. How much the Greenback ticket hurt Hancock was uncertain, but he was short by only 10,000 votes out of nearly 9,000,000 cast, and the third party polled 308,000 votes. The Democratic majority in the House disappeared, but the Senate was tied. And there were some hopeful signs from New York, where the party had once been so firmly anchored. A Buffalo Democrat who had been elected sheriff on a reform ticket was being groomed for mayor, and those who had heard Grover Cleveland speak thought he talked like a good Jeffersonian.

The party needed a new face. Unfortunately, Cleveland's war record was bad. He had dodged the draft by paying $150 for a substitute during the war. Actually, Cleveland had only a few salutary attributes—chiefly candor and honesty. Not much of a speechmaker, he said only one thing that stuck in the voter's memory: "A public office is a public trust." To voters who were sick of corruption in city hall, discredited cabinet members, conniving Wall Street bandits, and rampant bribery in legislatures and even Congress, Cleveland sounded like that rare breed of politician, an honest man. He also had a magic ingredient to go with his integrity—luck.

Jefferson's supporters hoisted this linen hand-painted banner, one of the earliest political artifacts still in existence, to proclaim their victory over John Adams and the Federalists in the 1800 election.

JACKSON TICKET

Honor and gratitude to the man who has filled the measure of his country's glory—*Jefferson*

FOR THE ASSEMBLY
GEORGE H. STEUART,
JOHN V. L. McMAHON.

Jackson and Jefferson were linked in an implied endorsement of a state assembly ticket after the 1828 election. Although Jefferson once called Jackson "a dangerous man," it fell to Jackson to carry the Democratic standard, and between 1824 and 1836 any voter who identified himself as a Jackson man was saying that he was a Jeffersonian Democrat.

Few presidents have worked through the labyrinth of state party politics as skillfully as James K. Polk. He was chief clerk of the Tennessee senate, served in the state legislature, went to Congress and rose to become Speaker of the House, and then returned to become governor. Perhaps no president in history was as faithful to his campaign pledges as Polk (he did not settle for 54°40′ in Oregon, however, as this poster suggests), yet modern historians have given him low marks as a president and party leader.

THE POLITICAL GYMNASIUM.

The 1860 presidential election was unique in that four major party candidates were serious contenders. This cartoon indicates some of the ludicrous aspects of the campaign.

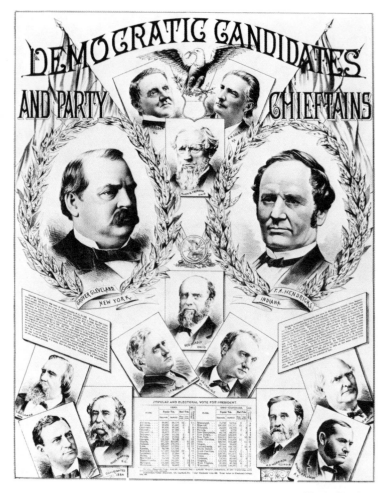

Democrats in 1884 promoted Cleveland as a party candidate who would command national support. To indicate the party had widespread support, North and South, Cleveland is shown with his running mate and other Democrats then occupying state gubernatorial mansions.

Soap! Soap! Blaine's only Hope!

BLAINE'S FUNERAL

DIED NOVEMBER 4th, 1884.

HON. JAS. G. BLAINE, and with him the REPUBLICAN PARTY, AGED 24 YEARS.

Conceived in Sin—Matured in Tyranny, and died of Chronic Disease of the Bloody Shirt.

PALL BEARERS.

JOHN A. LOGAN, JAY GOULD, EX. GOV. CORNELL, and JOHN I. DAVENPORT.

Undertakers, Hon. G. S. CLEVELAND, of New York, and THOS. A. HENDRICKS, of Indiana.

After Republicans lost the 1884 presidential election, gleeful Democrats held a mock funeral of the Republican candidate to bury the "bloody shirt" campaign cry that had helped defeat Democrats from 1864 onward. Although their report of the death of the Republican party, "aged 24 years," proved premature, Cleveland's victory was the Democrats' first in a generation, and he was the only Democrat in the White House between 1861 and 1913.

William Jennings Bryan was barely noted in this Washington *Post* cartoon of July 3, 1896, when the Democrats were split over the gold standard and the free coinage of silver. But after Bryan's ringing "Cross of Gold" speech, the hard-money wing was forced to accept the young Nebraskan as the party's standard-bearer.

Woodrow Wilson had to learn how to mingle with crowds and shake the hands of farmers and cattlemen as well as Wall Street financiers when he started his climb for the 1912 Democratic presidential nomination. Thus he overcame the opposition claims that he was a stuffy college president who lacked the earthy touch needed on the campaign trail.

In the official 1920 Democratic party portrait, presidential candidate James M. Cox and his running mate, Franklin D. Roosevelt, exuded respectability, but voters preferred the solidity of the Harding-Coolidge ticket.

During the Jazz Age, the would-be 1924 hit, "March to the White House," was the official campaign song distributed by the Democratic National Committee. Candidate Davis proved to be an able but unglamorous campaigner, however, and received only 28 percent of the vote.

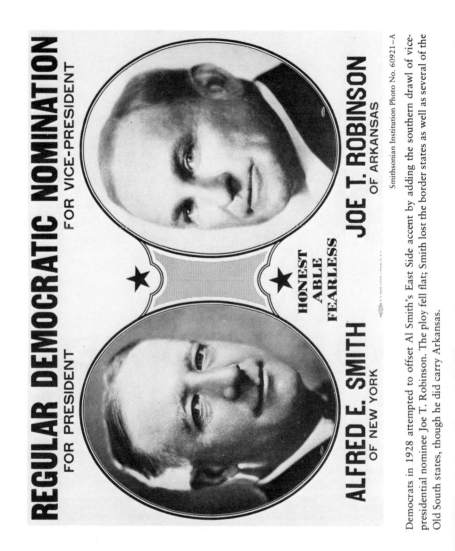

Democrats in 1928 attempted to offset Al Smith's East Side accent by adding the southern drawl of vice-presidential nominee Joe T. Robinson. The ploy fell flat; Smith lost the border states as well as several of the Old South states, though he did carry Arkansas.

When Franklin D. Roosevelt was inaugurated on a gray March 4, 1933, the section reserved for important spectators was almost empty, but there were plenty of anxious observers, and a worried nation hung on to Roosevelt's first official words for some gleam of hope.

A grave President Truman addressed the mourning nation on April 17, 1945, to reassure the people, who knew little about him, that FDR's policies were safe in his hands. "He never faltered—we never will!" Truman promised.

KENNEDY-JOHNSON

two great Democrats

John F. Kennedy surprised his admirers and confounded his enemies when he picked Lyndon Johnson as his running mate in 1960. The element of surprise was carried one step further when Johnson accepted Kennedy's offer and then helped carry crucial Texas in the closely contested election that followed.

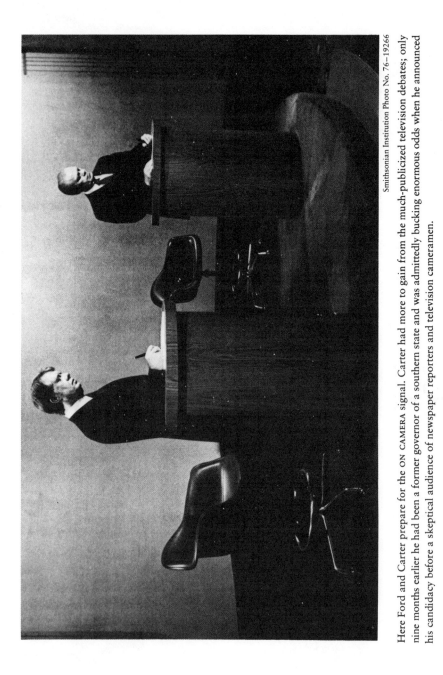

Here Ford and Carter prepare for the ON CAMERA signal. Carter had more to gain from the much-publicized television debates; only nine months earlier he had been a former governor of a southern state and was admittedly bucking enormous odds when he announced his candidacy before a skeptical audience of newspaper reporters and television cameramen.

SIX

Cleveland: Honest and Lucky

Garfield's assassination shook the country out of its lethargy, for his murderer appeared to be a demented product of the spoils system. President Chester A. Arthur did all he could to shake the taint of spoils that clung to his elegant person by appointing honest, capable men over the protests of hack politicians whose craving for patronage had not abated. The reform urge had never been stronger in grass-roots America, a fact that magnified Cleveland's potential even when he moved up from sheriff to the mayor's office in Buffalo. Cleveland was impressive for what he was not rather than what he was. He was not crooked, he was not a machine politician, he was not in favor of the lavish spending of public money.

Even these credentials probably would not have vaulted Cleveland into national prominence except for the coincidence of his election as governor of New York with a depression that hit the nation in 1882. The country, sad to say, had fallen into ruts of prejudice that played into the hands of corrupt bosses. State conventions and county caucuses dictated the whole tone of local politics. In Vermont there were towns where boys grew to manhood without considering what the Republican party stood for; all they knew was that every respectable citizen was a Republican. And in dozens of communities in Alabama, Georgia, Louisiana, Mississippi, and South Carolina, a prudent Republican kept his distance from the courthouse. Only an economic shock that hit pocketbooks, or revealed corruption proving that pocketbooks had already been hit, could shake voters from their lethargy.

There were abundant reasons why Americans were apathetic about their politics (unless they held office themselves). The preponderance of newspapers in the cities were staunchly Republican. Ranging from the New York *Tribune* to the Portland *Oregonian*, the leading newspapers in the hubs of commerce made no bones about their loyalty to the GOP. In many localities the best efforts of Democrats had to be saved for quadrennial elections, when faithful contributors could hire a versatile editor and a cheap printer. These newspapers appeared like mushrooms during presidential campaigns, to heat up the elections artificially. They contained overstatements, partisan propaganda, and journalistic politicking that became a part of the fun for Americans and bewildered foreign observers (who took the hyperbole seriously). The role of newspapers in politics expanded, however, after the New York *Times* blew the whistle on the Tweed gang, with its massive thievery (over $9 million spent for bogus courthouse repairs). The enormous circulation of the metropolitan dailies forced the public to pay attention to crooked politicians with voracious appetites for power and plunder.

In this setting Cleveland appeared as the Democratic godsend. Brooklyn's mayor Seth Low was more articulate and energetic, but Cleveland had the knack of appearing to be a babe in the woods who still knew how to handle the crooks. Tammany Hall leaders, skeptical of a do-gooder in Albany, were soothed into silence, and Cleveland won the governor's race in 1882 by a handsome plurality. Meanwhile President Arthur improved his respectability but alienated the Republican Old Guard. New York, with its huge slice of electoral votes and congressional delegation, had replaced Virginia as the seedbed of the Democracy (lest we forget, Seymour, Tilden, and Greeley were all New Yorkers). The Republicans were so entrenched, however, that Cleveland must have been honest when, after winning the gubernatorial election, he dismissed suggestions that he aim for a higher post. "I have no idea of re-election or any higher political preferment."

Then the effects of another depression hit the nation late in 1882 and lingered on during Cleveland's first year in Albany. Disillusioned voters gave the Democrats a majority in the House of Representatives. Bankruptcies multiplied, factory smokestacks grew cold, and the lines of wage earners at soup kitchens lengthened. Cleveland proposed no social remedies, however; instead he vetoed popular bills that would have cut carfares in New York City to a nickel and aided Catholic schools. Instead of backfiring, Cleveland's defense of his vetoes made him into a champion of strict construction of the Constitution, a fact that impressed businessmen. Despite a nasty battle with Tammany's new boss, "Honest John" Kelly, Cleveland weathered another veto of a popular maximum-hours law for streetcar operators (which would have cut working days from sixteen hours to twelve). The breach with Kelly was serious but not hopeless, for if Cleveland wanted to win reelection as governor he would need the 60,000 votes Tammany could deliver.

After twenty-eight years of frustration, the only hope for a Democratic victory in the 1884 presidential contest depended upon Republican ineptness combined with resentment over joblessness, depressed farm prices, and labor unrest. Republicans contributed to their downfall by dumping the incumbent president in favor of loyal but venal James G. Blaine, whom orthodox Republicans regarded as the white knight from Maine. But Democrats saw so many chinks in Blaine's armor they prepared to capitalize on his shady past. Gathering in Chicago, the Democrats listened to Boss Kelly warn that Cleveland could not carry his home state; other Tammany-inspired attacks on Cleveland brought catcalls from the galleries and caused a Cleveland supporter to send a thrill through the convention when he shouted, "We love him for the enemies he has made!" Cleveland won the nomination on the second ballot.

Cleveland's good luck held up when Joseph Pulitzer, the dashing St. Louis newspaper publisher, moved to New York and took over the tottering *World* in 1883. After Cleveland's nomination, Pulizer threw the *World*'s support behind the Democratic standard-bearer—no mean endorsement considering the *World*'s phenomenal success and Pulitzer's talent for picking winning causes. Over 200,000 *World* readers saw the first regular political cartoons lambast Blaine and his supporters as Babylonian revelers at Belshazzar's "feast of Special Privilege." Thomas Nast's pen-and-ink jabs at Tammany were scarcely more effective. After a huge dinner at Delmonico's the *World* told readers: "Beaten by the people, hopeless of an honest election, Blaine's appeal at the banquet of the millionaires was for a corruption fund large enough to buy up New Jersey, Connecticut, and Indiana, and to defraud the people of their free choice for President." Pulitzer told his editors to pull no punches. Democratic newspapers across the land quoted the *World* gleefully. For the first time since Polk's administration, a strong Democratic newspaper of national circulation threw the Republicans on the defensive.

Another journalistic break favored Cleveland when the nation's most disciplined laborers, the International Typographical Union, boycotted the New York *Tribune*. The ITU, correctly calculating that the *Tribune* was the nation's leading Republican newspaper, asked the party's leaders to rebuff Whitelaw Reid's wage policies. When Republicans hemmed and hawed, the ITU ordered a boycott of "the *Tribune* and James G. Blaine" forthwith. In November Cleveland won New York state by less than

1,200 votes; perhaps the 3,500 ITU members made the difference. Before the final news about New York sent Cleveland toward the White House, however, the campaign sank to the level of street-gutter politics. A sizable group of distinquished citizens who were normally Republicans became mugwumps to repudiate Blaine and his unsavory dealings while he had been Speaker of the House. Then a Buffalo newspaper leaked the story of the birth ten years earlier of a baby whom the mother claimed had been fathered by bachelor Cleveland. The Democratic nominee's reported fondness for a social glass and a few hands of poker was excused as a manly indulgence, but the Republicans hoped to discredit Cleveland completely by spreading full details of the New Yorker's admission in court of his parental responsibility. Eager to counterattack the Democrats' charge that Blaine was "the continental liar from the state of Maine," the Republicans came up with their campaign ditty:

> Ma, Ma, Where is my Pa?
> Gone to the White House, Ha! Ha! Ha!

Such a "moral lecher" was unfit to be president, the Republican newspapers argued. But Cleveland defused the incident by frankly admitting the story was basically true.

Did such an honest man deserve to be in the White House? No, said the sanctimonious *Independent*. Cleveland's "election would argue a low state of morals among the people, and be . . . a disgrace to the nation." But *Nation* magazine held that whatever Cleveland's drawbacks, "Blaine's vices are those by which governments are overthrown, states brought to naught, and the haunts of commerce turned into dens of thieves." Still the question rang out, could an honest man beat a crook?

Nobody could be sure, as long as New York was in doubt. Then came the famous incident that took Blaine by surprise. The Republican was welcomed at a rally by a bluenosed minister who assured him: "We are Republicans, and don't propose to leave our party and identify ourselves with the party whose antecedents have been rum, Romanism, and rebellion." Soon the slogan Rum, Romanism, and Rebellion came to haunt Blaine, for it was an insult to Catholics and contained overtones of bloody shirts and booze bottles. If the loss of ITU support was not enough, surely this historic gaffe put the quietus on Blaine's chances in New York and, hence, on his chances for the presidency. Although Blaine won New England (except Connecticut), and most of the mid-Atlantic states, he lost New York and the Solid South. A 28-year drought had been broken. Republican postmasters who had hung six presidents' portraits in their offices made ready to depart.

Cleveland's enemies whispered that the new administration would be delivered over to former rebels; southern blacks were warned that the new president might try to force them back into bondage; and Wall Street bulls expected the worst. Instead, Cleveland reminded voters in his inaugural address that every voter "exercises a public trust" and owes "the country a vigilant watch and close scrutiny" of officeholders. In what now seems the halcyon days of low-key federal government, Cleveland was speaking of a federal payroll of less than 130,000, and most of them were either customs officers, postal clerks, or postmasters. The spoils system, much changed since Jackson's day by recent civil service reforms, led to the dismissal of perhaps half the Republican holdovers. The assistant postmaster general, Adlai E. Stevenson of Illinois, was eventually placed in charge of the replacement process and thus earned the gratitude of the party faithful who believed Cleveland had been nudged into action by Stevenson. Some crocodile tears were shed for the ousted postmasters and their friends, but the nation was not shocked; Cleveland had promised to uphold the new civil service act, and his open contempt for office seekers proved he was determined not to become a hack politician. He made an avowed enemy of the spoils system, William C. Endicott of Massachusetts (and the "very Brahmin of the Brahmins"), his secretary of the navy. Senators Thomas F. Bayard, Sr., of Delaware and Lucius Q. C. Lamar of Mississippi, both respected for their moderation, took key posts as secretary of state and attorney general. The other Cleveland appointments were similarly judicious. Wall Street began to breathe easier, in fact, a bit too regularly to suit some of Cleveland's supporters, who feared that the country was fast verging toward a plutocracy in which wealth had replaced majority rule.

Gradually Cleveland showed that he was not a Democrat who looked with favor on every other Democrat. He was socially at ease with, but inclined to suspect, politicians—even those who helped him. He turned down a courtesy call from Tilden that was meant to place the 1876 candidate's friend in the best paying of all federal jobs (that of customs collector of New York harbor, worth $50,000 a year); and although some eight thousand low-paying postmasterships went to Democrats during his first year, the pace of turnover was not fast enough for Cleveland's critics. Toward his vice-president, Thomas A. Hendricks, Cleveland showed too much reserve, so that the Indianan reacted by saying: "I had hoped that Mr. Cleveland would put the Democratic party into power in fact as well as in name." In rebuttal to criticism that he was not appointing Democrats fast enough, Cleveland reportedly asked a vexed senator if he ought to "appoint two horse-thieves a day, instead of one."

After Cleveland settled into office, he made his stand on the money issue clear enough to alienate the soft-money crowd. He warned that if the coinage of silver continued under existing laws, people would soon begin hoarding gold. In fact, the Treasury held $165 million in silver dollars and was piling up more every day; and Cleveland hinted that unless the law was changed, citizens would soon learn that the one "who suffers most by mischievious legislation in money matters, is the man who earns his daily bread by his daily toil."* In short order, Cleveland urged that the Bland-Allison Act be suspended to stop the coinage of more silver dollars. Nothing was done, however, for Congress was straddling a teeter-totter, the Senate being controlled by Republicans and the House majority being held by Democrats.

Cleveland had in his makeup much of the Jeffersonian view that in a republic the chief purposes of government were to keep taxes low and prevent powerful interest groups from obtaining special privileges. He had been quick to use the veto when he was mayor and governor, and as president he maintained his reputation for saying no. When Congress passed a $10,000 appropriation bill for seeds to aid Texas farmers hit by a drought, Cleveland's veto message made his stand clear: "Though the people support the Government, the Government should not support the people." When the federal Treasury showed a surplus, Cleveland's instinct was to follow the Democratic tradition by cutting back on tariffs. He dramatized the situation by making tariff reduction the only theme in his 1887 annual message, a speech certain to set the tone for the forthcoming presidential election. Old-time Democrats who saw a low tariff as a kind of Eleventh Commandment cheered when Cleveland dismissed with a wave of the hand the intense public discussion "dwelling upon theories of protection and free trade. It is a condition that confronts us, not a theory." As expected, the House passed the bill calling for lower duties, but the Republican-dominated Senate rejected it.

Cleveland was eager to fight for reduced tariffs, but his party leaders were more cautious. Pennsylvania Democrats traditionally were out of step with the party's historic support for low tariffs, and many New York businessmen with investments in factories competing with European industry were wary of lower duties. The Democratic mayor of New York made a public declaration of

*Cleveland was quoting Daniel Webster, who had called for "sound currency" in an 1834 speech.

his anti-Cleveland attitude: "Cleveland is no statesman and I don't believe in his re-election." New York Governor David Bennett Hill took a similar stance. Their rancor stemmed mainly from Cleveland's views toward patronage. They wanted wholesale firings of incumbent officeholders and their replacement by Democrats; but federal jobs were a side issue after the tariff squabble beclouded the campaign for Cleveland's reelection and Republicans accused the president of favoring "free trade."

Tears might have welled in the eyes of Democrats who applauded Cleveland's insistence on a campaign pitched on the tariff issue, but concentration on a single issue hurt the president with other Democrats, who insisted that a huge increase in circulating silver dollars would keep the country prosperous. Cleveland also managed to step on the toes of practical politicians by his vetoes of bills passed by Congress conferring private pensions on Civil War veterans. These bills were passed to reward veterans politically allied with congressmen; and all pretense of merit was submerged since deserving veterans easily qualified under the existing liberal pension laws. When Cleveland vetoed the notorious Dependent Pension Act, which had rolled through Congress, the screams of wounded Democrats were almost as loud as those from the Republicans. Undoubtedly Cleveland was right in vetoing the bill, but it was a rash thing to do with his reelection looming.

At the St. Louis convention in 1888 a silver gavel, presented by the Colorado miners as a token "to that party which restored silver to the monetary plane from which it was degraded by the Republicans," called the delegates to order. Cleveland's enemies stayed at home and his friends readily maneuvered his renomination by a unanimous vote. The platform, reported by Henry Watterson, endorsed Cleveland's tariff message "as the correct interpretation" of the 1884 plank on the thorny issue—a frontal attack on those who said Cleveland had overstepped his authority. Civil service reforms and the exclusion of Chinese laborers were hailed, but the platform's boldest thrusts were saved for the "demoralizing surplus in the National Treasury." Andrew Jackson's shadow was discernible as the platform declared: "All unnecessary taxation is unjust taxation." The $60 million surplus had been "drawn from the people and [out of] the channels of trade" by Republican-sponsored "extravagant taxation." "The Democratic remedy is to enforce frugality in public expense and abolish needless taxation."

Republicans eagerly accepted the tariff issue as the crucial issue of the campaign, and they had a trick up their sleeves. A dispute with Canada over some fishing rights had furnished Cleveland with a chance to twist the British lion's tail—always good sport in an election year. Then the British minister in Washington received a letter, allegedly from an Englishman who had become a United States citizen, which questioned whether a vote for Cleveland "would do England a service . . . and [work] against the Republican system of tariff." The letter was a put-up job, but the British minister fell into the trap and answered that Cleveland was a safe bet to "manifest a spirit of conciliation." Late in October the Republicans published the letter and the British minister's reply to prove that Cleveland was, in effect, Queen Victoria's candidate for president. Thousands of handbills and editorials dinned the fatal message that Cleveland was England's choice. Democrats in the Irish wards from New York to San Francisco seethed. Cleveland reacted (under heavy pressure) by demanding the recall of the British minister, but the damage had been done.

The 1888 returns showed only a hairline difference in the popular vote, with Cleveland ahead by less than 60,000 votes out of 11,000,000 cast. The electoral count told another story, however. A shift of 7,189 votes in his home state (where prohibitionist Clinton Fish got 30,231 votes) would have made all the difference. But besides New York he also lost Pennsylvania and wound up with 168 electoral votes to Harrison's 233. The defection by New

York's machine had hurt Cleveland, for Governor Hill won reelection handily while Cleveland's backers spoke of "treachery" in Tammany Hall. The Solid South plus the old reliables New Jersey and Connecticut had fallen short again.*

Cleveland's four years in the White House proved that courageous presidents do not a party make. In fact, a headstrong man in the White House can alienate powerful interest groups, since loyalty and courage have not always been compatible partners in party politics. Cleveland's conversion to the low tariff cause, which should have appealed to the Midwest but in fact did not gain him a single corn belt state, should have been a lesson to the next generation of Democrats.

Meanwhile, Tammany Hall was triumphant, and as Americans increasingly left their farm homes for city dwellings, the pace of machine politics quickened. Precinct captains who knew the comings and goings of voters in their bailiwicks continued the time-honored customs of petty patronage, holiday favors, and having a reputation as an all-around good fellow, so that established patterns of patronage emerged. Although New York was by no means typical, the ethnic character of voting permitted the Democratic bosses to divide the spoils so that the Americans of Italian descent had drayage (and later sanitation), the Irish moved into the expanding police department, and the Jewish voters were as a matter of course left with public education, the field they seemed best qualified to handle.

Benjamin Harrison's victory had been far from a landslide, but in Congress the Republicans won clear majorities, which they viewed as a mandate on the tariff issue. Congressman William McKinley from Ohio (a state fast becoming "the mother of presi-

*The effect of Cleveland's tiff with Germany over Samoa is an indication of increasing voting behavior by country of origin. The German Americans in St. Louis and Milwaukee gave Cleveland a majority in 1884 but switched heavily to Harrison in 1888.

dents" since Virginia had defaulted after Tyler's tenure) fashioned a tough high tariff bill which Iowa farmers applauded while they watched the price of corn drop. McKinley said, "A cheap coat makes a cheap man," and thousands of GAR members nodded in agreement. As Wilfred Binkley showed, the midwestern Republicans stayed with their party in spite of tariff rates or soft-money issues, so long as the prices paid for corn and wheat were fairly stable. When grain prices fell, the Democrats made inroads; but these were only temporary gains that were easily lost when wheat climbed back to a dollar a bushel or better. As for the South, the Democrats by 1888 knew they had the Old Confederacy before the campaign began, so they concentrated on winning the border states and New York. Except for Connecticut, New England—so far as the Democrats were concerned—was a lost part of the continent.

A notable instance of rare Democrat-Republican agreement occurred during Harrison's administration when publicity focusing attention on sugar, beef, and other trust agreements forced Congress to act. Senator John Sherman, who was a Republican but something of a maverick, introduced an antitrust bill that glided through Congress. The "everybody line up" pension bill Cleveland had vetoed sailed through Congress, causing the federal outlay for veterans' benefits to leap from $87 million to $159 million in a decade. The idea that Uncle Sam had a Santa Claus standing behind him was becoming more fashionable.

Then the cash situation at the country stores grew tight, and corn prices fell. McKinley's sky-high tariff schedule had hardly been printed when voters reacted with a surge of Democratic ballots (even McKinley went down) that gave the Democrats their greatest majority since prewar days—235 seats in the House to only 88 Republicans. Still the Senate was in Republican hands, which kept a tariff revision off limits. Among the newcomers in the House was a brash young orator, William Jennings Bryan, whose voice boomed to the farthest corner of the cavernous congressional chamber. Any man who could talk so long (his maiden speech was allowed to go on indefinitely) and so forcefully was a man to watch. In those days, oratory was related only to lung power, logic, and the audience's stamina. Bryan had two of these on his side constantly.

Some things were changing, but the move was glacial. The old system of courthouse selection and legislative caucuses grated until the boom for primary elections began to catch on. Increasingly, outsiders insisted that each party's nominee ought to be selected by all the voters, not by the self-anointed few who sippped brandy or bourbon and picked candidates at their leisure. Most of the pressure for direct primaries came from obstreperous outsiders like Ben Tillman in South Carolina and Robert LaFollette in Wisconsin, whose ideas clashed with those of the party's entrenched clique. There was even some radical talk of selecting presidential candidates through primaries. Time was on the side of these outsiders, but for the moment the old creaking party machinery was working well enough to satisfy the lethargic majority, which could occasionally be aroused enough to strike down innovations.

The seekers of change thought their opportunity was at hand in 1892, when Cleveland's supporters mustered old friends for another assault on the high-tariff walls. Cleveland, a bit heavier and apparently wiser, launched his drive for a second term at the traditional January 8 banquet celebrating Jackson's New Orleans victory. While various candidates scrambled for position, Cleveland wrote a public letter to make it clear that he would accept the party's nomination at the Chicago convention. His hard-money prejudices may have helped turn back Bryan's plea at the Nebraska convention in March; at any rate Cleveland's friends headed off a clear-cut endorsement for the free coinage of silver. The party was not ready to march in cadence, however, for Watterson arrived from Kentucky and concluded that Cleveland was "washed up," and the Tammany Hall crowd was pumping for Governor Hill. At a time for great speechmaking and slogans, the party platform that was brought in by William F. Vilas of Wisconsin bespoke of tradition. The Democratic party representatives "do reaffirm their allegiance to the principles of the party, as formulated by Jefferson and exemplified by a long and illustrious line of his successors in Democratic leadership, from Madison to Cleveland." Republican tariff rates were denounced "as a fraud, a robbery of the great majority of the American people for the benefit of the few." The platform also condemned the treatment of Jews in Russia and Catholics in Ireland. But Watterson, who had influence in the South, was so against Cleveland that he predicted his nomination would lead the party "through a slaughterhouse into an open grave."

Like several newspaper prophets before and since, Watterson was wrong. Cleveland won the nomination on the first ballot after an endurance contest sent the voting into the wee morning hours. Cleveland was not present, of course, for convention etiquette demanded his absence. But in his acceptance letter he spelled out his terms—a fair tariff but no free trade. He had learned a few lessons, and among them was an ability to listen to his closest advisers. Luckily for Cleveland and the Democrats, the Republicans renominated Harrison, who took an anachronistic, tough stand on the Monroe Doctrine, and shilly-shallied on the gold-silver issue. Both parties tried to ignore the devastating Homestead strike that broke the back of labor organizers.* In the lackluster campaign that followed, Cleveland won New York, lost Pennsylvania, barely lost Ohio, and won the election through majorities in Illinois, Indiana, Missouri, and Wisconsin. For the first time since Lincoln's election, the Democrats had proved they could forge a national

---

*Marked by bloody pitched battles at Carnegie's Homestead, Pennsylvania, steel plant, the strike collapsed after the national guard was brought in to restore "law and order."

alliance based primarily on the farm vote and thus win a presidential election. Of course a farm depression made the difference. In Mississippi, where cotton dropped to six cents a pound, Cleveland had 40,288 votes to Harrison's 1,395.

The Populist party's platform in 1892 called for a sixteen-to-one ratio for the coinage of silver, a graduated income tax, postal savings banks to guard small depositors against bank failures, and the return by railroads of their unused land grants. Populists in the South tried to unite black voters with the yeoman white farmers, but the shocked whites first recoiled, then reacted by passing election laws that required challenged voters to "read and understand" the Constitution or some other document. The ruse was enough to frighten away most black voters, making the Democratic party "lily white" in the Old South and most of the border states.

Cleveland had barely settled in the White House for his second term when the country slipped into a recession that became a severe depression. Wheat fell below fifty cents a bushel, the ratio of silver to gold reached twenty-six to one in 1893, and Cleveland called a special session of Congress to remedy the crisis. Instead of repairing the damage, however, Congress repealed the silver purchase act, which conservatives believed was "destroying the value of the dollar." The president's stand on silver angered the western and southern Democrats, who were finding it hard to locate any kind of loose dollar. Then Cleveland alienated organized labor by using federal troops to crush the Pullman Palace Car Company strike in July, 1894. When the Treasury stock of gold was endangered by panicky greenback holders who cashed their currency in for hard money, only a grand gesture from banker J. P. Morgan (his syndicate underwrote a $62 million bond issue) restored some confidence on Wall Street, if not on Main Street.

Fortunately for Cleveland the business of taking public opinion polls to gauge a president's popularity had not been devised, for his rating would have surely been one of the all-time lows. With the best of intentions Cleveland had managed by his policies to alienate farmers, laboring men, miners, and railroad workers. Ben Tillman, a senatorial candidate in South Carolina, told howling audiences that if they sent him to Washington he would stick a pitchfork into "that old bag of beef," and thus he won the nickname Pitchfork Ben, which stuck until his colorful career ended. The young Nebraskan Bryan was furious with Cleveland's monetary policies and rallied behind the free-coinage banner of his Democratic colleague, Richard P. Bland of Missouri. Even Pulitzer's New York *World*, thoroughly disenchanted with Cleveland, called for new leadership in the Democratic party.

Cleveland's brief moment of glory during his second term came when he sent a message to Congress concerning the dispute with Great Britain over the Venezuelan boundary. The president invoked the Monroe Doctrine, but when Lord Salisbury insisted that the matter did not concern the United States, Cleveland bluntly told the country that either the British could arbitrate the dispute or fight. The nation applauded Cleveland, for a change, and the British ultimately signed an arbitration treaty.

Some hotheads in Congress wanted the United States to rattle a few sabers in Spain's direction after a Cuban rebellion drew a sympathetic response from the press, but Cleveland wanted no part of a new quarrel with a European power. He had problems enough at home as the election year snows melted but left him on thin ice with his party. Cleveland sent disciples to argue at state conventions for sound-money (gold-standard) platforms and candidates; but, except in Massachusetts and Michigan, the president's advice was pretty much disregarded. Clearly Cleveland had lost control of the party, and when his friends hired a special train to carry sound-money Democrats to the Chicago convention, they knew they had lost before their cabs reached the convention hall. A party split into two warring factions was faced with the opposition of a sound-money Republican who had written the tariff bill calling for the highest duties in the nation's history. William McKinley's candidacy had the approval of many gold Democrats who frankly said they would freeze in hell before they voted for a silver radical Democrat. Gleeful Republicans watched the infighting at the convention and ventured the prediction that they could "elect a rag baby," so torn were the Democrats over the gold-silver issue.

The battle finally came to a head when the convention considered the money plank for its platform. The New England, upper Midwest, and Pennsylvania delegates favored a hard-money plank. "Pitchfork Ben" Tillman made a bitter speech aimed at Cleveland, the banks, and the gold faction. More desultory debate followed, until the thirty-six-year-old Nebraska congressman, William Jennings Bryan, gained the floor. His famous speech was probably the most galvanizing address ever made in a convention. "I come to speak to you in defense of a cause as holy as the cause of liberty—the cause of humanity," Bryan began. He extolled the laboring man over the stockbroker, the crossroad merchant over the New York businessman, and he contrasted miners with "the few financial magnates who in a back room corner the money of the world."

Bryan's speech was pointed toward the farmers and the dwellers in small towns. "You come to us and tell us that the great cities are in favor of the gold standard. I tell you that the great cities rest upon those broad and fertile prairies. Burn down your cities and leave our farms and your cities will spring up again as if by magic. But destroy our farms and the grass will grow in the streets of every city in this country." Lest Jefferson's thoughts on the superiority of the yeoman farmer to the city-bred wage earner be forgotten, Bryan almost read the sound-money Democrats out of the party by invoking the founder's image. "I stand with Jefferson rather than with them, and tell them as he did that the issue of money is a function of the government, and that the banks should go out of the governing business."

The gold Democrats knew they were bested and moved for the aisles as Bryan spoke to the assembled thousands (without any microphones, remember) with words sure to bring cheers from a throng of old-time Democrats. The year 1896 was, he said, "1776 over again." The sound-money men wanted to follow England and surrender America's political independence to maintain the gold standard. "We reply that instead of having a gold standard because England has, we shall restore bimetallism and then let England have bimetallism." The din rose as Bryan flung his challenge: "Having behind us the commercial interests and the laboring interests and all the toiling masses, we shall answer their demands for a gold standard by saying to them, 'You shall not press down upon the brow of labor this crown of thorns; you shall not crucify mankind upon a cross of gold.'" That did it. The rest of the convention was a formality, except that the two-thirds rule meant that the silver Democrats had some arm twisting to do after the fourth ballot. In the sweeping up that followed, the new Democratic National Committee took on some new talent, including Ben Tillman and Josephus Daniels of North Carolina. At his summer home Cleveland heard the tidings with dismay. "I am not fretting except about the future of the country and party," he told a cabinet member, "and the danger that the latter is to be compromised as an organization."

Bryan stood by his platform, which filled two newspaper pages, with the famous money plank planned as his cudgel. The controversial plank denounced the 1873 coinage law as "demonetizing silver without the knowledge or approval of the American people"—an act that resulted in "the appreciation of gold and a corresponding fall in the prices of commodities reproduced by the people . . . the enrichment of the money-lending class at home and abroad" and the "impoverishment of the people." This act had resulted in a gold standard, which was "a British policy" leading to "financial servitude to London." The nation's ills could only be cured by the free coinage of silver in a ratio of 16 to 1, with the silver dollar made "full legal tender, equal with gold, for all debts, public and private." There was more about lower tariffs, trusts, and the territories. But what the Republican newspapers soon told readers was that a radical young Democratic congressman was out to make the dollar worth about fifty cents. With no apology whatever, the Republican press took Bryan's "Cross of Gold" speech as a signal to crucify the Democratic candidate.

What hurt the Democrats most, perhaps, was that their own spokesmen echoed the Republican charge. "Lunacy having dictated the platform," said the New York *World*, "it was perhaps natural that hysteria should evolve" a candidate as unlikely to win as Bryan. A political party could "survive being made odious," but "there is peril in making it ridiculous. The nomination of the 'boy orator' for the White House at this junction of the nation's affairs . . . comes perilously near taking this fatal step." The defection of the *World* hurt the Democrats, for New York journalism, as the fountain of wire association stories and editorial direction generally, set the tone for much of the country. Bryan's only friend in Manhattan was William Randolph Hearst, the brash young westerner who had bought the *Journal* and made it a sensational rival to the *World*. In Chicago the *Tribune* was firmly entrenched as the Republican oracle, overwhelming its rivals by reaching breakfast tables in nearly every midwestern whistle-stop.

Governor Peter Altgeld, the first Illinois Democrat elected since Civil War days, was being flayed along with Bryan, but for different reasons. Altgeld had tried to stem the tide of irrationality that followed the 1886 Haymarket bombings in Chicago, which most of the press attributed to anarchists. Seven policemen had been killed, and a decade later the incident, which damaged organized labor by innuendo, was still a party bogeyman. Governor Altgeld pardoned three of the convicted bombers, convinced their trials had been rigged. For this he was regaled in the Republican press as a dangerous radical, and young Theodore Roosevelt told reporters he fully expected to meet Altgeld someday on a battlefield pitting anarchists against the decent people of America. The hysterical tone of these attacks hurt Bryan immeasurably.

Against a backdrop of the Haymarket executions and a cruel depression, the election in 1896 represented a sharp break from the past. Democrats raised about $1 million for the campaign, while their frightened opponents poured nearly $7 million into the Republican party coffers. The alarmed financial community was aghast that Bryan might conceivably win, and the Republican presses poured forth a deluge of campaign literature that inundated marginal areas with the message that anarchism would surely follow Bryan's election. McKinley, tutored by an iron-and-steel magnate, Mark Hanna, spoke softly from his front porch in Canton, Ohio. Bryan, still attempting to capitalize on his "Cross of Gold" speech, lived in a railroad car that sped from state to state in a whistle-stop tour the likes of which the country had not seen.

Midwestern farmers, squeezed between low prices for their products and their gold-dollar mortgages, rebelled at the logic of supporting a candidate committed to a policy of easier money and more foreign trade. Buffeted by the uncertainties of weather, insects, and a glutted world grain market, farmers were looking desperately for stability, not anarchy. The archconservative Omaha *World-Herald* of the 1970s was outspoken for Bryan in 1896 (he had once served on its staff), but such influential midwestern stalwarts as the Des Moines *Register* and Chicago *Tribune* assured farmers that their desertion of the party of Lincoln and Grant would spell economic ruin, and the farmers believed them. It was about the last time the bloody shirt would be waved; but wave it did, and millions of voters implicitly cheered by voting against Bryan.

The election proved what the 1890 census returns had already shown—that the nation was turning into an urban-dwelling citizenry remote in interests and dreams from the Jeffersonian farmers. Not only was the census tilting toward the cities, but the supply of public land available for homesteading was nearly exhausted. McKinley's electoral vote was not of landslide proportions (271 to 176), but the states with large cities and most of the corn belt went for him. Boston's Italian American voters apparently were as afraid of the silver-tongued Democrat as his neighbors in Iowa were. Outside the South, Bryan carried only his home state, Nebraska; South Dakota; Missouri; Kansas; and the mining West (Idaho, Montana, Nevada, Utah, Washington, and Wyoming). In the popular vote, McKinley had a 600,000-vote plurality.

In the debris of the 1896 debacle the Democrats found a new scapegoats. First, there was Wall Street, which saw that McKinley's managers had unlimited funds. Except in the South, the press had been overwhelmingly anti-Bryan. A journalistic juggernaut pictured the nation as certain to fall into a bottomless depression if the free-silver candidate—"the wretched, addle-pated boy" as the New York *Tribune* called Bryan—became president. Bryan had said the Democratic party wanted "to make the masses prosperous." The Emporia (Kansas) *Gazette* shot back: "That's the stuff! Give the prosperous man the dickens! Legislate the thriftless man into ease . . . put the ragged, greasy fizzle who can't pay his debts on the altar . . . [and give everybody] the chance to get something for nothing."

McKinley swept into office with the feisty Theodore Roosevelt for a vice-president and a safely Republican Congress. Cleveland left the White House a discredited man. "The Democratic party which he has deceived, betrayed, and humiliated, long ago stamped him as a political leper and cast him out as one unclean," the Kansas City *Times* gloated. "The reproaches of the entire American people accompany him in his retirement." The Atlanta *Con-*

stitution declared Cleveland left office "under a greater burden of popular contempt than has ever been excited by a public man since the foundation of government." Pretty strong, but Cleveland went his way without looking back. Within two years there was talk of drafting him to run in 1900.

Meanwhile the nation's attention was diverted away from monetary policy and the tariff quarrel by the Cuban revolution, which gave Hearst's New York *Journal* a chance to dabble in propaganda and guide American foreign policy through editorials and jingoistic journalism. For a variety of reasons the United States finally declared war on Spain, and as wars go it was short, easy, and therefore popular. The Democrats who were disturbed about American involvement in Cuba and the Philippines gave a hint of what the chief difference would be in the 1900 campaign by asking that all-important question, was the war really justified? The first shot fired at an American ship by the Spaniards would compel every patriot to support his flag, the New Orleans *Times-Democrat* asserted, "but he will know all the time that he has been driven into an unjust and unnecessary war, to satisfy the demands of men who, for political purposes solely, have desired to plunge the republic into a foreign war."

Spain proved to be far weaker than anybody imagined, as the worst war casualties came from mosquitoes instead of Mauser rifles, and the whole business was so mercifully short no draft was needed. Bryan, as titular spokesman for the party, was concerned about the peace treaty. Had we gone to war to help free Cuba or to join in the race for colonies that was already causing the major European nations to jockey for power? Cleveland added his voice to Bryan's in opposing the acquisition of territory in the Orient, but at the last minute the 1896 standard-bearer urged ratification of the peace treaty and thus weakened the newly formed Anti-Imperialist Leagues (which seemed to attract more Democrats than Republicans). Still the treaty squeaked by the Senate with a margin of two votes, after the only Democrat on the five-man peace treaty commission spoke against Philippine annexation.

The country was moving back into a period of prosperity with no real ground swell of public opinion forming on foreign policy issues. The full dinner pail was an issue everybody understood, and times were good in 1900. Gold from the Klondike poured into the channels of commerce, thinning the ranks of the unemployed, and the prices for cotton and wheat moved upward. Cleveland finally had to write a public letter to squelch talk of his running again, but in most Democratic circles McKinley's popularity made the quest in 1900 seem beyond hope. One of the few optimists in Bryan's camp was William Randolph Hearst, who accepted the presidency of the National Association of Democratic Clubs in May. Hearst listened to Democrats who pleaded for a strong Democratic newspaper in Chicago, and on July 2 Bryan pressed an electric key in Indianapolis that sent the presses of the new Chicago *American* whirling. There was only one hitch. Bryan and Hearst could not agree on the main issue for the forthcoming campaign. Hearst favored a declaration of war against the coal, steel, and other trusts, and Bryan wanted to make antiimperialism his stalking-horse. Despite the obvious displeasure of the New England wing of the party, Bryan's nomination seemed certain by the spring. Bryan almost slipped as he climbed into the saddle, however, for his denunciation of American territorial acquisitions was a pale campaign issue compared to the fervor generated by his "Cross of Gold" speech. Then a boom for Admiral George Dewey almost upset the Bryan bandwagon and probably would have if the hero of Manila Bay had not revealed his ineptness through a couple of public utterances. After Dewey's boom fizzled, Bryan easily won the nomination. Then the old party dispenser of plums, Adlai E. Stevenson, was chosen as his running mate. Bryan insisted on retaining the 1896 platform plank of free silver, but he kindled a few sparks of enthusiasm with his plea for a lengthy plank denouncing "territorial expansion when it takes in desirable territory which can [never] be erected into States in the Union." Hearst liked the part promising action against trusts—"Trusts that are the legitimate product of Republican policies . . . fostered by Republican laws [and] . . . protected by the Republican administration, in return for campaign subscriptions and political support."

Bryan campaigned fervently. The outcome was foretold by the complacence of the opposition, because the Republicans depended on the popular war and prosperity to keep voters loyal. Working men were warned that a Democratic vote might bring the dreaded breadlines and thin pay envelopes. Bryan piously talked about protecting "our brown brothers" in Mindanao, while Republican editorials exhorted voters to cast a ballot for "McKinley and a full dinner pail." The specter of the Democrats as radical reformers with wild-eyed, impractical schemes that would dilute the nation's currency was constantly drummed into voters by the dominant Republican press. When Hearst counterattacked, the opposition branded the publisher as a bird of similar feather (and after McKinley's assassination in 1901, much of the blame was heaped on the transplanted Californian's rancorous attacks on the dead president). "From coast to coast this newspaper has been attacked and is being attacked with savage ferocity by the incompetent, the failures of journalism, by the kept organs of plutocracy," the *Journal* charged. "One of the Hearst papers' offenses is that they have fought for the people, and against privilege and class pride and class greed and class stupidity . . . with more force and talent and enthusiasm than any other newspapers in the country." This was true, and the aged Hearst of a half-century later was in no way identical to the Democrat who was aiming at the presidency as he blew out the thirty-eight candles on his birthday cake.

Hearst's flirtation with the Democrats in 1896 had been logical. He and Bryan were both young men on the make, and as the son of a Democratic senator from California, Hearst had grown up attached to "the party of the people." The Bryan–Stevenson ticket lost, but Hearst had been loyal and sometimes almost single-handedly kept the nominees from being totally ignored in metropolitan America. Although they were swamped by an electoral vote of 292 to 155 and lost by nearly 900,000 votes in the popular ballot, Bryan and the Democrats owed Hearst a favor. A seat in Congress (from a Tammany-controlled ward) was his first reward. With the twelve thousand Democratic clubs he nominally headed as a base, Hearst moved toward the White House by encouraging the nationwide formation of William Randolph Hearst clubs.

Hearst's detractors, who formed an enormous legion, scoffed at his pretensions; but we need to be reminded that in 1903 "Hearst, more than any other man, was the absolute expression of all the blind need and ignorance and resentment which troubled the worker and farmer."* The New York *Evening Post* condemned Hearst's drive for the Democratic nomination. "There never has been a case of a man of such slender intellectual equipment, absolutely without experience in office, impudently flaunting his wealth before the eyes of the people and saying, 'Make me President.'" To show that he had spunk, freshman Congressman Hearst tried to introduce a bill calling for an investigation of railroad rebates that kept coal prices high. Regular Democrats had no liking for the ambitious upstart, which meant that his pet bill went nowhere, a situation that applied throughout his frustrating years in Washington.

Hearst vowed to be back, expecting that his newspaper war on the trusts would cause a surge of public opinion the convention delegates in St. Louis could not ignore. Bryan, after two losing battles, was thought to favor Hearst in return for past favors; his endorsement could have stopped the building sentiment for Judge Alton B. Parker. Parker, an able but colorless conservative, had

*Louis Filler, *Crusaders for American Liberalism* (New York: Harcourt, Brace, 1961), 137.

the New York Democrats from Albany and Tammany pulling for him—an embarrassment to Hearst since he now resided there. Parker delegates made jibes at Hearst's backers, claiming they were branded with dollar signs, while Bryan's known anti-Parker stance was liberally interpreted as a backhanded boost for Hearst.

Bryan, a bit flabbier but still the spellbinder, shocked the convention by placing a nonentity in nomination. The custom of long demonstrations after a nominating speech was gaining popularity, and Hearst newspapers joyfully noted that their chief's rally lasted thirty-eight minutes. One minute would have been sufficient, however, for when the 997 delegates started voting, only 194 went to Hearst. Parker, carried by a surge of support by hard-money Democrats, was soon the nominee.

Of course, Democrats never did anything the easy way, and Parker fell in with tradition. After two violent clashes over the soft-money plank, the convention shied away from the silver-gold issue completely. Informed of his nomination, Parker shot back a telegram to the delegates declaring he would not run unless the party came out for a gold-backed dollar. Bryan nearly had a stroke when he heard the bad news, but Hearst's men saw a slim ray of hope for their man. "The Democratic party can always be relied on to make a damn fool of itself at the critical time," Senator Tillman observed with a sad shake of his head. The New Yorkers talked Parker into toning down his remarks, and the convention adjourned to send a divided party back to campaign halfheartedly for a man whom few knew and fewer thought could beat the high-riding Theodore Roosevelt. Their expectations were met as Parker, a dismal campaigner, won the South's 140 electoral votes and nothing more. The Democrats' only solace was that in South Carolina, Parker had 52,563 votes to Roosevelt's 2,554. Across the nation, Roosevelt's majority was over 2.5 million votes.

The national Democratic party had fallen to pieces. Bryan, still in his forties, was willing to work, but his ideas on silver and imperialism had been rejected by the voters. Issues were sub-merged by personalities, and Roosevelt was having a grand time as the darling of the Republican press. The presidency had be-come, more and more, a nationwide popularity contest. The party loyalty of yesteryear was lacking in Democratic wards, where the glamour of Roosevelt's candidacy was in sharp relief against Par-ker's prissy stand on hard money. Nationally, the party still ex-pected people such as August Belmont, the New York financier who had been at the 1860 convention, to keep the coffers filled (they never were, and Bryan had scrimped to get by on $650,000 in 1900). Locally, the city machines were apolitical in many re-spects; patronage flows could be managed despite the loss of a governor's race if the right people were still on influential boards and commissions. Indeed, the brazen power of the machines had provoked Lincoln Steffens' sensational magazine articles in *Mc-Clure's*. The articles jolted Roosevelt into coining the word *muck-raker* as a pejorative term for a nosy reporter ("adversary jour-nalist," in 1970s parlance).

As one of the first muckrakers, Steffens perceived that political parties were changing from groups of voters united by a philo-sophical bond into warring camps that often knew not why they warred. He saw that machine bosses used party labels for selfish personal gains, bolted to the opposition when an opportunity beckoned, and never thought about what was best for the people's interests. Starting with the corrupt Democratic machine in St. Louis, Steffens investigated and exposed political machines in Chi-cago, Minneapolis, Pittsburgh, Philadelphia, and Boston. In St. Louis a young Democratic lawyer, Joseph W. Folk, had been machine-elected as a circuit attorney on the assumption he was "safe." Once in office the conscientious Folk uncovered a web of corruption managed by the Democratic machine (which had been elected on a reform ticket). What Steffens found was that grafting politicians cared little for the party label they wore, as long as their corruption was underwritten by the businessmen of the community; in Philadelphia or Pittsburgh the machine was nominally Republican, and a Democrat won control of Minneapolis running as a Republican. Payoffs for votes on streetcar franchises, Steffens learned, were eagerly accepted by men elected as Democrats, who were turned out by Republicans, who then took higher bribes in the name of reform.

New York was, at the moment, in the hands of the "goo-goos," or good government crowd, that had followed Seth Low to defeat Tammany in 1901. Low brought in civil service reform and an honest set of officials, but after two years the party bosses contrived his defeat. The frustrated reporter admitted that Tammany was "hardly known by its party name—Democracy—having little standing in the national councils of the party and caring little for influence outside of the city." At least, Steffens conceded, Tammany leaders "have their hold because they take care of their own." Tammany favors ranged from a job on the city payroll, to picnics on the Hudson, to seeing that an arrested man had a friend in court. Sadly, Steffens concluded, the urban voters did not care much whether a Democrat or a Republican was in power. He quoted a Philadelphia ringleader for a kind of epilogue: "The American people don't mind grafting, but they hate scandals."

No scandals rocked the White House while Theodore Roosevelt lived there. The indefatigable TR was the newspaperman's pal, a generous man with the quip and a buoyant mood that suited the country. No politician who so captured the nation's affection that the toy teddy bear was named after him needed to worry about disgruntled voters, though his foray into trust busting ruffled some of the GOP stalwarts on Wall Street.

Bryan was waiting in the wings when the Democrats girded themselves for a forlorn-hope campaign in 1908. Among the 1,001 delegates attending the convention there was a sprinkling of women. These active ladies were dead-earnest advocates of a constitutional suffrage amendment and were the first women ever accredited by a major-party convention. Their enthusiasm was hardly contagious, although the party faithful made all the required speeches hailing imminent victory for the Democracy.

In fact, shaken by the muckrakers' disclosure, voters looked to Republicans to follow through on reforms promised or underway in the life insurance, coal, railroad, and security industries, among others. Roosevelt had paid some attention to saving the public lands and listened to the long-suffering conservationists. Bryan, still a relatively young man, somehow came across as the tired politician with no new answers. Whatever suspense the campaign contained came from a short-lived recession that frightened the party's backbone—the farmers and workingmen. A "currency famine" had reminded people that the Republicans' claims of being the dinner pail party were not 14-carat promises.

Roosevelt, bowing to the third-term pressure, threw his support to cabinet member William Howard Taft. The rotund Ohioan swamped Bryan in a campaign notorious for its lackluster appearance. Bryan still worked hard, but the thrill in his voice was missing. The suffragettes, who demanded the vote and paraded down Fifth Avenue in bloomers, drew the derision of sidewalk commentators; but they had a good deal more going for them than Bryan's tired messages on silver coinage. And the tidal wave of Americans shifting from farms to cities was flowing strong. The census figures soon showed that a nation 95 percent agrarian in 1800 had grown to a country with forty-two million in its cities and barely fifty million people still on farms or living in villages. The stream of immigration had also been diverted from northern Europe and the British Isles to southern and eastern Europe. This new wave was reflected in the Italian, Russian, and Yiddish newspapers founded between 1880 and 1910; and unlike the earlier immigrants, these new Americans did not rush to join political parties. Their hesitancy stemmed from their Old World experience, for they had come from lands where politics operated out of fear rather than persuasion.

Bryan was ill-prepared to handle the new forces taking shape, and the apathetic American male voters eagerly accepted Roosevelt's endorsement of Taft. Bryan captured only the South along with Nebraska, two mining states, and the newly admitted Oklahoma. In spite of 6.4 million votes this was less than a movable feast for a man who during three presidential campaigns had been the walking embodiment of the Democratic party.

Even worse were the Democrats' future prospects. Bryan was finished, but so was nearly everybody else. The Democrats desperately needed a messiah for 1912, but most of the promising young men in the North and Midwest for a generation or so had been Republicans. The increasing agitation for the direct election of senators, for an income tax, for a ban on the sale of ardent spirits, and for voting rights for women were all issues that made thousands of voters discomfited in the conservative America of 1908. The agitation for constitutional amendments provoked the fictitious Chicago bartender, Mr. Dooley, into giving newspaper readers a fair assessment of the nation's feelings.

I injye th' right to get money, but I niver have had anny money to spind. Th' constichooshion guarantees me th' right to life, but I die; to liberty, but if I thry bein' too free I'm locked up; an' to th' pursoot iv happiness, but happiness has th' right to run whin pursood, an' I've niver been able to three her yet. . . . I'd give all th' rights I read about for wan privlege. If I cud go to sleep th' minyit I go to bed I wudden't care who done me votin'.

SEVEN

New Freedom, New Deal, and New Problems

Princeton University was no hotbed of liberalism during the first decade of this century. Republican fathers sent their sons there to learn French and history and how to make money; but perhaps President Woodrow Wilson, formerly a Princeton professor, was forgiven his Democratic affiliation, since he had opposed Bryan in 1908 (particularly after the Peerless Leader had returned from Europe and called for state ownership of all railroads). Wilson, a native Virginian who spoke and sometimes thought like a Yankee, impressed the money men in New York when he lamented Bryan's continued hold on the Democratic party. As Bryan's comet fizzled, Wilson's star rose, boosted by his after-dinner remarks in praise of the conservative edge of the old Jeffersonian party. Encouraged by important men on Wall Street to run for the New Jersey governorship on a reform platform, Wilson easily succumbed to their entreaties. He then proved to be a maverick and scored an astonishing victory in the 1910 general election by pledging to fight "boss rule."

Bryan was finished as a popular candidate, and until Wilson's reform record in New Jersey began to attract attention, the Republican press more than once suggested that what the Democratic party needed was a quiet but decent burial. Democrats bounced back to control the House after the 1910 elections, however, and Speaker Champ Clark was a different breed of politician from his autocratic predecessor, Joe Cannon. A bill lowering the tariff on textiles passed Congress only to be vetoed by Taft. Taft's men also wrecked the conservationists' plans to halt giveaways of the public domain (some 180 million acres had been handed to the railroads alone); and Democrats saw a campaign issue forming as Taft's secretary of the interior approved enormous land concessions to private industry. No land grant had ever been made by Congress to a corporation or syndicate under a Democratic administration.

In addition, there was the eight-hour day, which the mine workers had talked about for decades until the American Federation of Labor also took up the cry. Cannon would not allow discussion of the radical labor demand while he was Speaker. Remarkably, the House Democrats suddenly showed the kind of imagination that had excited so many voters in 1896, except their program was not a shopworn monetary theory. They struck at the old House rules that made Speakers potentates, and pushed for an eight-hour day for government employees. Probing for a method to halt the cyclical boom-and-bust currency shortages led to legislation that evolved into the Federal Reserve System. The once-taboo subjects of a graduated income tax, a tax on inheritances, votes for women, and the popular election of senators were brought out into the open by congressional debate. To the horror of customers at Delmonico's, a famous New York restaurant patronized by millionaires, an amendment to the Constitution permitting income taxes (struck down previously by the Supreme Court) passed Congress but was less than eagerly received by the state legislatures. If the income tax amendment were ratified, the excuse for a high tariff as necessary to support the federal government would fade. Journalistic exposés of the fortunes accumulated in a tax-free atmosphere by Rockefeller, Morgan, and

Carnegie no doubt prepared the nation for a major overhaul of the taxing structure. Jolted by charges that the Senate was a rich man's club, Congress passed along another constitutional amendment early in 1912 calling for the direct election of senators. And state after state enacted direct primary laws to end the choosing of candidates by the favored few.

Thus the political climate of opinion was changing and ripe for a fresh face to match the swirl of ideas that overwhelmed Taft and his Republican supporters. Totally lacking the political intuition of his predecessor, Taft managed to alienate Republicans right and left, but he still held his honored place with the Republican kingmakers when a disillusioned Roosevelt announced he would fight for the 1912 party nomination. After a bloody Chicago convention, both Taft and Roosevelt were in the race—one as a regular Republican, the other as a bolting "Progressive." The screams of anguish from regular Republicans awoke Democrats to their opportunity. All they needed was a candidate who combined the mystery of a Pierce, the conviction of a Polk, and the intellect of a Jefferson.

Neither Speaker Clark nor majority leader Oscar Underwood of Alabama filled the bill. Only the parvenu from New Jersey, Woodrow Wilson, met all the demands; yet the Democrats loved their two-thirds rule, and if Wilson or any other upstart was going to win the nomination, he first had to cross the field of fire at the Baltimore convention. Clark had the misfortune of attracting Hearst into his camp, for the newspaper publisher was now regarded as a discredited opportunist by old-line Democrats. Underwood's chances were hurt by his southern background; the party had not picked a candidate from the South since the disastrous Breckinridge convention of 1860. Wilson's only other serious rival was Governor Judson Harmon of Ohio, a sound-money Democrat who had served in Cleveland's cabinet. There was no love lost between Bryan and Harmon, a fact that counted later; Bryan's blessing proved to be crucial after the balloting seemed interminable.

On the tenth ballot Clark's supporters counted 556 delegates and sensed victory, for not since 1844 had a candidate with a majority faltered in the home stretch. But Bryan held a final trump. As Clark's strength seemed to be rising, Bryan boomed out his intention of switching from the Missourian to Wilson. Bryan leaped off Clark's bandwagon for the simple reason that Wall Street's staunchest allies were climbing aboard.* When the balloting resumed, after a merciful Sabbath respite, the Illinois machine boss moved his state into Wilson's column. On the forty-sixth ballot, Wilson finally had his two-thirds majority. Hearst fumed. He blamed Bryan for ruining Clark's chances and said Bryan's "ruthless methods" meant "that a nomination delivered to any Democrat by this convention would be of but little value."

While Hearst and Clark ranted, the matter of a platform still confronted the delegates. Mr. Dooley once insisted that "all platforms is alike" because the Republicans took all credit for good things until "they was nawthin' left f'r the dimmycrats but th' 'we denounce and deplores'"; but the 1912 planks were hickory tough. The Republican high tariff was assailed as "a system of taxation which makes the rich richer and the poor poorer," whereby the farmer sold in a free market but bought in a protected market, thus getting the short end of both deals. This plank, which could have been written by a member of Jackson's Kitchen Cabinet, demanded "a tariff for revenue only." Constitutional amendments for an income tax and direct election of senators were endorsed, as was the presidential primary, which a few states had already adopted as an experiment in direct democracy. The use of injunctions to break strikes was denounced as a Republican legal strata-

*Eugene H. Roseboom, *A History of Presidential Elections: From George Washington to Richard M. Nixon* (New York: Macmillan, 1970), 368.

gem; workers were promised their essential right "to organize for the protection of wages and the improvement of labor conditions, to the end that such labor organization . . . should not be regarded as illegal combinations in restraint of trade."

The climax of the 1912 platform came in recognition of the goals of the muckrakers: "The Democratic party offers itself to the country as an agency through which the complete overthrow and extirpation of corruption, fraud, and machine rule in American politics can be effected." A smiling and waving lanky college president, looking something like a Sunday school superintendent, promised to use the platform as his official White House guide. Wilson the candidate soon proved to be a different man from the boardroom conservative who had thought a few years earlier that labor needed tight controls and bankers could be trusted with loose reins. His experience in Trenton had sobered Wilson, changing him into a zealous convert to the progressive cause. He blasted high tariff walls as "the entrenchments of Special Privilege," assailed protective duties as "the mother of trusts," spoke of the Democratic party as a haven for the common man, and insisted that individuals, not corporations, were the only possessors of rights and privileges in a democratic society.

Perhaps Wilson could not have won against a united Republican party. The point is hardly worth pursuing, for the Taft regulars snarled at the Bull Moose wing and groped toward inevitable defeat. The Democratic nominee cut all his past ties with New York bankers and gloried in a campaigner's remark that the issue "clearly joined for the people . . . is Wall Street vs. Wilson." With his finger on the public pulse, Wilson dropped his professorial approach to the nation's problems (he had once thought the president ought to be akin to the British prime minister) and was ready to use the powers of the presidency for a positive role in government. This was a 180-degree turnaround from the traditional and suspicious Democratic view of executive power; but Wilson saw an opportunity to make government an active frontline fighter in the war on trusts, corruption, and poverty, rather than a passive observer. If any lesson from the muckrakers' exposés had been learned by Wilson, it was that graft cannot defy an honest, dynamic leader who had earned the people's trust.

In some ways the 1912 campaign was a bridge between the old Democratic party and an emerging new force that claimed ties to Jefferson and Jackson but felt bound to follow instincts rather than traditions. Thereafter the people would hurl themselves into cities at a fast pace, leaving forever the easygoing tempo of a rural nation where crops, horses, and weather were dominant topics of conversation. The automobile, motion picture, streetcar, electric light, telephone, and new wireless telegraphy heralded a technological revolution that would be accelerated by war and a business boom into an era of unparalleled comfort, anxiety, and social upheaval. Similarly, in politics the dire :t state and presidential preference primaries cut into the power of the old leadership and promised a fulfillment of the Jefferson-Jackson ideal of majority rule for the good of all.

While the winds of change blew, the biggest obstacle facing the Democrats still was mounted by the Republican claims that they alone could keep the nation prosperous. The New York *World*, back in the Democratic fold, assured voters Wilson was a safe bet, as did the Baltimore *Sun*. In an effort to avoid the taint of contributions from corporations, the Democratic National Committee appealed for $1 contributions from "100,000 earnest citizens." Even so, the campaign expenses had to be borne by large contributors since less than a third of the $1.1 million spent by the Democrats came from small contributors. Replacing the old Democratic patrons a new batch of millionaires like brewer Jacob Ruppert and financier Bernard Baruch pledged large sums. Most of the money was spent in New York, where forty-five electoral votes seemed to hold the key to the election.

Wilson's managers spent too much money, but they did one thing right—they pointed their man at Theodore Roosevelt and ignored Taft. With the former president as his target, Wilson stressed the ties Roosevelt had with big business. "The new [Progressive] party legalizes monopolies and systematically subordinates workingmen to them," he told a Labor Day audience in Buffalo. (Wilson spent a lot of time in New York, looking at those forty-five electoral votes as a lover beams on his mistress.) In upstate New York, where Democrats traditionally had hard sledding, a raft of endorsements from the leading newspapers helped relieve the tension.

As a southern man of northern principles, Wilson failed to dent the Negro voter's prejudice against the Democrats. Historian Arthur Link noted that a considerable sum was spent courting the black voters and was "for the most part wasted." A newspaper published for Negro readers in Manhattan put the matter bluntly: "The *New York Age* does not see how it will be possible for a single self-respecting Negro in the United States to vote for Woodrow Wilson . . . he has most of the prejudices of the narrowest type of Southern white people against the Negro."* Wilson walked right by the blacks and stayed out of the Republican strongholds to concentrate on the cities where large numbers of laboring men were registered voters. He also threw his hottest bolts at the high tariff walls and asked his audiences of factory and mill workers if their pay envelopes reflected the blessings of a protective tariff, to which the managed response was always a booming "no!"

The huge crowds who waited for hours to see and hear Wilson in St. Louis, Kansas City, and Chicago were carrying their own message. The people wanted to see the man who was the object of so much newspaper publicity. The media, mainly owned by Republicans, had made Wilson into a potential giant killer even as

*Quoted in Arthur S. Link, *Wilson: The Road to the White House* (Princeton, N.J.: Princeton University Press, 1947), 501–502.

their properties endorsed Taft or Roosevelt. Perhaps 200,000 people had seen or heard Wilson during this fall tour of the midwestern states. During the final days of the campaign, party bosses had little need to exhort loyal precinct workers to make sure of the crowds; throngs in Pittsburgh, New York, and Philadelphia pushed and shoved each other to have a glimpse at the man who might be the next president.

Half of Princeton, New Jersey, was asleep when Wilson learned that he had become the second Democrat to win the presidency since Buchanan left the White House. In the popular vote Wilson was over two million ballots ahead of Roosevelt, and Taft ran a poor third (Socialist Eugene Debs was a relatively strong fourth). In the electoral college it was a Democratic landslide—Wilson had 435 votes to 88 for Roosevelt and 8 for Taft. Even Maine had gone Democratic, along with thirty-nine other states (Arizona and New Mexico had filled out the Union), leaving the Republicans Vermont and seven other GOP bastions. Wilson had lost California by only 174 votes and had routed the Republicans in New York. New England, which had not gone for a Democrat since Pierce, gave Wilson substantial leads. As Bryan said, "Let every Democratic heart rejoice." Congress was also handed over to the Democrats, which meant that the southerners of long tenure would head the key committees. If nothing good happened to the country during the next four years, it would be easy to pin the blame on the Democrats.

The nation soon saw that the Democrats meant business. "No one can mistake the purpose for which the Nation now seeks to use the Democratic party," Wilson said in his inaugural address. Prodded by Wilson, the Democratic Congress launched a legislative program that combined party loyalty with a faithful effort to make the 1912 platform part of the law of the land. The most drastic overhaul of the tariff since 1857 gave consumers lower prices on wool products, paper, sugar, and lumber. The Federal

Reserve banking system swung into action to prevent future panics caused by artificial currency drains. The Clayton Antitrust Act put some teeth into the decrepit trust-control legislation. The Federal Trade Commission was created to see that businessmen eschewed the corruption that was supposedly a trait limited to politicians. Other legislation aided the farmers through low-interest loans and broadened the scope of the eight-hour workday law.

These were heady days in Washington as the Democrats labored to keep their platform promises without publicly proclaiming that the conservative wing of the party had been silenced into submission. Between Cleveland, who thought strikes were illegal and had used troops to break them, and the White House occupant who only sixteen years later told Samuel Gompers that the latchstring was always out, there was a gulf that could only signify a major shift in the party's structure. Labor was moving in to share the spoils of victory with the farmer, and the businessmen would have to move over for both. Moreover, the Democrats had taken the initiative away from the Republicans in the state legislatures, who, prior to 1912, had been far more receptive to organized labor's demand for workmen's compensation laws.

Wilson proved to be not only a talker but a doer. Jefferson had disliked public speaking so much he sent his annual messages to Congress, where they were read by a clerk. This practice was followed by all his successors until Wilson strode into a joint session of Congress, explained the nation's expectations, and pointed out what Congress should do in response. Wilson's cabinet was headed by Bryan, who took over as secretary of state in an obvious bow to seniority (and perhaps for his grand gesture at the Baltimore convention). William Gibbs McAdoo, who had organized financing for the engineering marvels that tunneled under the Hudson River, was named secretary of the treasury. Josephus Daniels was appointed secretary of the navy, with Franklin D. Roosevelt as his assistant. Franklin K. Lane of California was chosen as secretary of the interior. Albert Burleson, a seasoned congressman and artful politician, was picked as postmaster general. There was some shuffling and a few replacements, but this Wilson cabinet took America into the war ahead and, without scandals or furor, gave the country eight years of honest leadership.

Unlike Cleveland, who had no ambitions to control the Democratic party, Wilson used his cabinet and his trusted adviser, Colonel Edward M. House, to keep patronage under control without alienating standpatters or moderates. In some cases this meant dealing with the very forces that had opposed Wilson at the convention, but Wilson wanted a strong majority in Congress and he figured that the only way to achieve it was by cementing party loyalty through patronage. When his convention supporters complained that Wilson had betrayed his friends to placate his former enemies, Wilson recalled an anecdote about an indifferent organ player in a frontier church where a sign was posted: "Don't shoot —he is doing his damnedest." After his friends advised him to stop taking potshots at the New Jersey machine, Wilson resigned himself to working with the bosses he had denounced in the fall of 1912 so that he could have a Democratic Congress elected in 1914.

Urban America, now the dominant force in the nation's political life, showed in the 1914 elections that the city dwellers' romance with the Republicans was no summertime affair. Despite all the reform legislation and a prosperity that Republicans said the Democrats could not sustain, the GOP cut the Democrats' House majority to twenty-five. The elections were held while across the Atlantic war clouds foretold a major shift in European politics. But here at home, without the old and safe southern wing, Democrats would have been struggling to uphold Wilson's reform program. After Germany rolled the Allied armies back to the suburbs of Paris, Wilson urged Congress to start a revitalization of the nation's naval and military strength, but congressmen from German American districts in Wisconsin and Missouri had to be persuaded. The first Democratic leader-president since Polk had a direct telephone line installed from the White House to the Capitol, and he sent young men from one end of Pennsylvania Avenue to the other, scurrying for vital votes on appropriations issues that were too close for presidential comfort.

In many respects Wilson was imitating Theodore Roosevelt by joking when a joke was needed, sternly rebuking when a show of anger was called for, and holding his personal popularity high as an asset for his party's use. But Roosevelt saw virtue in the corporations and delighted in the company of railroad presidents, whereas Wilson encouraged federal agencies to serve as watchdogs on "unfair competition" and let it be known that huge conglomerate empires such as the Standard Oil Company of New Jersey would henceforth proceed under government scrutiny. Still, Wilson did not slam the door on businessmen and bankers who came calling at the White House during a brief recession, and he listened sympathetically when informal agreements were substituted for full-scale trust-busting actions.

The Democrats in Congress began to show real affection for Wilson. He switched from the reform wing to the standpatters in Virginia, supported Underwood in Alabama, and made friends in border states by allowing the old Clark supporters to name their friends to postmasterships and clerical jobs. Perhaps to keep the southerners happy Wilson kept the Negroes at arm's length, allowed federal jobs in Washington to remain on a segregated basis, and in various ways let it be known that his New Freedom was the same old deal for blacks. Booker T. Washington was the foremost of the Negro leaders who confessed their disappointment with Wilson and the Democrats in general.

Even so, the Democratic party that had come out of its cocoon in Wilson's administration was hardly recognizable in the sweep of power now emanating from the White House. True to Jefferson-

Jackson antecedents, the Democrats still labored to keep tariffs low; and the old bank issue had been buried in the vault where the Federal Reserve now kept its currency. But under Wilson the Democrats dropped the conservatism of Cleveland, made overtures to organized labor, and sought alliances in the North and far West to phase out the exclusive delta-prairie entente that had kept the party afloat but rarely victorious.

The European war caused the Democrats to fall back on a traditional position. In 1915 factory orders from the Allies sent Americans to work in record numbers, but shipping their products to Europe brought a long-forgotten Democratic foreign policy plank out of the closet. A German fleet of submarines attacking the British naval blockade aroused the same cry used by Jefferson and Madison, as Wilson reminded the belligerents that freedom of the seas was an old idea that Americans had easily interpreted as fighting words. "Free ships make free goods" had been a Democratic slogan in 1809. Wilson revived the saying as he warned Germany, after the dramatic sinking of the *Lusitania* killed 1,200 (including 128 American citizens), that unrestricted warfare by U-boats was a grave threat to American lives and property.

The nation was so shocked by the *Lusitania* torpedoing that Wilson might have talked Congress into declaring war in May, 1915. Instead he chose to warn Germany of the country's commitment to neutrality. Then, with a presidential election coming up, Wilson mended his party fences in preparation for the quest of a second term. Striving to make his party's structure sound, he worked with local leaders, congressmen, and the national committee to solidify his leadership. He deftly chose positions, legislation, and appointments that would command party support. Certain of his strength through party cohesion, Wilson nominated Louis Brandeis for the Supreme Court early in 1916. Brandeis was the first Jew ever appointed to the high court, and his confirmation brought out the need for party loyalty in the Senate. Congress passed Wilson's much-desired Child Labor Act, which barred goods made by youngsters from interstate commerce. He spoke before the American Federation of Labor convention, which no previous president had ever dared to do. And laws were enacted to end the so-called dumping of cheaply produced foreign goods to undercut the American competitors. The record was impressive, and Wilson knew it.

At the St. Louis convention, jubilant Democrats wasted no time in renominating Wilson amid speeches reminding audiences that the president was a defender of American rights on the high seas and the rights of the farmers and laboring men at home. A delirious throng shouted and beat drums for twenty minutes in the demonstration that followed. A common theme running through the oratory was "He kept us out of war!" Thenceforth, that motto was emblazoned in Democratic newspapers and on party banners until it seemed that Wilson and Peace were synonyms. Unmistakably, the nation wanted to steer clear of the bloodbath that was draining Europe of its youth and treasure.

Confident that a united party could name a winning ticket, the Republicans nominated Supreme Court Justice Charles Evans Hughes, a brilliant lawyer but a poor platform speaker. Considerable sums went into the Republican campaign coffers to help Hughes by electing a GOP Congress. To counter Wilson's "Peace with Honor" campaign the Republicans reminded voters that the current prosperity was war created but that they had given the nation decades of good times since Lincoln's day. German Americans were wooed away from the Democrats by Republican allusions to Wilson's bellicose stand over the *Lusitania*. Irish American voters, angry over the Easter Sunday tragedy in Ireland, were told that Wilson was pro-British (a rare thing, that, a Democrat who was pro-British). The Preparedness Day bombings in San

Francisco gave organized labor a black eye with the general public and probably damaged the Democrats, who were avowedly pro-labor in the major cities. These defections hurt.

To offset the Republican inroads in Pennsylvania and New York, the Democrats organized a western headquarters in Chicago. A women's bureau was added to encourage the participation of a voteless (in all but twelve states) and militant segment of the populace. County weeklies, still one of the great sources of newspaper readership in America, were assiduously courted to counter the heavy imbalance of Hughes endorsements by large-city dailies. William Randolph Hearst, ever the maverick, threw his coast-to-coast chain of dailies squarely behind Hughes. Wilson heard that on Wall Street the betting odds were ten to one against him. "They used to control the finances of the nation," he joked, "now they only control the betting odds." He left much of the speech making to others, including energetic young Franklin D. Roosevelt.

The Republicans came close. When Wilson went to bed on election night, it appeared that he had probably lost. Hughes won by a huge margin in Pennsylvania and was far ahead in New York. Illinois was close until the wee hours, when Hughes went ahead to stay. Except for the South, the outlook at 10 P.M. on election night was disheartening; but Senator Thomas J. Walsh and his friends in Chicago kept saying, "Wait until we hear from the West." Telegraph keys clacked out a message of hope as Montana, North Dakota, Colorado, Utah, Idaho, Washington, and finally California put the lid on Wilson's reelection, with a 600,000-vote plurality over Hughes. The electoral count: Wilson 277, Hughes 254. The Democrats won California by less than 4,000 votes, but that was all Wilson needed.

The victory was Wilson's personal triumph and was not because of a Democratic party endorsement of any magnitude. The Democratic margin in Congress was cut to a mere ten votes. Voters had not been impressed with the party record so much as with

Wilson's promise to keep the country at peace. Within six months he had to break that pledge, an action the country forgave in the excitement of April, 1917, but remembered in the gray dawn of November, 1920. The 1916 Democratic platform had called for votes for women but was silent on the proposed "ban on booze" in the Eighteenth Amendment, which gave the nation a delayed hangover after Congress sent it to the states late in 1917. The suffragettes kept busy until Congress finally sanctioned the women's voting rights amendment in June, 1919. Nearly all other domestic issues were swallowed up by the war, which found the nation essentially unprepared both emotionally and militarily for the tremendous exertions required before the armistice of November, 1918. Party differences were shuttled aside as Wilson appointed Republicans to cabinet and subcabinet posts in a determined effort to "make the world safe for democracy" by feeding a large share of its population and offering a 14-point program to preserve the postwar settlements.

Wilson threw himself into the fray as commander in chief and diplomat extraordinary, forgetting sometimes that he was also the head of the Democratic party. One result was that in the 1918 elections, the Republicans capitalized on the voters' disgruntlement over rationing, wartime restrictions of various sorts, anger at the administration of the draft laws, and similar petty annoyances that would have spelled trouble for any party then in power. Only days before the German surrender, the Republicans won a majority in Congress again to place an implacable foe of Wilson's foreign policy in a key Senate role.

Democrats, dazzled by Wilson's drive and intellectual zest, applauded when the president broke another precedent by going to Europe to direct personally the treaty negotiations. When the League of Nations concept emerged as Wilson's brainchild, a tremendous power struggle in the Senate also took shape, and there Wilson ultimately was beaten by a combination of miscues, prejudices, and party defections. Wilson had met his match in a dozen senators who squirmed as Henry Cabot Lodge read the 268-page Treaty of Versailles to a sleepy Foreign Relations Committee. Wilson apparently had no idea that the league might prove unpopular. Democratic newspapers charged that such blatant partisanship would ruin the hopes of a prostrate Europe. "The peril which the enemies of the League foresee," said the New York *Evening Post*, "is only the imperilment of their own ideas." Republican senators William Borah and Hiram Johnson attacked the treaty by taking the scalpel to its 440 articles, moving the Democrats from amusement and resignation to final despair. Some Democrats who originally had supported Wilson grew restive as the debate wore on; in time they detected a shift in public sentiment against the League of Nations and moved into the opposition camp.

Wilson, bewildered by the threatened rejection of his dream, took his case to the people in September, 1919. He moved large audiences in the West with his tearful recollection of American military cemeteries in France and spoke of his vision of a world with no more wars. Before the tour was over, however, the president suffered a paralytic stroke. His special train raced back to Washington.

Wilson never fully recovered. The Senate revised the treaty, angering the stricken president so that he begged Democrats to do the impossible—reject the revision and support only the original version. Thus partisan politics obscured any effort to determine whether the country really wanted to crawl back into a shell or instead to practice the internationalism that was Wilson's gospel. From his sickbed Wilson made a final plea for rejection of the Senate version of the treaty, and on the crucial vote Republicans Joseph S. Frelinghuysen and Lodge were joined by enough Democrats to gain a 49–35 majority, seven votes short of the necessary two-thirds margin. Wilson's stubborn plea placed the southern Democrats in company with intransigent Republicans Borah and

Johnson and the liberal George Norris. The party loyalty Wilson had nurtured during his first term was dissipated during the last years of his second. Wilson's scorn for the "wilfull little group of men" in the Senate had to include a few of his erstwhile supporters. Wilson's physical condition was not public knowledge, since the press shielded him as an act of courtesy which nevertheless misled the people. The treaty vote came in March, 1920, with the Democratic convention scheduled for San Francisco in June. Wilson's wife, ignoring the advice of Wilson's closest friends, encouraged him to consider running for a third term. Preposterous as it was, nothing could nudge Wilson into a public statement disavowing any plan of renomination. Thousands of loyal Democrats, who only knew the vigorous president whom they had cheered in 1912 or 1916, assumed that he would seek vindication at the polls, and they went to San Francisco committed to his support. In his own official family, McAdoo (now also in Wilson's real family, as a son-in-law) was talked about as a nominee along with the attorney general, A. Mitchell Palmer. The old American penchant for a war hero was missing when the party hopefuls had gathered for the 1920 Jackson Day banquet at the Willard Hotel in Washington. (General John Joseph Pershing was popular but apolitical.) Even Bryan had been there, still hoping, no doubt, for some kind of miracle. Optimism reigned, the Washington *Post* reported under the headline "Many See Wilson as Logical Candidate to Carry Treaty to People."

McAdoo, assuming that Wilson might finally bow out, spoke of withdrawing from contention. But, because bad news always travels faster than good, the word about Wilson reached the hotel lobbies in San Francisco. Even the busboys in the crystal-domed Palace Hotel dining room must have heard of the president's pitiful condition. Wilson, incapable of deciding for himself, did nothing and was not among the fourteen nominated as a marathon of balloting loomed. The nominees included Governor Alfred E.

Smith of New York and John W. Davis, a New Yorker but native West Virginian. McAdoo had a slight lead at the outset, but Governor James Cox of Ohio steadily moved into the lead and finally had the necessary two-thirds majority after a weary forty-third roll call. Franklin D. Roosevelt was picked for the vice-presidential nomination, a tribute to his enthusiasm and good looks (as well as a nod to the eastern wing, which had not been excited about the newspaper publisher-turned-politician).

The convention had its nostalgic moments. William Jennings Bryan was still making speeches (he had quit Wilson's cabinet to protest Wilson's *Lusitania* note) and calling for strict enforcement of the Prohibition laws. The old war-horse was rebuffed when his dry plank came to a vote of the full convention and lost, 930 to 156. A Democratic lady from Tennessee was picked as vice-chairman of the national committee, which was revamped to give each state two members, one of which had to be a committeewoman. The Democrats wanted the women to remember the party that had spearheaded the drive for women's suffrage—the Nineteenth Amendment finally was ratified in August, 1920—while Republicans had dragged their feet.

The selection of Cox was fitting, delegations agreed, because he represented the moderate wing of the party with its midwestern roots at a time when the country seemed in a hurry to forget the recent past. Wilson's preoccupation with the war and the peace treaty, followed by his failing health, meant the White House had defaulted in its responsibility to nurture a crop of qualified Democrats who would keep the embers of Wilson's New Freedom alive. In truth, the New Freedom was dead and its chief exponent, now weary and embittered, soon would be in his grave, too.

After the wartime binge of high prices, which paid for everything from wheat to Model-T Fords, Wall Street cooled off and the nation's economy dipped. The Republicans, sensing the voters' mood as petulant, looked for a candidate who would not ruffle the hackles raised during the treaty fight. They found their man (through a deal arranged in the famous smoke-filled hotel room) in Senator Warren G. Harding, also of Ohio. He was a perfect fence-straddler, having been absent when the vote was taken on the treaty. Harding spoke of carrying America "back to normalcy," and although nobody knew exactly what that meant, it sounded pretty good to over sixteen million voters. Roosevelt had warned them not to be taken in by the "Republican shell game" of deceiving people about the League of Nations; but in the final weeks talk about the league issue seemed to be hurting the Democrats in the cities, on the farms, and throughout the Midwest.

Cox was hit so hard he was spun into obscurity. The Harding landslide deprived Democrats of every state except the South, which was not solid any longer, Tennessee having defected for the first time since Reconstruction days. There was other bad news from the border states; Kentucky stayed with Cox, but Maryland, Missouri, Oklahoma, and West Virginia went in the Harding column. The electoral vote was 404 to 127, and Harding's plurality over Cox was a record-breaking seven million votes. Democratic incumbents in Congress fell by the score, and except for the southern delegation, the party had little to lean on for the forthcoming Congress.

Sick in mind and body, Wilson put on his silk hat and accompanied Harding to the inauguration. The New York *World* observed that morning, "Mr. Wilson is leaving the White House, but his spirit still dominates the scene." It sounded good but it was not true. The New Freedom had been dismantled, and the Harding landslide had demoralized Democrats so completely that for the next twelve years they stumbled through two presidential and six congressional elections without leadership or much hope. The Democratic party needed a statesman, but the best talents of the country seemed headed for law offices, laboratories, and industrial boardrooms during the 1920s.

Not that the party lacked issues. Harding's legendary incompetence left in its wake the Teapot Dome scandals, a cabinet officer sent to prison, and a trail of corruption that crisscrossed Pennsylvania Avenue. Senate Democrats were better at finding evidence of graft than at placing the Harding scandals before voters. Everybody who touched the sordid Teapot Dome business came away with dirty hands, including McAdoo, who had been an attorney for one of the oil magnates involved. McAdoo's legal work had nothing to do with the scandal, but his chances as the standardbearer in 1924 were blighted by the association. Al Smith, the Catholic governor of New York, was considered a strong contender despite the Ku Klux Klan bigotry raging in the country. The racketeering already associated with Prohibition made many Democrats ready to admit that the Eighteenth Amendment was a gross failure, but the party chieftains feared a public stand on the volatile issue. The governor of Texas predicted that repeal would be as easy as trying to change the Ten Commandments. Although farm prices had begun to slip from their 1918 highs, the boom on Wall Street and a general wave of urban prosperity made Harding's successor seem invulnerable. When Calvin Coolidge said "the business of the United States is business," he was talking the cash register politics that caused campaign contributors to dig deeply.

With Wilson dead and McAdoo brushed by the tar from the Wyoming hills, the party failed miserably by turning its back on a southerner, Senator Underwood, who might have rejuvenated the New Freedom he had helped a decade earlier. Instead, bickering between Klansmen in the party's southern wing and Catholics from the large city machines turned the Madison Square Garden convention in 1924 into a public donnybrook.

McAdoo fought back at the whispers about his retainer from the convicted oil man and won support in the South and West, and Governor Smith had friends in the states with huge blocs of electoral votes. Smith, a product of the East Side of Manhattan, was a popular governor who had guided significant social legislation through the labyrinthine Albany legislature. Nominated by Franklin Roosevelt, who called Smith "the Happy Warrior," the New Yorker exuded competence. But his Catholic background frightened party leaders, particularly those below the Mason-Dixon Line, where the Klan had spread a gospel of race prejudice and religious intolerance. A bitterly debated resolution denouncing the Klan finally lost by a single vote. There was less acrimony over a plank urging that the League of Nations issue be removed from party politics so that the nation could give its attention to any viable means of "outlawing the whole war system."

McAdoo led the early balloting but fell into a deadlock with Smith. Weary delegates voted, tried to sleep, and stuck by their men for nine days, until the 102nd ballot, when a "grey horse," John W. Davis, moved into the lead and finally became the nominee. Davis' nomination was a psychological slap at Smith, for the two had little in common beyond their party affiliation. In manners, dress, language, and political philosophy Smith was everything Davis was not. Learned in the law, Davis had served in Congress when the Democratic party was at high tide during Wilson's first term. He left the House to serve as solicitor general, and in that post he scored some notable victories in a couple of civil rights cases before the Supreme Court. He upset the Oklahoma "grandfather clause" law that deprived blacks of their votes, and he knocked down the infamous Alabama convict leasing system.* Sent by Wilson to England as our ambassador in 1918, Davis spent some time at the Versailles treaty conference. When the Democrats shuffled out of power in 1921, he hung up a gilt-edged shingle on Wall Street, an unlikely camping spot for a presidential aspirant in the Democratic party.

*Ironically, Davis represented the diehards in the monumental 1954 *Brown* v. *Board of Education* case, which overturned laws sanctifying racial discrimination.

The platform said that the Republicans were "concerned chiefly with material things; the Democratic party is concerned chiefly with human rights." But voters seemed more concerned about material things, too, judging from the way Coolidge led from the outset in the *Literary Digest* straw poll. Not given to wordiness, Coolidge spoke of "a government of common sense" in his acceptance speech and promised to enforce the Prohibition laws. The nation's leading newspapers hailed Coolidge's short speech, which the Los Angeles *Express* said "deserves a place with the great state papers of America." A dissenting view came from the Baltimore *Sun*, which said the president's words made "an artful appeal to the materialistic instincts of the voters."

As the underdog, Davis could not be a taciturn, front porch campaigner. Accepting his role as a compromise candidate, he made speeches that were too logical to ignite any fireworks during the campaign. He hit at the Republicans' "robber tariff," but only the old-timers were still excited about the tariff. More to the point was the income revelation law, which passed by the grace of House Democrats. Howls of anguish and alarm followed when Secretary of the Treasury Andrew Mellon released the names and incomes of the country's wealthiest men, implying that this was what was in store for the whole country if Davis won. Actually, much of the Republicans' spleen was vented on a liberal GOP senator from Wisconsin, Robert La Follette, who bolted his party to run for president under the Progressive party banner. La Follette, who to his party's embarrassment had pushed the Teapot Dome investigation, made heavy inroads into the Democratic vote, carried Wisconsin, and in California made Davis a poor third.

The voices of both Coolidge and Davis were heard between cracks of static on Atwater-Kent radios—a much-heralded and disappointing innovation in campaigning. Both men looked and sounded like characters out of Sinclair Lewis' *Main Street*. Except for the names, the Republicans might have used the 1896 campaign literature, so similar was the GOP liturgy of economy and national prosperity. The "black bag" corruption of Harding's administration was quickly forgotten by voters, whose main interests seemed fixed on Jack Dempsey, Red Grange, Mary Pickford, and Babe Ruth.

Internally, the Democrats still seethed over the McAdoo-Smith fight. The campaign droned on, with Coolidge holding his peace and Democrats complaining they had run out of money. A new magazine, *Time*, closed the book on the lackluster Coolidge-Davis contest with one sentence: "Election day brought the campaign to an abrupt demise." Coolidge swamped the Democrats everywhere but the South, with a total popular vote of 15.7 million—6 million ahead of Davis. Most embarrassing of all was the fact that Davis had only 28 percent of the popular vote to Coolidge's 54 percent and La Follette's (on the Progressive ticket) 16 percent. The Democratic party has never been so badly beaten, not even with the fiascoes of Parker in 1904 or McGovern in 1972.

The Democrats were down but hardly out. The national party was in disarray, but in Chicago, Jersey City, Kansas City, and New York the Democrats ran well-oiled machines that survived Republican landslides, good government reform movements, and even endless internal bickering. A strong coalition of immigrants and Irish Americans in Chicago held the rock-ribbed Chicago *Tribune* at bay. Frank Hague, a member of the Democratic National Committee, decided who served in what offices in Jersey City. Tom Pendergast handled Kansas City in similar fashion and took a pugnacious county official named Harry Truman under his wing. Tammany still ruled in New York, where the inner brass had boosted into office a handful of young liberals. With Tammany's help, Al Smith bucked the Coolidge trend to defeat Theodore Roosevelt, Jr., in the 1924 governor's race. Smith, Robert F.

Wagner, and James J. Walker were Tammany favorites whose interests ranged from a 48-hour workweek for women to a bill legalizing Sunday baseball. After the 1924 debacle the New York Democrats made their move. Tammany boss Charles F. Murphy died, leaving Smith in control. He backed the popular Jimmy Walker in the 1925 mayor's race and began building a national organization to eradicate Klan support from within the party. Increased crime associated with rum running and bootlegging caused Prohibition to rise as an issue that would be pivotal in 1928. Smith made an unequivocal stand in 1920 when as governor of New York he tried to have the state's ratification of the Eighteenth Amendment repealed. Convinced that the people had made a gigantic error and wanted to admit it, Smith became an avowed Wet. No issue fermented between 1924 and 1928 as did the eastern Democrats' drive to repeal the Eighteenth Amendment, for it clearly separated party followers in the South and West from their big-city brothers. Moreover, it was a declaration of war on the Ku Klux Klan, which by 1927 had between three and four million members, most of them from rural and small-town America.* "Science had abolished the God of their fathers," Oscar Handlin observed, "strange influences emanating from the city had weakened the family and destroyed traditional standards of authority; intemperance created bad habits; and corruption spread through politics and business." A vast number of Klansmen considered themselves Democrats. Smith was bound to bring out the worst in that wing of the party which burned crosses and wore white hoods in search of an all-white, fundamental Protestant past. The Know-Nothing party was long dead, but the spirit still moved in Atlanta, Indianapolis, and Little Rock.

Smith had a disarming frankness that was a political asset in

*David M. Chalmers, *Hooded Americanism* (New York: Doubleday, 1965), 291.

New York but little help in the Central Valley of California, where the Hearst newspaper was warning readers of a Yellow Peril taking shape in the Orient. Smith liked to admit he favored the underdog, and his record on social legislation proved it. As for being president, he confessed that New York had so much power in national politics, any man elected governor (as he was four times) could sit "on the steps of the capitol at Albany with his spyglass trained on Washington."

Knowledgeable Democrats were heartened when Coolidge said he did not choose to run in 1928; this meant they would not be facing an incumbent. The Klan's popularity suddenly waned after KKK officials were imprisoned for a variety of felonious activities. But the Prohibition issue was touchier than the city Democrats realized. "If you think this country ain't Dry," Democrat Will Rogers warned, " you just watch 'em vote; and if you think this country ain't Wet, you just watch 'em drink. You see, when they vote, it's counted; but when they drink, it ain't. If you could register the man's breath that cast the ballots, that would be great. But the voting strength of this country is Dry."* It turned out that Rogers knew a lot more about America than Smith. The party platform lacked Smith's forthrightness. As in 1924, the plank only pledged Democrats to support the law. There was more humor in that plank than in some of Rogers' newspaper jibes.

Democrats trooped to Houston in 1928 because Jesse Jones lived there. Jones, a wealthy cotton broker, promised to pick up the unpaid bills, and party finances were such that Houston had no formidable opposition. The New Yorkers' special train chugged into the Houston depot full of enthusiastic Democrats wearing straw hats with red, white, and blue bands booming Smith. Sidewalk salesmen hawked neckties emblazoned with SMITH AND——above a generous stein of foaming beer, and bands played "On the

* Quoted in Oscar Handlin, *Al Smith and His America* (Boston: Little, Brown, 1958), 125–46.

Sidewalks of New York." Franklin D. Roosevelt, wheeled into the convention, acted as Smith's floor manager. After the favorite sons went through the motions, Smith's name rattled through the hall and a noisy demonstration was carried across the nation on the radio. The Happy Warrior was going to have his chance.

A consummate campaigner in his own backyard, Smith proved to be less of a spellbinder on the campaign trail. His East Side accent grated on soft-drawling southerners, and his flamboyant wisecracking style offended midwestern farmers. The Klan, though dying, was alive enough so that burning crosses in Oklahoma and Montana lighted the tracks of Smith's whistle-stopping train. Protestant ministers raised the specter of "a Pope calling at the White House" and questioned the morals of a man who was so blunt in his opposition to Prohibition. The national Republican party nominated a safe and sane Iowa native, Herbert Hoover, and steered clear of an anti-Catholic propaganda. This did not deter dozens of state and local GOP committees, however, from passing out crude handbills and pamphlets detailing imagined horrors that would descend if Smith reached the White House. Virtually conceding Smith's loss, the New York *Times* said editorially that some consolation would be derived from a large popular vote for the Democrat "even if he should fail of election." "No thinking man, no political manager," would ignore an avalanche of votes for Smith since this would prove that voters wanted something "done to repair or avert the immense harm wrought by prohibition." A heavy Smith vote would also, the *Times* claimed, prove that voters rejected "the miserable and unAmerican spirit of religious intolerance . . . in our public life."

The same October 21, 1928, issue of the *Times* also told another story. Although large commodity surpluses were beginning to pile up on farms and in warehouses, International Harvester stock sold for 309, J. I. Case for 395. Other industries also had soaring shares; DuPont reached 435, RCA 237, General Motors 221, and Montgomery Ward 349. The country was on a spree that was leaving the farmers holding the sack; but most of the population was living in cities and towns and they had not yet heard the Macedonian cries from rural America, where folks still read by kerosene lamps and used wood fires for cooking and heating. (The farm bloc in Congress was a bipartisan coalition of Democrats and Republicans battling shoulder to shoulder to see that agrarian interests were not totally submerged by spokesmen for labor and industry.)

In the final days of the campaign the widely read *Literary Digest* dropped another load of bricks on the Democrats. The popular magazine announced that its final 1928 poll gave Smith only four states in the South and showed that the rest of the nation would go for Hoover by a 63-percent majority if the sampling proved correct. Which was almost the case. Smith did not lose the entire South; he only lost half of it. But he did gain Massachusetts and Rhode Island (states with large Catholic populations). Hoover had called Prohibition "a noble experiment" and pointed to the bustling marketplace, and that had been enough to give him 444 electoral votes. The only solace for the Democrats lay in urban America. Reversing the 1920 trend, Smith had carried the twelve largest cities and had more votes than any other losing candidate in history.

Smith conceded that he had been soundly whipped, and tried to hide his bitter disappointment. Humorist Will Rogers said, two days after the voting:

FOR SALE—Would like to sell, trade, dispose of or give away to right parties franchise to what is humorously known as Democratic Party. Said franchise calls for license to enter in national elections . . . but if intelligent parties had it they would let various elections go by default when understood they had no chance. If in right hands and only used in times when it had an "issue" or when Republican party had split, think it could be made to pay, but present owners have absolutely no business with it. Under present management they have killed off more good men than grade crossings have.

Democrats needed to laugh. Smith's hand-picked national chairman conceded that America had reached "a permanent plateau of prosperity." "Prosperity absorbs not only all criticism but nearly all issues as well," party historian Frank Kent surmised. The opposition, triumphant on a dry platform, was drunk with power. On March 4, 1929, Hoover was inaugurated amid speculation that the Democratic party had become "the permanent minority" in the nation's political life. The Democrats were badly outvoted in Congress, had lost governorships in most northern strongholds, and could only point to Franklin D. Roosevelt's victory in New York for consolation. There, on the capitol steps in Albany, the man in the wheelchair had his spyglass pointed toward the Potomac.

Roosevelt had paid his dues in the Democratic party. Starting as a state senator, he had worked first in Albany and then in Washington (as assistant secretary of the navy), campaigned for Cox as his running mate, bargained to keep Smith from being overwhelmed, and then won the governor's race in 1928 when nearly all other Democrats lost. A tough campaigner who struggled to conceal the physical damage he suffered from a poliomyelitis attack in early manhood, Roosevelt had a Harvard accent but an understanding of the common man when he surveyed audiences of workers and farmers who were worried about wages and milk prices. During the summer and early fall of 1929, Roosevelt probably dreamed of becoming president, but such a vision was farfetched. The Democrats were still in shock, ready to concede that Smith was their titular leader because nobody else had the urge to challenge him.

Politics was becoming a dull business, while the marketplace provided the nation with the thrill of speculation. Bucket shops sold stock on thin credit margins with few cautionary words about risks. RCA stock had shot up to 520, even though the company had never paid a dividend. General Electric had climbed a shocking 200 points in nine months. Each day the smiles on Wall Street grew broader. Skyscrapers were abuilding. When stock prices faltered and made a sharp plunge, a battery of university professors told newspaper reporters the sell-off was a "temporary correction . . . affording a buying opportunity for quality stocks." Then, without any warning, all the accumulated steam in the overheated economic boilers blew off the safety valves almost overnight. Black Friday on Wall Street gave way to Gloomy Monday, and Ghastly Tuesday, October 29, 1929, when sixteen million shares were dumped in a selling panic. Nobody could have been thinking about the 1932 presidential elections that night. They were too worried about what would happen on Wednesday. The next morning readers of the New York *Times* were reassured by John J. Raskob, the Democratic National Chairman, that the setback was temporary. "My friends and I are all buying stocks," he said.* More millions of shares were available for them, as the avalanche of selling continued.

Gradually, the dismal ticker tape news from New York went humming out across the land. Bewildered citizens soon worried about their savings in banks, which led to more panic, bank closings, called-in loans, foreclosures, and factory layoffs. When automobile sales plummeted, Henry Ford cut back on production to send a scare through the working men in Detroit. Half-finished buildings were abandoned by bankrupt construction firms. Factory orders dwindled. The Bank of the United States in Manhattan was forced to lock its doors, leaving 400,000 desperate depositors

---

*Raskob, a Catholic and personal friend of Al Smith's, had broken with precedent after the 1928 campaign and established a permanent national committee office in Washington. He remained as chairman until replaced by James A. Farley.

wondering if they had lost everything. Before the end of 1930, some 1,300 banks had failed.

What the nation needed was a combination of a George Washington and Houdini, to restore confidence and perform magic. But Hoover, for all his abilities, was overwhelmed by the magnitude of the crisis. He first assured citizens that the country's business was "on a sound and prosperous basis." When that proved to be untrue, Hoover called on the Federal Reserve to lower interest rates and thus promote industrial expansion. But the Republican Congress turned the tables by passing the Hawley-Smoot Tariff Act, which raised the duties on most imported goods to the highest levels in history. That forced many European industrial nations out of the American market, helping to bring on their own depression a year later. Twelve million Americans looking for work were confronted with NO HELP WANTED signs.

In New York State, Governor Roosevelt responded to the crisis by calling on the legislature to pass relief programs for the unemployed and establish a pension plan for the aged. The country was turning into a nation of skeptics, many of whom agreed with Will Rogers' earlier quip about Roosevelt: "If he had retained his splendid qualities and stayed with the Republican end of the family, he would have been President." The dean of political columnists, Walter Lippmann, dismissed Roosevelt as "a pleasant man who, without any important qualifications for the job, would very much like to be president."

Wheat fell to thirty-five cents a bushel, cotton was offered at six cents to few buyers, and in the Southwest parched farmlands were foreclosed as the dust storms whirled past abandoned homes and broken windmills. "Brother, Can You Spare a Dime?" became a popular song—people could still sing—and with pork chops selling for fifteen cents a pound it was possible to eat well, provided a dollar bill was still in the family sugar jar. In these circumstances the Democrats headed for the Chicago convention convinced that the country was tired of "Hooverizing." The beleaguered president, stirring himself, called for low-interest loans to homeowners and farmers and an enlarged scale of relief programs (to be administered by the states and cities); and he asked fortunate Americans to make sizable contributions to charitable groups providing emergency meals and beds for the wandering jobless.

On the other hand, some things were unchanged. Democrats still had their Jackson Day dinners in Washington early in January and charged five dollars a plate as they had in 1912. Smith, believing the party owed him a third crack at the presidency, told the gathered faithful that Prohibition had to go. "Why, rum, booze and beer are running all over the United States untaxed," he said, "and the only man that is going to be safe during March when you have to make all those income tax figures up is the bootlegger." Roosevelt had not been so forthright about where he stood on repeal. "Why in hell don't he speak out!" an angry Smith blurted. The Washington *Post* noted that Roosevelt would not be at the Jackson Day dinner but that a trip to the capital then was unnecessary, because "the Democrat most acceptable to the greatest number of Democrats in all sections is Franklin D. Roosevelt."

Victory-hungry Democrats gathering near the Chicago stockyards thought they detected the winds of change shifting their way. Roosevelt had won important primaries but had lost the big ones. William Randolph Hearst saw a Roosevelt boom forming and tried to head it off by coming out for Texan John Nance Garner, Speaker of the House of Representatives. Hearst created a boomlet for Garner as "a plain man of the plain people . . . another Champ Clark." Because the first Champ Clark had failed, it was predictable that with Hearst backing him Garner would also wither in the Chicago heat. The campaign for the nomination took a strange twist when the Hearst newspapers vaulted Garner into the thick of the fight by an upset victory in the California presidential primary. Meanwhile, Al Smith broke with Roosevelt and became the

Tammany candidate, which meant that Roosevelt would go to the convention with only a portion of his own state's important votes. A sign of the times was the fact that the only other serious candidate was Newton D. Baker, who had been in Wilson's wartime cabinet.

The Roosevelt demonstration began with an organist playing "Happy Days Are Here Again!," a tune that has since become a Democratic theme song. When the roll was called, Roosevelt had been stymied by the two-thirds rule, for he had 666 votes on the first ballot but needed 770 to win the nomination. Smith was second, trailed by Garner and Baker. By the third ballot there were fears that Roosevelt's support might give way, that a dark horse might suddenly rear up. Here, so the story goes, old Hearst picked up his telephone in far-off San Simeon and talked with James A. Farley, Roosevelt's manager. Perhaps it was then that the word went out. When the fourth roll call began, William Gibbs Mc-Adoo (now a Californian heading his delegation, senatorial candidate, and friend of Hearst) announced that his state was switching 44 votes from Garner to Roosevelt. The bandwagon rolled, and in quick order the party had a Roosevelt-Garner ticket. At long last, so Hearst believed, he had become a real power in the making of a president.

In the ensuing campaign, Roosevelt soft-pedaled his "forgotten man" theme, which, before the convention, had gained much attention but also drew fire from Smith and others as a "demagogic appeal to the masses of the working people of this country . . . setting class against class and rich against poor." Instead, Roosevelt fell back on the traditional Democratic cudgels—demands for a lower tariff, a balanced national budget—and said he was pleading "not for a class control but for a true concert of interests." He even took a stand on repeal; he was for it.

Plenty of forgotten men showed up at the polls on election day—enough to give the Democrats the presidency, control of

Congress, and more statehouse executives than anybody could remember. In his acceptance speech at the Chicago convention, Roosevelt had said: "I pledge you, I pledge myself, to a new deal for the American people." Voters took Roosevelt on faith, convinced that Hoover could not cope with the misery that was engulfing the nation. The victory was not for the Democrats so much as for the desperate fear resulting from the Republicans' failure to keep their promise of prosperity. Indeed, since Monroe had weathered the 1819 panic, no incumbent president has been able to withstand the loss of confidence that arose during a depression.

Roosevelt realized the nation was groping for a sign of restored hope, and he set about in spectacular fashion to make the New Deal a reality. During the famous hundred days Roosevelt used his party leadership as had no president since Jefferson to enact with unaccustomed rapidity social legislation, farm bills, credit measures, and public works programs that were daring, innovative, and breathtaking in their blow to old party ties. Blacks in the cities, once considered safe Republican voters, deserted the GOP in a mass exodus of combined hero worship and gratitude for the attention New Dealers paid to exploited Negro laborers and sharecroppers. Farmers, patronized by the so-called farm bloc but in reality weakened by their blind loyalty to Republican laissez faire policies, found their populist instincts channeled into action by the free-wheeling Henry A. Wallace, a converted Iowa Republican who, as secretary of agriculture, educated Roosevelt about pigs and corn prices. Roosevelt's electrifying bank moratorium gained him friends in the business community who were near the precipice of bankruptcy, and he picked up more support when insured bank deposits and a regulated securities market injected stability into what had been near chaos on Wall Street.

The honeymoon did not last too long, but during the first six months or so the Democrats made enough friends in Washington to last a generation. And it is doubtful if any political party in our history had as much balanced leadership or preached party loyalty with as much conviction as was the case during Roosevelt's White House tenure from 1933 to 1945. Roosevelt came as close as any man could in trying to combine the roles of Washington and Houdini. At the same time, he paid homage to the Democratic party in ways others had not dreamed of. The Jefferson Monument for the party's founder, long talked of but only a drawing board sketch, rose east of the Capital Mall. The Jefferson-Jackson Day dinners had long been a party fixture, with the one held in Washington serving as a famous annual sounding board and gathering of the clan. From 1827 to 1935 the dinner tickets had cost a nominal sum, usually five dollars, but with Farley as postmaster general and party wheelhorse these affairs became an important fund-raising activity. Starting in 1936 the Democratic National Committee took charge and sent out one or more tickets to all party members in Congress (and in high appointive federal positions) with a $50 price tag. Two thousand Democrats contributed $100,000 to the party coffers at the 1936 dinner, where the president spoke. Thereafter, Farley and his followers raised the price to $100 (and much later, as a sign of the inflationary times, to $1,000). Budgetary deficits notwithstanding, the Jackson-Jefferson Day dinners also took a role in party affairs when two presidents used them as a forum to announce their retirement. Dinners held around the country coincided with the Washington gathering and attracted as many as 250,000 Democrats during the heyday of the New Deal. These affairs furnished state and local party committees with war chests for future campaigns and helped to pay old bills left over from past battles.

During the early New Deal years the party flourished as never before through the support Roosevelt and his appointees gave to Democrats at nearly every level of government. Loyalty to the party, often paid lip service at convention time, became a key tenet in Roosevelt's working guide to the presidency. Through Farley, and later through his successors (also postmasters general, which made that cabinet seat a party listening post), the national committee functioned as an adjunct of the White House staff. The committee's professional staff was paid by the party, but its eyes and ears focused on 1600 Pennsylvania Avenue.

Farmers were a dwindling part of the voting population, but through the New Deal program of price supports, rural electrification, and the farm loan program, the agrarians received more attention under Roosevelt than under all past presidents. If the direct subsidies and special favors to farmers were not within the Jeffersonian tradition, they fitted into the New Deal scheme as part of an effort to "help the common man help himself" out of the depression. Deftly Roosevelt supported parity prices for farmers while he assured city-dwelling consumers that their interests were not being overlooked. Indeed, the city-dwelling organized laborer in a sense had replaced the farmer as the yeoman Democrat. This fact was attested to by the Wagner Act and companion legislation, which assured minimum wages and protected unions from coercive tactics by setting fair arbitration standards. A generation of big-city Democrats relied on the Wagner Act—"Labor's Bill of Rights"—for their campaign pitch, as a testament of faith meant to stir loyalties at the polls on election day. On civil rights for blacks, however, Roosevelt was skittish. As Frank Freidel noted, Roosevelt "seemed ready to leave well enough alone in questions that involved white supremacy."

In the cities New Deal alliances were made with James Curley, Frank Hague, Ed Kelly, Pat Nash, Tom Pendergast, and a score of lesser machine leaders to control patronage and to assault the main citadel of distress—unemployment. Actually, the New Deal welfare program was replacing the bosses' Santa Claus image, weakening the old-fashioned paternalism among literate second- and third-generation voters. Roosevelt could not stomach all the local bosses, however, and his break with Senator Huey Long had long-range, shattering effects on Louisiana politics. Long announced early in 1935 he would seek Roosevelt's defeat at the 1936 convention, but the Kingfisher died that fall, the victim of an assassin.*

Roosevelt's critics, who always constituted a small army, claimed that his crushing defeat of Alfred M. Landon in 1936 was a personal, not a party, victory; in fact, the president carried his party along. Landon won only Maine and Vermont in the electoral college (the worst defeat in United States history), but Republicans running for Congress were also stunned by the Roosevelt landslide. In the House, the Seventy-fifth Congress had 331 Democrats, 89 Republicans; and in the Senate, 76 Democrats, 16 Republicans. The party that had been dismissed as a permanent minority in 1928 had risen spectacularly in the eight intervening years. As Roosevelt's cabinet member and confidant Harold Ickes mused a few days after the election: "The Democrats gained Governors and Senators and Congressmen where already they had too many. . . . The President pulled through to victory men whose defeat would have been better for the country."† Such frankness was probably confined to cabinet meetings.

Since nearly 80 percent of the newspapers had supported Landon and at least one poll had predicted a Republican victory, the question was raised, What accounted for Roosevelt's landslide? The answer was found in the depression (still lingering) and in the personality of FDR. The word was rarely used in Roosevelt's time, but he certainly had *charisma* to spare.

Perhaps too impressed by the magnitude of his victory, Roose-

*Roosevelt's supporter and the boss of Chicago, Anton Cermak, also was assassinated. Cermak was in Miami, riding in the same car with President-Elect Roosevelt, when an assassin fired in the car's direction and hit Cermak. Roosevelt was unharmed.

†Harold L. Ickes, *The Secret Diary of Harold L. Ickes* (3 vols.; New York, Simon & Schuster, 1953), I, 700–705. A reformed Republican who had once campaigned for Theodore Roosevelt, Ickes served as secretary of the interior from 1933 to 1946.

velt launched his campaign to increase the Supreme Court, where Republican-appointed justices were thwarting some key features of the New Deal. For the first time the Democrats in Congress balked, leading to some disenchantment between the Hill and the White House. Roosevelt finally gave up that fight (one of the few he lost) and became more involved in international affairs after August, 1939. Nonetheless, state party chairmen knew they could always have ten minutes of the president's calendar when they visited Washington, and New Deal opponents within the party learned to mute their criticism on even-numbered years.

Although Roosevelt was accused of being an intense partisan, much of his party loyalty was a response to the intemperate attacks leveled at him by the press from the summer of 1933 onward. Convinced that Republican publishers had carried their detestation of his policies too far, Roosevelt inaugurated his famous fireside chats to go over the heads of the newspaper moguls and reach the people directly through their four-tube radio sets. Public reaction to these informal talks was so favorable that Roosevelt lessened his rancor against the lords of the press.* A notable exception was the Chicago *Tribune*, in which Roosevelt's old Harvard classmate Robert McCormick turned all his editorial guns on the New Deal. Roosevelt finally persuaded the wealthy Marshall Field to start an opposition newspaper in Chicago to counterattack the *Tribune*'s propaganda war. Thus the Chicago *Sun* was born in December, 1941, at a time when Roosevelt's problems suddenly shifted to a larger screen.

World War II forced Roosevelt out of the party arena into a global role. Between 1940 and the time of his death, Roosevelt tempered his control over the party by appointing a few Republi-

---

*FDR also used the presidential press conferences in unprecedented fashion to provide both a sounding board and a direct line to voters. His 998 press conferences between 1933 and 1945 were a tribute to stamina, political savvy, and his rapport with the newsmen.

cans of national stature to serve at the cabinet level or near it. Henry L. Stimson, Taft's secretary of war, returned to the identical position with Roosevelt as the war clouds gathered, and he served throughout the conflict. In foreign affairs, the Senate Republicans were invited to the White House and asked to declare a truce until the war ended. Led by Senator Arthur Vandenberg of Michigan, the Republicans magnanimously responded, giving Roosevelt all the aid and comfort he needed to keep the conduct of international affairs out of partisan politics.

While Roosevelt was at his active best, he was a vigorous campaigner, or at least a brave one. During one campaign, when whispered doubts of the president's physical fitness reached the White House, Roosevelt managed to campaign in an open car during a cold, driving rain to show his mettle. He also had the knack of turning criticism into a joke, as in 1944 when he shaped remarks about his pet Scottie, Fala, into a boomerang and brought laughter to a national radio audience. The "No Third Term" campaign fell flat in 1940, as Roosevelt defeated Wendell Willkie handily, with 449 to 82 in electoral votes and a 4.9 million national plurality. In the midst of World War II the Republican efforts were slightly better, but with a minimum of campaigning Roosevelt beat Thomas Dewey by 3.6 million votes (and a 432–99 electoral tally) after he dropped Henry Wallace as his vice-president and chose Senator Harry S. Truman instead. The Republicans' charge that Truman was a puppet on strings pulled by Tom Pendergast fell flat.

Within six months Truman was president, determined to be as loyal to Democrats as they were loyal to him. Party whips kept Congress in line to support membership in the United Nations with virtually no opposition, and in the peace following August, 1945, the nation dropped its historical "no entangling alliances" stance for the first time by joining the North Atlantic Treaty Organization. By 1947 the so-called cold war with Russia ended all possibility of peacetime cooperation between the erstwhile allies and laid the groundwork for a "red scare" with menacing overtones. Democrats, sometimes overreacting to Republicans' chants of "softness toward Communism," increasingly backed away from liberal stances, particularly in the Midwest and South. But opposition to the UN and NATO was sporadic, with probably as many Democrats as Republicans afraid of a new international role for the United States.

To some degree the Democratic party had changed vastly, too. The old silver and tariff issues had long been submerged, to be replaced by new problems mainly involving civil rights, labor relations, foreign affairs, and the enlarged role of the federal government in a variety of programs once thought to be of strictly local concern. Truman was a farmer-turned-president with Jefferson's faith in the ability of the common man "to pursue and obtain Happiness and Safety"; but in the atmosphere of international tension prevailing after 1945, the president spoke not only for a party or a nation but also as the chief of a leading power among the western democracies.

The contrast between Truman and Roosevelt also showed the importance of party bonds. Like the only other Democratic president they had known, both believed their political philosophy had Jeffersonian roots that made them responsible to public opinion and party traditions. The rise of the mass media and the overshadowing of newspapers, first by radio and later by television, tended to weaken party ties and project candidates as personalities. In the quest for votes, superficial qualities of appearance and repartee overshadowed the candidate's intellectual capabilities or his character.

In this changing world, perhaps Truman was the last of his breed. Certain of his own integrity, humble about his intellectual makeup, and firmly convinced that the Democratic party would help him survive when a cold war crisis lurked around every bend, Truman waded into the postwar years with awesome confidence. He soon proved that he loved his party more than his party loved him.

EIGHT

The Care of Human Life and Happiness

The three decades that passed between the election of the "do-nothing, good-for-nothing" Republican Eightieth Congress and Jimmy Carter were notable for moon landings and a plethora of technological advances that were unmatched in the areas of human relations and political achievement. The technical and industrial skills of Americans which made victory in World War II inevitable were soon channeled into providing for the greatest orgy of conspicuous consumption in history. At the same time, Americans crowded into the cities in an unconscious effort to test Jefferson's surmise that a nation of city dwellers would make poor republicans. "I view great cities as pestilential to the morals, the health, and the liberties of man," the Founding Father had warned. Since the chief domestic problems of postwar America were concentrated in the poverty and inner decay of metropolitan centers, it was too late to wonder whether Jefferson had been right. The challenge facing the nation's political leadership was to prove Jefferson wrong about the cities but right about the ability of man to govern himself.

Many of the nation's problems stemmed from the complete change in the pattern of American life between 1890 and 1945. Automobiles, electricity, and the shortened workday transformed the living habits of an expanding industrial society. In Jefferson's day only 3 percent of the people lived in cities, but by Truman's time urban America had grown to 56 percent, and in Carter's first year 76 percent of the nation was city born and bred. The number of farmers fell to less than five million, out of a population of 205 million. In a nation of farmers there is always work to do, and unemployment is negligible when there is land to till, crops to sow, cattle to feed, fences to mend, and gardens to be weeded. But in an industrial society of wage earners, finding a job and holding on to it becomes an obsession. Thus Jefferson and the Democrats who followed him worked to please the farmers, confident that in securing their happiness the national welfare was served. By Wilson's time the number of farmers was declining and their sons were hurrying into towns and cities with bright lights and paved roads. The Iowan moving to Pasadena stayed with the Republican party, but the Hoosier dairyman who went to Louisville probably took a different course.

Whatever problems the Democrats encountered with farmers after 1912, the main party concerns centered in the cities, so that by 1946 the chief domestic challenge facing Democrats came down to a simple four-letter word: jobs. Truman learned to dislike Henry Wallace intensely, but at the end of World War II the old New Dealer spoke and wrote of his vision of "60 Million Jobs" while the president nodded approvingly. Keeping Americans on payrolls was his administration's main objective—ahead of low-interest rates, civil rights gains, farm parity—and it was right on a par with efforts to win the cold war with Russia. The 1946 Employment Act was "a landmark in national economic policy," which became the pillar of Democratic domestic programs.*

To some degree, the Democrats' emphasis on full employment

*Norman A. Graebner, Gilbert C. Fite, and Philip L. White, *A History of the United States* (2 vols.; New York: McGraw-Hill, 1970), II, 829.

was a carry-over from the psychology of the depression, when jobless breadwinners scavenged food from garbage cans. The old Democratic message of public frugality and a federal government of limited scope was out of harmony with the stark fact that out of a work force of 48 million Americans in 1933 nearly 15 million could not find work. After World War II the specter of another economic collapse haunted the business world, and a sneeze on Wall Street caused many federal officials, including some of Truman's cabinet, to seek remedies for double pneumonia. Truman's instinct was to seek programs that kept payrolls full, even if their cost made Jefferson's vision of a parsimonious national government seem old-fashioned.

A self-educated politician who read Jefferson carefully, Truman was a country boy himself and in a wistful moment might have regretted the fact that America had grown into an industrial giant. But as a practical politician he transformed his Jefferson ideals into a program tailored principally for urban America. Retaining his faith in the common man, Truman depended on the impetus of the New Deal to provide congressional support for slum clearance, full-employment legislation, and a bold program to end racial discrimination.

Perhaps FDR had once dreamed of a Democratic party committed to a liberal credo, a modern mixture of republicanism with progressive goals that would force out the mossbacks and cleanse the party of its foot-dragging conservatives. But for Truman it was current results, not the drafting board future, that counted. His efforts to phase out discrimination against Negroes' civil rights drew fire from southern Democrats. A wave of strikes in the automobile and steel industries, followed by settlements that conservatives branded as inflationary, caused the president's popularity to dip in the influential public opinion polls. Truman, untroubled by doubt, kept on his course. Within his own party a ranking congressman from Virginia baited organized labor as being dominated by radicals "tinged with communistic theories" and abetted by federal officials. Dozens of Democrats shook their heads in agreement when Representative Howard W. Smith warned that union leaders—labor bosses—were threatening to establish a plutocracy run by organized-labor chieftains. For his part, Truman was more worried about his party's veering to the right than about the troubles caused by a Dave Beck or John L. Lewis.

The collective danger signals foretold the election of a Republican-dominated Congress in 1946. Riding on a wave of HAD ENOUGH? signs, the GOP outnumbered Democrats in the House, 246 to 188, and captured enough Senate seats to hold a 6-vote majority there. A rash of antilabor bills went into the legislative hopper, including the Taft-Hartley Act, which outlawed the closed shop, trimmed the unions' powers in jurisdictional disputes, prohibited union campaign contributions, and forced union officials to swear that they were not Communists. Truman, realizing the role that unions had come to play in the Democratic party, unhesitatingly vetoed the bill. The Republicans easily overrode the veto, aided by a sizable assist from southern Democrats. The vicissitudes of Truman's civil rights proposals in this climate of opinion were easily predicted. Northern Democrats stood by Truman but shared his frustration as White House plans for increased social welfare programs were pigeonholed in congressional committees. Republican-oriented newspapers gloried in the Democrats' frustration. Front page editorial cartoons in the Chicago *Tribune* and Des Moines *Register* depicted a wild-eyed Truman cut adrift by his party and paddling frantically in all directions. "To err is Truman," punning columnists chortled.

Even in his party, Truman found it hard to find loyalty of the kind that had sustained Roosevelt in his dark moments. In the cacophony of dismal straw poll reports and criticism from the South, party leaders in the Midwest and Far West spoke of dumping Truman in favor of a popular apolitical figure at the 1948

Philadelphia convention. George C. Marshall, Dwight D. Eisenhower, and Supreme Court Justice William O. Douglas were mentioned during these trial-balloon days. Truman appeared to ignore the criticism, well knowing that he could have the nomination if he wanted it. Never much of a theorist, he did not argue whether Hamiltonian doctrine had replaced Jeffersonian ideals; it was enough for him to know that he believed the federal government should "serve the interests of all and not the few," particularly the "privileged few." That much of the 1948 party platform raised no outcry, but when Truman supporters called for repeal of the Taft-Hartley Act, they lost hosts of friends in the South. The final insult to the southerners was a plank calling upon Congress to send the president a civil rights bill that would insure all citizens the right to vote, "guarantee them equal opportunities for employment," protect their personal security, and provide "equal treatment in the service and defence of our nation." Drafted by Hubert Humphrey and offered as a substitute by northern liberals, the 1776-sounding plank was supposed to be Truman's undoing. Apparently Truman was ready to settle for less, but once the fight was in the open, he stuck with the liberals.

The plank barely passed, but not before southern Democrats had heaped invectives on their northern fellow-delegates. A hurried effort to replace Truman led to the nomination of Senator Richard Russell of Georgia. On the first ballot, Truman had 947 votes to 263 for Russell. Eastern television stations carried Truman's defiant acceptance speech at 2 A.M. Insofar as the leading newspapers and public-opinion polls saw the situation, Truman had wasted his time. The outraged southern dissenters met in Birmingham a week later, nominated a ticket with a South Carolina senator and Mississippi governor as standard-bearers for the States' Rights or Dixiecrat party. When the ultraliberal Progressive party chose Henry Wallace as their nominee, the fragmented Democrats appeared to have fallen into the same trap they had baited for Republicans in 1912.

Truman's loyal guard dwindled, but he displayed prodigious energy as he began a whistle-stop campaign in West Liberty, Iowa, where he warned voters that only the Democrats could keep the nation prosperous. He also spoke disparagingly of the Republican-dominated Eightieth Congress, which had voted down a grain storage program intended to aid midwestern farmers. Large crowds urged the president, "Give 'em hell, Harry"; and Truman did, buoyed by the increasing turnouts. Pollsters, however, continued to insist that Republican Thomas E. Dewey's White House tenure was all but a *fait accompli* to be confirmed on election day. Party coffers were distressingly empty as pessimistic predictions drove potential Democratic contributors into hiding. Nobody could recall when an incumbent president had been such an underdog. To make matters worse, a southern faction grabbed control of four states' election machinery and ran the Dixiecrat ticket electors as the regular Democrats and thus kept Truman off their ballots. A national victory for their ticket was impossible, but the Dixiecrats could conceivably throw the election into the House and there make a deal with the northern Republicans. Such things had happened before.

Truman drank his glass of buttermilk on election night and went to bed. When the returns came in, telling a story far different from the pollsters' predictions, bicarbonate of soda was perhaps the drink ordered by state chairmen and bosses who had allowed the party machinery to rust. They failed to read the faces of the crowds and instead had believed the media forecasts of a Dewey landslide. Truman's gutsy appeal to union members and Negroes (he was the first president ever to campaign in Harlem) had been underestimated. There had never been such a political upset in our history. Amazingly, Truman had lost New York,

Pennsylvania, and four southern states but still won by carrying twenty-eight states to Dewey's sixteen and by winning 303 to 189 in the electoral college. Truman, running simply as the Democratic candidate, would have lost; but Truman, the president whose judgment and courage had earned the voters' respect, won. The Democratic registration figures (gaining steadily from 1933 onward) showed that three out of every five voters considered themselves Democrats; but, in practice, ticket-splitting and the fear of ousting an incumbent during good times gave presidential campaigns a different set of rules from those in the days of Jackson, Polk, and Pierce.

The Democratic majority that captured Congress on Truman's coattails was less enthusiastic than the chief executive about carrying forward the New Deal philosophy. Truman's Fair Deal program, which drew only polite applause, urged Congress to consider expanded medical insurance, increased social security payments, a repeal of the Taft-Hartley Act, and an increase of the minimum wage to seventy-five cents an hour. The Washington *Star* called Truman's message to Congress "the most frankly socialistic [speech] ever presented by a president." Congress gave Truman the minimum-wage increase and a housing bill, but it balked at repeal of the Taft-Hartley Act and flatly rejected a civil rights investigative commission. A full parity program for farmers never made it through both houses, but increases in corporation and income taxes did. One result was that Truman had a budget surplus during his second term—a rare thing in the memory of voters.

Truman had locked horns with Republicans who were eager to find evidences of Communist influence in various federal agencies. At one time he branded their investigations "a red herring" and became impatient with charges that Communist agents held responsible federal posts. Truman's ire was most aroused by Republican Senator Joseph McCarthy of Wisconsin, who made sweeping charges of espionage in the State Department. Russia had the atomic bomb (after 1949), and Truman's doctrine of containing Communists in eastern Europe led to the Marshall Plan and United States participation in the North Atlantic Treaty Organization. Then North Korea invaded South Korea, prompting Truman to order American forces into the fray as part of a United Nations force. The president's bold action sent a tremor through the nation in 1950, for it seemed that another world war might erupt at any moment. Tires and sugar were hoarded, and Truman's popularity began to ebb again. Yet when he startled a Jefferson-Jackson Day dinner audience early in 1952 by announcing that he would not seek renomination, the party faithful suddenly realized how much affection they held for their pugnacious chieftain.*

Truman's decision left the field open for a galaxy of senators who were ready to prove that they were self-made men, born in a log cabin (or reasonable facsimile thereof) and committed to the principles of FDR. But Truman had his own candidate, albeit a reluctant one, in Governor Adlai Stevenson of Illinois (grandson of Cleveland's vice-president). Presidential primaries were gaining new stature, and the victory of Senator Estes Kefauver over Truman in early March (Truman had ignored the contest and lost by 4,000 votes) heralded a new era of media coverage—or overcoverage—of potential White House occupants. Kefauver went on to win a number of presidential primaries, including a shocking upset in California; but when the tumult died at the Chicago convention, Truman's will prevailed. Despite the president's urging and support from the city machines, Stevenson had to be drafted. He was governor of the host state, but still he broke with tradition by appearing at the convention to welcome the delegates (an

*The Eightieth Congress had passed an "anti-Roosevelt" constitutional amendment—the Twenty-second—which limited presidential tenure to two terms. The amendment, which excluded Truman, was ratified in 1951.

unheard-of thing for a genuine candidate to do). But Stevenson finally bowed to pressure and an amateurish draft movement to become the most articulate presidential candidate offered to voters since Lincoln's time.

The Republicans held a mock draft of their own, with a huge boost from the national media, and finally pitted Dwight Eisenhower and Richard Nixon against Stevenson and Senator John J. Sparkman of Alabama (the memories of 1948 were forgotten in a love feast of sorts). Stevenson's good humor and logical speeches gave the campaign an air of suspense, but in fact the contest was a mismatch. Democrats who had moved into the middle income brackets also moved into the suburbs, where they took on (as Wilfred Binkley noted) "the political coloration of their new neighbors and began voting Republican." College graduates who obtained degrees through the "GI Bill of Rights" tended to identify with the Republicans and to be more active in political campaigns in suburban America. In these areas Stevenson was badly beaten, as well as in every section except the Old South (and West Virginia).

Eisenhower's popularity was so immense that he could have easily won without the kind of campaign that Senator McCarthy preferred to wage, with his charges that the Democrats belonged to "the party of treason." The Korean War dragged on as Republicans reminded voters that Democratic presidents had involved the country in three wars in the twentieth century, presumably while Republicans carried big sticks but kept the nation at peace. A convention fight over a loyalty pledge had left a bitter aftertaste in some southern states and may have caused the crack in the Old South that sent Virginia, Tennessee, Florida, and Texas into the Republican column.

Democrats who had seen Stevenson as a leader in the Roosevelt-Truman tradition were as disappointed as their candidate, who remarked on election night, "As Lincoln once said, it hurts too much to laugh, and I'm too old to cry." At long last, the Democrats' appeal to keep the good times coming had left most voters unmoved. The Congress carried into office by Eisenhower's landslide (55 percent of the popular vote and 442 electoral votes to 89) was barely Republican, however, and the promise to apply the brakes to many New Deal and Fair Deal programs could not be kept unless the southern Democrats joined an informal alliance with the GOP leadership. A political marriage of convenience was arranged, thus ending the Democrats' reliance on the South as a steady, reliable voting bloc. From 1952 onward, the labels in the Old Confederacy counted for little.

Republican campaign rhetoric during the 1952 contest was not carried through after the election. Eisenhower had once called the Tennessee Valley Authority project an example of the "creeping socialism" he would seek to end, but the remark fell into Willkie's basket of "campaign oratory" and the TVA stayed put. Any social legislation offered by the Republican president made it through Congress only when Democrats came to the rescue, a fact perhaps responsible for the election of a Democratic Congress in 1954 (232–203 in the House, 48–47 in the Senate).

Before the Democrats took over, the Senate had had its fill of Senator McCarthy. He had not relented when the Democrats left the White House but was still insisting that "softness on Communism" remained a chronic malady in national government. A wave of loyalty oath laws and guilt-by-association charges, mainly hitting Democrats, followed in the wake of this "red scare." But finally the Wisconsin senator's accusations fell on Republicans as well as Democrats and brought a Senate resolution amounting to censure. Thereafter, the chief advocate of anticommunism as a campaign issue was Vice-President Nixon.

President Eisenhower was strangely detached from the controversies that swirled through Washington during his first term, and he seemed headed for an easy reelection campaign when he suffered a severe heart attack in September, 1955. His rapid recovery dimmed the Democrats' hopes that another candidate might replace the president on the Republican ticket. Even so, Stevenson and Kefauver battled the snow and sleet of presidential primaries for what proved to be a sacrificial honor. Truman lifted the veil on his thoughts when he called Stevenson "a defeatist" and vainly boosted Governor Averell Harriman of New York as the nominee. Stevenson won on the first ballot.

The inner workings of the Democrats' convention power structure were made public when Stevenson took the unusual step of throwing the vice-presidential spot into the delegates' laps by announcing that he had no choice for a running mate. Senator John F. Kennedy had provided some unaccustomed eloquence in nominating Stevenson, and the party leaders in Congress (who controlled, so they thought, the convention) quickly settled on Kennedy as their nominee. However, the delegates reacted to the awesome gavel-wielding power of Speaker Sam Rayburn by choosing Kefauver for the second place. But in coming close, Kennedy's ambitions suddenly flared. The handsome junior senator from Massachusetts was quick to perceive that the flow of power was ebbing before a new force, and he was soon making marks on his 1960 calendar.

The Stevenson-Kefauver ticket was different from the usual party balancing act. Both candidates were committed liberals, and though Kefauver was from the South he was not beloved by most southern Democrats because of his stands on civil rights and labor legislation. Eisenhower, whose father image had grown instead of diminished after his heart attack, stood above the din of partisanship. Party registration figures meant little in a personality contest. On the eve of the election Eisenhower offered no encouragement to the French and British who moved into the Suez; the Union Jack came down in the oil-rich shiekdoms where it had once been the symbol of power. Voters seemed unconcerned about such matters; they gave Eisenhower 57 percent of the vote and all but seven states in the electoral college. Even Louisiana, which had not been carried by a Republican since Reconstruction days, went for Eisenhower. Equally upsetting for Democrats was the postelection revelation that only 35 percent of the nonunion workers and 40 percent of the low-income voters had voted for Stevenson. Democrats came in a poor second in New York, Pennsylvania, and growing California. In Grosse Point, Michigan; Beverly Hills, California; and Scottsdale, Arizona, support for the Stevenson-Kefauver ticket was hardly discernible.

In the congressional races, however, the Democrats were again in charge (234–201 in the House, 49–47 in the Senate), and two of the most powerful men in the country were Texans—Speaker Rayburn and Senate majority leader Lyndon Johnson. When a recession hit the country in 1957, they fought it by guiding legislation through Congress that benefited unemployed workers, brought defense contracts to blighted industrial areas, and fed more funds into the vast interestate highway building program. Johnson also bullied a civil rights voting act through a reluctant Congress. When the Soviet Union launched a space vehicle into orbit in 1957, the nation's shocked reaction was a probe of the tardiness of American scientists in matching the feat. Meanwhile, huge grain surpluses in the Midwest spelled trouble for Republicans who had promised farmers 90 percent of parity a few years earlier.

Congressional elections in 1958 caused some soul searching among editorial writers, political speech makers, and confused voters. The difficulties attending the Supreme Court decision (*Brown* v. *Board of Education*) that decreed an end to segregation in public schools, the spectacular orbit of Sputnik, and the layoffs in heavy industry raised a doubt about the nation's direction and well-being. The Republicans had balanced the federal budget in both 1956 and 1957, but too many people were out of

213

work and the farmers were disgruntled about weak commodity prices. The GOP marshaled support for a series of right-to-work laws (banning the union shop) in semi-industrial states—an action that hurt unions more than their leaders cared to admit. And if Russia really was a threat to world peace, then what was the impact of Soviet advances in atomic power and space exploration? These doubts and troubling unemployment led to a huge gain for Democrats in the fall elections. In the Senate they added 15 seats (now 64 to 34), and the House counted 282 Democrats to 154 Republicans.

A subtle change came in the shift of voting powers away from the old machines into new hands as teachers' unions, police and civil service bargaining agents, and other forces cut up the past patronage patterns. The DeSapio, Lawrence, and Daley machines saw their power erode as second- and third-generation Democrats moved into the suburbs or into different neighborhoods with indifferent records of party loyalty. The presidential nominating convention was still the great gathering of the clan, but the old practice of allotting seats by electoral votes was changed after World War I in favor of larger delegations for the most loyal states. Then, after 1936 extra seats on delegations were added for states that went Democratic in the previous elections. The southern defections in 1952 and 1956 gave the Midwest and North a better position in the forthcoming campaign. The convention delegations, once handpicked by the courthouse crowd or brought out of the statehouse stables, were coveted by a rising group of politically active and younger breed of Democrat. The swelling ranks of the middle class, whose votes controlled most elections, demanded more of a voice in party affairs, and they began to attend county central committee meetings, which had once been occasional, poorly attended gatherings of "good old boys."

Clearly, this was a time of discontent in America. Many of the newcomers in politics were college-trained, middle-income parents who had first tasted participatory politics in parent-teacher meetings or local zoning hearings. Perhaps they had never heard of Edmund Burke's admonition in a similar period of unrest: "When bad men combine, the good must associate." But they were an aroused citizenry of the kind Jefferson dreamed of when he considered the functions of the press and the schools in a republic. Energetic, perceptive women rubbed elbows with the old gentlemen in straw hats as they questioned past practices at caucuses, scanned registration lists, and volunteered for committee posts that once went vacant year-in, year-out. The zeal of this new Democrat (and a similar revival of interest was taking place in Republican ranks) shocked the old courthouse gangs into anger at first, then into dismay, and sometimes into outright disaffection. In some states, such as California, the movement took the form of a well-organized club program that brought old party regulars to heel; while in others the experience was akin to that in Virginia, where the tradition-disdaining new Democrats plowed into the old Byrd machine and eventually caused a revival of the Republican party by the offended and realigned conservatives.

With these forces in motion the presidential primaries began to take on a significance matching the hopes of their earliest backers. At the turn of the century, primaries in Wisconsin and elsewhere were regarded as the democratic panacea for boss rule. On the other hand, the momentum and the hoopla conferred by television coverage of the early primaries probably distorted their value. "The Democrats of New Hampshire, where the first primary is usually held, are all fine people," Clinton Rossiter said, "but neither so fine nor so wise that they should be able to make or break a presidential aspirant all by themselves." From 1952 onward, however, the primaries spread to other states as direct democracy was extolled in the legislatures and applauded in the television newsrooms.

No group of Democrats understood the changing face of pol-

itics more than the staff assembled by Senator Kennedy in preparation for the 1960 campaign. Drawing on the talents of bright,
attractive young volunteers and financed by a sizable family fortune, the Kennedy campaign had a storybook quality. He almost
singlehandedly challenged the Democrats to become the kind of
party Roosevelt envisioned and, had he lived, this might have happened. What did happen was that Kennedy simply overawed the
other campaigners.

Old prejudices died hard, or at least people thought they did.
Kennedy was a Catholic. Would a repetition of Al Smith's debacle
follow, if Kennedy became the nominee? Although Kennedy was
the epitome of the Ivy League elite, with his tailored suits and
proper pronunciations, he quickly learned something about poverty when he campaigned in West Virginia. In this strongly Protestant state, which the stop-Kennedy forces chose for their battle-
ground, the 43-year-old senator soundly defeated the darling of
the surviving New Dealers, Senator Humphrey. Humphrey then
withdrew from the race. Kennedy went on to win the primaries in
every state where his name was on the ballot.

Stevenson avoided the primary battles and worked with a hard
core of liberals, hoping that in an impasse he would be beckoned
for a third try. An uproarious Stevenson demonstration shook the
Los Angeles convention when the most famous member of the
Illinois delegation suddenly took his seat. Soon Mrs. Eleanor
Roosevelt entered the hall, and the emotions of Democrats spilled
over so that it seemed possible the hard-working Kennedy might
be upset by the momentary recollection of past battles waged and
lost. Senator Johnson's supporters refused to wilt, and innuendoes
about upstarts "who needed a little gray in their hair" abounded.
But the tough Kennedy workers moved state delegations into line,
and the matter was settled in short order when the Daley machine
turned its back on homestater Stevenson and swung behind New
England's favorite son. Kennedy won on the first ballot, then did

the unexpected by pulling Lyndon Johnson on board his band-wagon as the vice-presidential nominee. The Republicans confidently offered voters a balancing-act ticket that teamed Richard Nixon with Henry Cabot Lodge.

Sparked by youthful volunteers, the Kennedy organization took over their party's national machinery. Experienced politicians wondered if the amateurish doorbell ringers could produce votes, and the polls gave Nixon an early edge. Worried most by the Catholic issue, Kennedy went into the lion's den as a Daniel of old, spoke to the Houston Protestant ministers, and declared his commitment to absolute separation of church and state. But the South still stood orf, and Kennedy wanted the Old Confederacy to offset the western states where Nixon seemed so strong.

Then the Reverend Martin Luther King, the black civil rights leader, was convicted of obstructing justice in a Georgia court and sentenced to four months at hard labor. While Republican strategists pondered their next step, Kennedy made a much-publicized telephone call to King's wife condemning the injustice of the sentence. The media leaped on the incident, and while southerners generally condemned Kennedy for "butting in," he made a solid point with voters in other sections of the country who perceived that he was not a trimmer. This highly publicized event, along with the television debates, which Kennedy seemed to win by projecting a feeling of self-assurance (and a robust appearance, contrasted with Nixon's haggardness), may have decided the contest.

With prime-time television programs costing over $150,000 in a single evening, the party's financial structure was burdened, and costs mounted until a staggering $14 million had been spent. The press was endorsing Nixon, but television was showing a confident, youthful Kennedy in the final days of the campaign. Publishers might have gnashed their teeth, but the impotence of newspapers in national elections had become an established fact.

The election was one of the closest in history. The 64 percent turnout of registered voters was the highest since the 1908 election, but Kennedy's margin of victory was a mere 118,574 votes out of the 68,000,000 cast. Still, Kennedy had 300 electoral votes to Nixon's 223, and until the Illinois vote went Democratic the outcome had been uncertain. There were charges that irregularities in Cook County tilted the state toward Kennedy. One of Mayor Daley's lieutenants recalled: "When we carried the state for Jack Kennedy, they say we stole all the votes. When the Republicans win the votes, they don't steal them. . . . [Look at] one Republican precinct in Oak Park. That precinct had 600 registered voters. On election day they cast 610—595 Republicans and five or six Democrats. Now, not a word was said. If that was a Democrat, the precinct captains would all have been in jail." Nixon's aides chose not to press the matter. In New York, Nixon had more votes than Kennedy in the straight Republican-Democratic columns, but 406,000 Liberal party votes gave Kennedy the final edge.

The Congress elected for Kennedy's first term was Democratic, but the House margin was cut; and Sam Rayburn's death (a year later) raised doubts about the leadership vacuum, since Johnson had also left the Senate to become vice-president. Their successors were men of less abrasiveness, and also of less persuasion. There were promises to keep in civil rights, labor laws, and relief for tax-burdened urbanites. Kennedy also knew from his experiences in 1959–1960 that the party's machinery was in need of a drastic overhauling, and if the president bore any grudges, he concealed them with considerable charm. During the campaign Kennedy had made it clear that he intended to punch holes in the myth that there was no real difference between the two major parties. "If the Democratic party is charged with disturbing the status quo, with stirring up the great interests of the country, with daring to try something new—I plead guilty," he said. Kennedy made his campaign manager the national party chairman, with orders to strengthen the party where it was weakest, in the far West and Deep South.

Kennedy started his White House tenure with a flair that was reminiscent of Roosevelt's 1933 plunge into the presidency. Harvard professors and big-city bosses found a welcome, new ideas were passed along to young staff members eager to serve their chief, and in short order a Peace Corps was offered to the underdeveloped nations as proof that Americans wanted to share their knowledge along with their largesse. Kennedy's wit, his deft handling of the press corps, and his phrase making sent his popularity zooming during his first twelve months in office. When the governors of the fifty states were invited to the White House, only fifteen were Republicans, so complete had been the sweep of Democrats in the preceding elections. Yet in terms of solid accomplishments, Kennedy had trouble with his Democratic Congress. His decision to send an American space team to the moon was accepted almost without a murmur of protest; but when Kennedy's civil rights bill went to the Senate, Democrat Sam Ervin of North Carolina called the bill "the most sharp and decisive measure in this area since the Reconstruction Acts of 1867." The bill never made it through Congress.

In the 1962 elections the Kennedy charm had failed to provide extra leverage in Congress. In the House, Democrats lost three seats but gained two in the Senate. As Kennedy looked ahead to the 1964 campaign, he considered the weak spots and determined to make a drive for southern support by making a goodwill tour of Texas. Accompanied by Vice-President Johnson he scored a triumph in Fort Worth, then headed for Dallas. His murder on November 22, 1963, dealt the nation a reeling blow from which full recovery was not evident fifteen years later.

Lyndon Johnson, the young New Dealer-turned-New Frontiersman, led the nation in mourning but soon made it clear that his watchword, "Let us continue," was more than a slogan. The first bona fide southerner in the White House since the other Johnson, he was able to wheedle a bared-teeth civil rights bill out of Congress, aimed at racial discrimination in public accommodations. Even an 83-day filibuster in the Sente could not kill Johnson's bill, which finally passed, 73 to 27. White House pressure reestablished the Democratic consensus in Congress, making 1964 a banner year in tallying the accomplishments of the Democratic president who worked with his congressional majority on domestic programs aimed at betterment for the trailing minority of Americans.

In the realm of foreign affairs, the American commitment in Vietnam grew from a tiny pinprick into a deep gash. Johnson's interest stepped up after a minor naval engagement in the Gulf of Tonkin brought Congress to the edge of surrendering its legislative function; a resolution that passed unanimously conferred on the president broad powers "to take all necessary steps" to uphold the southeastern Asia defense treaty. The Republicans soon picked Senator Barry Goldwater as their nominee, choosing a candidate who gloried in the cold war with Russia and China. The choice left to voters was clear-cut. Johnson campaigned sparingly, and (for what it was worth) the Democratic platform promised to seek a detente in Soviet-American relations. "We cannot and we will not play the war game of bluff and bluster," Johnson told an Albuquerque audience. The polls, so unreliable in 1948 and so hedging in 1960, gave Johnson a commanding lead in September that the final vote confirmed—43 million votes to 27 million for Goldwater. The Republicans captured only Arizona and five southern states. In Congress, 295 Democrats faced 140 Republicans in the House, and 68 Democratic senators were opposed by 32 Republicans.

The victory went to Johnson's head. He became more enmeshed in the struggle to end the Vietnamese war and showed less concern for growing problems of urban discord, unemployment among blacks, and growing signs of inflation amid spotty recessions. Johnson handpicked Hubert Humphrey as his vice-president, and to the Minnesotan much of the party business now fell. Lacking Kennedy's personal charm and somewhat suspicious of the media, Johnson fell back on Senate cronies to keep alive his Great Society program to fight poverty, provide medical care for the aged, and pass the greatest educational appropriation in history. To Johnson's credit, he did bestir himself on behalf of a civil rights voting bill in 1965 after the Selma, Alabama, march for freedom dramatized the remaining barriers to Negro voting rights. Literacy tests and poll taxes were swept away, so that the future of Negro political power rested in the hands of blacks for the first time in history. A gigantic appropriation for improving the lot of low-income groups in the cities was hailed as proof that the war on poverty was being won.

The trouble was that the war in Vietnam was not being won, and Johnson failed to recognize the high price demanded of the people with regard to their sons and their patience. Unrest on college campuses followed an unprecedented race riot in Los Angeles that ended in the arrest of four thousand blacks and the loss of $140 million in property. Growing concern over the use of drugs by young Americans, attended by upward curves in urban crime rates, contributed to the national malaise. The high cost of supporting the Vietnam war helped undermine the dollar in international monetary dealings, but Johnson reaffirmed his belief (in 1967) that "by seeing this struggle through now we are greatly reducing the chances of a much larger war—perhaps a nuclear war."

Were the Democrats becoming, as their opposition had so long insisted, the war party? Johnson said not, explaining that it was better to fight a small police action than engage in a major war with the Chinese or Russians. But resistance to the draft grew, leading to some arrests and sending thousands of young Ameri-

THE DEMOCRATS *From Jefferson to Carter*

cans into hiding or into Canada for a refuge. Johnson's tone became more strident as he saw the situation deteriorate. Meanwhile, Democrats began to question the president's leadership. "Dove" candidates in the 1966 congressional elections did not fare well, but Republicans gained forty House seats and four in the Senate. Almost at the moment Johnson was assuring Americans that the end of the Vietnamese agony was in sight, the war took a different turn, and the Communist forces (of the Democratic Republic of North Vietnam) swept southward against crumbling resistance from American-supported Vietnamese armies. A disillusioned and humiliated president, nearly beaten in the New Hampshire primary by an antiwar candidate, shocked the nation by announcing he would no longer seek and would not accept the presidential nomination.

President Kennedy's younger brother, now a senator from New York, leaped into the race. Bearing the Kennedy name and the same dynamic appeal, Robert Kennedy seemed headed for the Democratic nomination until he was shot during the celebration of a primary victory in California. His death in June, 1968 (following the April assassination of Negro leader Martin Luther King), was a sledgehammer blow to the liberal Democrats who had been eager to end the Vietnam war and attack domestic problems related to racial tension, urban decay, and black unemployment.

Still, the Democratic party had resources that were at the ready reserve. Vice-President Humphrey had avoided the primary fights, but he suddenly emerged as the best-known and most-respected Democrat in the nation. His nomination at the Chicago convention was marred by the near riots caused by overzealous antiwar demonstrations, which the television cameramen covered in depth —perhaps too much depth if overall significance was a factor. The manhandling of demonstrators by the Chicago police also was

222

marked down as a strike against the Democrats, on the vague ground that the mayor of Chicago was a Democrat.

After their near disaster with Goldwater the Republicans turned back to Richard Nixon, who appeared in the role of a peacemaker. Both parties had hawkish Vietnam platform planks, but Nixon promised to end the war and told voters to hold him responsible if he broke his pledge. Humphrey, the tiring darling of the old liberal wing of dispirited Democrats, spent his days answering hecklers and trying to explain away the Johnson stand on Vietnam. Meanwhile, Governor George Wallace of Alabama held his own presidential nominating (American party) convention and threw a wrench into the Democratic machinery by threatening to carry the whole South for his splinter group. In the final days of the campaign, polling groups hedged by calling the election a toss-up.

Could the Democrats win New York, Pennsylvania, Michigan, and Texas and still lose the election? Yes, the 1968 results showed. Except for the Wallace defection in five states, Nixon took nearly everything that was left, straight across the country from New Jersey to California. Although in the popular vote Nixon led by less than 320,000, he had 302 electoral votes to Humphrey's 191. There was no doubt about the bedraggled coattails of Lyndon Johnson's presidency; Humphrey had ridden them in pain and anguish to a close but humiliating defeat. When Johnson moved out of the White House, he left behind a remarkable record of domestic accomplishments that seemed of little consequence beside the disillusionment attending the Vietnam war. Few Democratic presidents had ever forced Congress to accept so many bills for housing, civil rights, medical aid, slum clearance, and educational benefits; but the nation seemed more worried about events on the other side of the globe and troubled that they had not been told the truth all along.

Nixon won, but he still had to deal with a Democratic majority in Congress. Four years of internecine national government followed. On the domestic front, Nixon was indifferent toward civil rights legislation but made little effort to undo the other Democratic programs already in progress. Instead he turned his attention to foreign affairs. No Democratic president could have initiated the talks with Communist China which Nixon carried out (early in 1972), if not brilliantly, at least with surprise and a minimum of criticism. The war in Vietnam went on, but peace talks were resumed.

A real power vacuum existed in the Democratic party, however. The old machine bosses were dead or dying; their organizations were crumbling under the exigencies of black unrest, urban sprawl, and generously conceived welfare programs. On one hand the nation had a president who took all of the party's functions into his own closet, where only a trusted few could gain admittance; and on the other hand the Democrats lacked a strong leader who could guide them back to the pathway of victory, if not righteousness (Nixon had proved there could be a fork in the road). As James MacGregor Burns noted, "The paramount fact about American political parties is their organizational weakness at all levels, from local to national." Never was this more true than between 1968 and 1972, when the Democrats offered only the shadow of opposition.

For decades the Democrats had proclaimed that theirs was the party of hope, that in depressions and wars they had lifted the people's spirits with a message exuding Jeffersonian confidence in the common man's ability to work out his problems: What one man could do, the nation as a whole could accomplish. Almost by default the Democrats permitted the level of public debate to slip into a slough of despond, mired down by platitudes, often superficial, and always tinged with fright. Could the Vietnam war be ended by an act of Congress? What was really happening in the big-city ghettos? Would college students stop shouting their slogans and go back to class?

In these discouraging days the Democrats turned the party reins over to theoreticians who convinced the leadership that the old courthouse gangs and city bosses were to blame for many of the nation's problems. In a search for scapegoats the theorists found them in the old-fashioned state central committees, which were dominated by white, middle-aged, and middle-class males. Without consulting the rank and file, a stamp of disavowal was placed on machines already creaking and groaning, barely able to operate in such former strongholds as Kansas City or New York.* With the best of intentions the Democratic party chieftains permitted a drastic revision of the rules governing the selection of national convention delegates. The new plan opened the door on smoke-filled rooms, but as it turned out, it also blew away most of the apparatus for a winning campaign, including an electable candidate who could attract the growing mass of so-called independent voters. Quotas for women, blacks, and other minority groups permitted open caucuses from the precinct to state levels, to reject incumbents (white and male) in favor of a broader slice of the general population. The old bosses and courthouse chairmen were successfully challenged and often purged; Democrats of long standing were mystified by the turn of events. A heavy media emphasis on the primaries also gave the candidacy of Senator George McGovern a momentum that accelerated as his enthusiastic followers, many of them newcomers to party ranks, captured precinct, district, and state conventions operating under the new quota rule.

---

*The mortgage default of Tammany Hall in 1943 was more than a financial embarrassment. Tammany's troubles signaled the end of a once-potent force in the national party structure and the breakup of a stabilizing element in the city government of Manhattan. New Yorkers mystified by police and teacher strikes might ponder why such problems never bedeviled New York in Tammany's heyday.

By the time of the Miami Beach convention in 1972 the front-runner Senator Edmund Muskie (Humphrey's running mate in 1968) had faded as McGovern captured primary after primary. The South Dakotan won the nomination easily and picked Senator Thomas Eagleton for the second place on the ticket. Senator Edward Kennedy's refusal to seek the nomination, and the paranoid actions of certain Republicans who feared that Kennedy might somehow become the candidate, were part of a web that began entangling Nixon in the Watergate disaster. But even the scent of scandal seeping into the late summer campaign could not aid McGovern's faltering campaign, which struck its first snag with his discarding of Eagleton (when the Missourian's treatment by a psychiatrist was revealed) after first expressing "1000 percent confidence" in his vice-presidential choice. Many a Democrat in 1972 paraphrased the boss who in 1900 had viewed Bryan's prospects and said, "I am a Democrat still—very still." By mid-October McGovern's defeat was predicted by the polls with a confidence that reminded some of the 1948 straw ballots, but this was not to be the year of the miracle.

The outcome was devastating. McGovern won only one state (Massachusetts) and the District of Columbia. Thus he became the first Democrat to lose the entire South, and the parallels between the 1936 and 1972 landslides only proved that a major party candidate could practically forfeit and still the party would survive. Nixon had 521 electoral votes to McGovern's 17. In the popular vote count, McGovern lost by nearly 18 million and had only 37 percent of the total. (Nixon had almost 61 percent, slightly ahead of Roosevelt's 1936 total.)

Nixon had proved that McGovern was a loser of classic dimensions, but the Congress that was elected showed the emerging realignment of the parties still favored the Democrats. Except in the bluestocking districts, the cities habitually sent Democrats to Congress. And Iowa, which Senator Jonathan P. Dolliver said would go Democratic when hell froze over, had a senator and two representatives who were Democrats. For twenty years the South had been voting for Republican presidential nominees; but the congressional seats went to Democrats, so that the seniority system gave them a stranglehold on the key committee assignments determined by what seemed almost lifetime contracts for the incumbents. During only four of the past forty years had the Republicans mustered a majority in Congress.

The Democrats had made 1932 one of the pivotal points in our political history by making the Great Depression the same kind of historic crossroads that the Civil War had been for the Republicans. Whatever the concern over slavery, foreign affairs, or tariff barriers, it seemed that nothing registered on the voters' minds as much as prosperity. What the Democrats had done was take the "good times" issue away from the Republicans by convincing the majority in national elections and congressional races that *they* were the trusted preservers of jobs, bank accounts, and whatever else fell under the rubric of social security for the breadwinners.

The national committee had learned a few lessons from the 1972 fiasco. At Kansas City in 1974 an interim convention was held, and the rigid quota system was relaxed. Acknowledging that the formula had caused havoc at Miami Beach, the committee made another change in convention rules which spelled the end of the kind of draft movement that had made Stevenson a candidate in 1952. Henceforth, the rules committee decreed, a person's name would not be allowed to go before the nominating convention without the nominees's written consent. This meant that the early declarers, the primary battlers, and only the avowed candidates could ever become the Democratic nominee, so long as the rule prevailed.

The old axiom—No senator ever becomes president, and Harding is only the exception that proves the rule—had been shot full of holes by events after Roosevelt's death in 1945. Only one president since that time had not been a senator, and during off years the scurrying of would-be candidates sometimes left the Senate an empty chamber. Early in 1975 a national magazine listed the Democrats most likely to succeed in the coming presidential marathon, and all but two were senators. What effect the resignation of Richard Nixon would have on party strategy was uncertain, since the titular leader (McGovern) had lost nearly all of his following. Nobody paid much attention to the short, soft-spoken former governor of Georgia who was the longest of long shots. "My name is Jimmy Carter, and I am running for president of the United States," he said in disarming candor. When had the last former governor of a southern state been a Democratic nominee? Well, in 1844, when Polk had come out of nowhere.

Television helped Carter by offering free time to the underdog from Plains, Georgia, who did not have backing from the CIO political action committees. Not a single large city machine was interested in him. From the first slogging through the New Hampshire snows down to the final run at the 1976 New York convention, Carter's unsophisticated campaigning proved more effective than more carefully organized efforts by aspiring senators or the last-minute rush by the governor of California. Projected as the first real farmer to seek the presidency since Jefferson, Carter assumed that the time-honored Jeffersonian theme of restricting the growth of the federal government would earn him enough votes to win the nomination and the election. After winning the nomination easily, he chose Senator Walter Mondale of Minnesota for his ticket mate, then devoted his energies to holding the cities in the Democratic column through intensive campaigning in metropolitan areas. The campaign trail that began in Des Moines would end in Manhattan.

How much the Democratic cause was aided by Gerald Ford's pardoning of Richard Nixon cannot be known. President Ford agreed to television debates with Carter, but the format and style lacked the fire of the 1960 exchanges. A heavy Republican vote in the suburbs and the fractured South almost deprived Carter of victory, and the issue was in doubt until Ohio finally fell into the Democratic column (by 9,000 votes out of 4 million cast). New York, Pennsylvania, Texas, and Ohio gave Carter the comfortable lead needed to offset Republican votes in the Midwest and West, with 297 electoral votes to Ford's 240. And, perhaps temporarily, the South had returned to the Democratic fold.

There is an old saw to the effect that one is well advised to bring a lot of money when traveling or going into politics. Certainly politics had become an expensive national pastime, for Democrats spent perhaps $55 million in all their 1976 contests and wound up on election night with the usual deficit. Much of the money came from fund-raising activities and contributions from various lobbying and interest groups. Aided by a change in the income tax laws, both parties had their major financing come from the federal treasury. Large gifts by individuals were outlawed by post-Watergate legislation, but whether the federal government should be the chief source of funds for political campaigning remained a moot question. The costs of prime television time and direct-mail advertising had grown to outlandish proportions. Traditional lapel buttons and bumper stickers gave way to newer and far more expensive campaign techniques that centered in the television studios. Certainly more money was spent on one 30-second spot announcement in 1976 than on all the presidential campaigns from 1796 to 1828 combined.

The Democratic party that acknowledged Carter as its new leader on January 20, 1977, was unlike the close-knit circle of friends and followers that had created the party in 1796 to turn the country around by delivering the presidency to Jefferson. Philosophically, the Democrats of 1977 were the great-great-grandsons of Americans who had labored fervently for freedom of the seas, low tariffs, a balanced federal budget, a small federal bureaucracy, a small standing army, low interest rates, and a diplomatic corps of modest size and budget. These early party guidelines had long since been superseded; the sands of party loyalty had been shifting for generations, and as new problems arose, the Democrats in power found Jefferson's maxims comforting, and sometimes practical. The glaring exception, of course, was the high cost of running the complex federal government. Thus the rising generation of Democratic leaders barely spoke of Jefferson's concern for a balanced budget; instead they emphasized the Founding Father's commitment to human rights.

Probably the most Jeffersonian president of the twentieth century has been Harry Truman, and in voting for Carter in 1976, Americans may have been expressing a desire for another earthy, plain-talking, active chief executive. Carter's small-town background and his unconventional campaigning as an underdog gave him a Truman-like quality that appealed to voters searching for an honest man of conviction, a courageous leader who might profit from his mistakes and also admit his failures. Perhaps, too, voters recalled that the best presidents have in all times been men who worked with their party, using its machinery as a responsive means of promoting the general welfare. Generally speaking, the presidents who have been weak party men have been poor presidents. Would Carter know how to restore vigor to the party and thus build a firm base for implementing his program in Congress? Surely the majority in 1976 thought Carter would prove to be in the Jackson-Truman tradition.

Carter's first four years in office would answer many questions concerning his ability to use the Democratic party for the national good. Meanwhile, party platforms had become campaign relics; too much emphasis was placed on the candidate's photogenic qualities, too little on the qualities of his mind. For good or ill, Carter became the party's leader and symbol, his ideas became the platform, his staff became the party's staff. His early decision to run for the presidency, his total reliance upon state conventions and presidential primaries, and his attacks on a burgeoning federal bureaucracy were in themselves proof that the Democratic party was undergoing a transformation. The party Jefferson had founded was barely recognizable in 1978, except for the rhetoric at party gatherings, and whether Carter had a real commitment to basic Jeffersonian Democracy was by no means certain. But when Carter said he wanted to serve a nation "as good as its people," he seemed to imply that the people must be trusted. Jefferson would have been pleased.

In one sense, however, the country and its leaders had let Jefferson down. The great exponent of a democratic faith had no doubt that an enlightened, free people would see to it that life, liberty, and fair play would become dominant national traits. Jefferson never considered "the possibility that a free citizenry may also be a politically indifferent citizenry," a fact that has often permitted special interest groups to ravage the nation's natural resources, vote themselves gifts from the public treasury, and mock the idealism expressed by every president from Washington to Carter. Yet Jefferson himself had feared the power of venal politicians. "To special [interest] legislation, we are generally averse," he said in 1817, "lest a principle of favoritism should creep in and pervert that of equal rights."* When Harry Truman said he would be a president "for all the people," implying that he would not truckle to any favored group, his defiance of lobbyists and pressure tactics struck a Jeffersonian chord. Carter's veto of pork barrel projects in 1978 gave a hint that he too was at heart a Jeffersonian, beleaguered by the kinds of interest seekers who have been flocking to the temples in Washington since 1800.

*James S. Young, *The Washington Community, 1800–1828* (New York: Columbia University Press, 1966), 27; Thomas Jefferson to George Flower, September 12, 1817.

The social gains made from Roosevelt's first moves in 1933 through the legislative record of the Ninety-fifth Congress formed a solid part of the Democrats' history of accomplishment; and most of them were so firmly fixed in the nation's political structure that the Republicans made no effort at revocation or repeal. Of course, the thought of a federal government employing 2.8 million people and paying over 8 percent interest on a national debt approaching $680 billion, would have numbed Thomas Jefferson. The overriding concern of nineteenth-century politicians for balanced budgets seemed too old-fashioned to discuss in an era in which politicians practiced the fine art of Keynesian economics, unmindful of budgetary deficits when human welfare was thought to be jeopardized. Although both parties have seemed willing to practice the British economist's not-to-worry advice on public spending, there has been a distinct difference in their programs to maintain national prosperity. In general, the Republicans have believed that the best way to keep America prosperous is through subsidies and tax incentives to business and industry; the Democrats have favored spending programs designed to create and sustain a vigorous consumer demand for goods and services. In practice, Republicans have talked tough about communism, making the Democrats squirm when defense budgets soared in the arms race with the USSR. Republicans think defense contracts help the nation's business and also strike a pose against Russian imperialism. Democrats have liked the jobs created by multi-billion-dollar defense budgets but have wondered if a sense of national priorities was not distorted when thousands of children started every day without breakfast.

A story making the rounds during the Great Depression was a kind of parable in those days of widespread distress: "Take a loaf of bread and give it to two politicians. The Republican will try to sell it, and the Democrat will go ahead and eat it." The point (or one of the points) was that Democrats in the New Deal days were more interested in people than in prosperity. Forty years later the Democrats still had that reputation. President Carter would have to prove that the reputation was deserved. Challenged by defiant oil sheiks abroad and a devastating inflation at home, could Carter help restore the nation's confidence by reminding the people that the Democratic credo rested on a belief that the wealth of the nation lay in the resources of its people—in their ideas, their labor, and their courage—and not in bank vaults, oil wells, coal mines, or even the fertile midwestern loams? Whatever Carter's course, the Democrats would always have a program as long as they looked beyond worries over a multitude of temporary problems to the beacon first lighted by Jefferson:

The care of human life and happiness, and not their destruction, is the first and only legitimate object of good government.

A political party founded on that premise, and committed to its fulfillment, should last as long as the nation endures.

Bibliographical Note

T rying to write a history of the Democratic party is a task that has frightened away all but the foolhardy or the zealous. The earliest histories appeared during every presidential election, were often thrown together with scissors and paste, and were hardly more than campaign tracts. From the whole of the nineteenth-century writings, only two works dealing with the Democrats cannot be ignored: Jabez D. Hammond, *The History of Political Parties in the State of New York* (Syracuse, N.Y.: Hall, Mills, 1852), and Martin Van Buren's *Inquiry into the Origin and Course of Political Parties in the United States* (New York: Hurd and Houghton, 1867). The winds of change blowing in 1912 signaled a different approach to political affairs, a fact soon confirmed by the publication of Charles A. Beard's *Economic Origins of Jeffersonian Democracy* (New York: Macmillan, 1915). Beard's sweeping approach demonstrated that scholarship and political ideas were compatible. In less than a decade, the role of parties was being scrutinized in the denouement of Harding's 1920 landslide. Arthur N. Holcombe, *The Political Parties of Today* (New York: Harper & Brothers, 1924), provided a brief, able study of both major parties and included the best survey of the Democratic party up to Wilson's last term. The 1920s were discouraging years for the Democrats, but the stirring 1928 campaign provoked two party histories—Frank R. Kent, *The Democratic Party: A History* (New York: Century, 1928), and Henry A. Minor, *The Story of the Democratic Party* (New York: Macmillan, 1928). Kent's book is written with a combination of prejudice and facts, whereas Minor's is fact-packed, though the prose is often emotional. Herbert Agar, *Pursuit of Happiness: The Story of American Democracy* (Boston: Houghton Mifflin, 1938), leans toward the visceral approach. Since 1938 the only attempt to present a broad-sweeping party history for the layman has been David L. Cohn's illustrated and readable *The Fabulous Democrats* (New York: G. P. Putnam's Sons, 1956).

The promise heralded by Beard's early work came to the foreground in Wilfred E. Binkley, *American Political Parties: Their Natural History* (New York: Knopf, 1943); Richard Hofstadter, *The American Political Tradition, and the Men Who Made It* (New York: Knopf, 1948); and Louis Hartz, *The Liberal Tradition in America* (New York: Harcourt, Brace, 1955). Binkley, Hofstadter, and Hartz deal with both major parties and their leaders, and their crisp writing, insights, and skilled interpretations continue to have impact for their balanced presentations.

More recently a scholarly flood has inundated the campuses but often left little choice for the lay reader. The best books dealing with the nation's party system include James MacGregor Burns, *The Deadlock of Democracy* (Englewood Cliffs, N.J.: Prentice-Hall, 1963); William N. Chambers, *Political Parties in the New Nation: The American Experience, 1776–1809* (New York: Oxford University Press, 1963); Joseph Charles, *The Origins of the American Party System* (Williamsburg, Va.: Institute of Early American History and Culture, 1956); Ralph N. Goldman, *The Democratic Party in American Politics* (New York: Macmillan, 1966); Richard Hofstadter, *The Idea of a Party System: The Rise of Legitimate Opposition in the United States* (Berkeley: University of California Press, 1969); Roy F.

Nichols, *The Invention of the American Political Party* (New York: Macmillan, 1967); and Clinton Rossiter, *Parties and Politics in America* (Ithaca, N.Y.: Cornell University Press, 1960). Arthur M. Schlesinger, Jr. (ed.), *A History of U.S. Political Parties* (4 vols.; New York: Chelsea House, 1973), contains the major historical documents for both parties with well-written introductions by a galaxy of distinguished scholars. Essays on major party developments are brought together in Wilfred E. A. Bernhard, Felice A. Bonadio, and Paul A. Murphy (eds.), *Political Parties in American History* (New York: G. P. Putnam's Sons, 1974). V. O. Key, Jr., *Southern Politics in State and Nation* (New York: Knopf, 1949), stands in a class by itself.

Special studies on the Democratic party range from monographs covering brief time spans to collected essays and include many regional studies of merit. William N. Chambers, *The Democrats, 1789–1964* (Princeton, N.J.: Van Nostrand, 1964), has a summary view with appended readings. Important books on phases of party history include Stuart Gerry Brown, *The First Republicans* (Syracuse, N.Y.: Syracuse University Press, 1954); Lance Banning, *The Jeffersonian Persuasion* (Ithaca, N.Y.: Cornell University Press, 1978); Norman Risjord, *The Old Republicans* (New York: Columbia University Press, 1965); Noble Cunningham, *The Jeffersonian Republicans: The Formation of Party Organization, 1789–1801* (Chapel Hill: University of North Carolina Press, 1957); Sanford Higginbotham, *The Keystone in the Democratic Arch: Pennsylvania Politics, 1800–1816* (Harrisburg: Pennsylvania Historical Museum Commission, 1952); Ronald P. Formisano, *The Birth of Mass Political Parties: Michigan, 1827–1861* (Princeton, N.J.: Princeton University Press, 1971); Joel H. Silbey, *A Respectable Minority: The Democratic Party in the Civil War Era, 1860–1868* (New York: Norton, 1977); Lawrence Grossman, *The Democratic Party and the Negro: Northern and National Politics, 1868–1892* (Urbana: University of Illinois Press, 1976); Horace S. Merrill, *Bourbon Democracy of the Middle West, 1865–1896* (Seattle: University of Washington Press, 1967); Roger L. Hart, *Redeemers, Bourbons and Populists: Tennessee, 1870–1896* (Baton Rouge: Louisiana State University Press, 1975); J. Roger Hollingsworth, *The Whirligig of Politics: The Democracy of Cleveland and Bryan* (Chicago: University of Chicago Press, 1963); Arthur S. Link, *Woodrow Wilson and the Progressive Era, 1910–1917* (New York: Harpers, 1954); Robert K. Murray, *The 103rd Ballot: The Democrats and the Disaster in Madison Square Garden* (New York: Harper & Row, 1976), about the 1924 covention; William E. Leuchtenburg (ed.), *The New Deal: A Documentary History* (New York: Harper & Row, 1968); Herbert S. Parmet, *The Democrats: The Years After FDR* (New York, Macmillan, 1976); and Robert A. Garson, *The Democratic Party and the Politics of Sectionalism, 1941–1948* (Baton Rouge: Louisiana State University Press, 1974).

There is no good overall study of political machines headed by Democrats, but there is a special work and a few biographies of bosses. Roy F. Nichols, *The Democratic Machines, 1850–1854* (New York: Columbia University Press, 1923), was a pioneer work. Gustavus Myers, *The History of Tammany Hall* (New York: Boni & Liveright, 1917), and Denis T. Lynch, *"Boss" Tweed* (New York: Boni & Liveright, 1927), have been revised by Leo Hershowitz, *Tweed's New York* (New York: Anchor, 1977). For the nominating process, James S. Chase, *Emergence of the Presidential Nominating Convention, 1789–1832* (Urbana: University of Illinois Press, 1973), and Paul T. David *et al.*, *The Politics of National Party Conventions* (Washington, D.C.: Brookings Institution, 1960), are helpful. Local Democratic politics are the focus of Roy V. Peel, *The Political Clubs of New York City* (New York: G. P. Putnam's Sons, 1935); Norman M. Adler and Blanche D. Blank, *Political Clubs in New York* (New

York: Praeger, 1975); and James C. Wilson, *The Amateur Democrats* (Chicago: University of Chicago Press, 1962), with the latter covering Chicago, Los Angeles, and New York.

A listing of works on the major personalities in the Democratic party requires some choices from an abundance of outstanding books. Merrill Peterson, *The Jefferson Image in the American Mind* (New York: Oxford University Press, 1960), is an important work surpassing everything except Dumas Malone, *Jefferson in His Time* (5 vols. to date; Boston: Little, Brown, 1948–).

Arthur M. Schlesinger, Jr., *The Age of Jackson* (Boston: Little, Brown, 1948), is of a classic dimension. The Democratic presidents between Jackson and Wilson have been treated unevenly. The noteworthy biographies are Robert V. Remini, *Martin Van Buren and the Making of the Democratic Party* (New York: Columbia University Press, 1959); Charles A. McCoy, *Polk and the Presidency* (Austin: University of Texas Press, 1960); Allan Nevins, *Grover Cleveland: A Study in Courage* (New York: Dodd Mead, 1932); and Horace S. Merrill, *Bourbon Leader: Grover Cleveland and the Democratic Party* (Boston: Little, Brown, 1957). Arthur S. Link, *Wilson* (5 vols. to date; Princeton, N.J.: Princeton University Press, 1947–), is a magisterial work that stands out, and John A. Garraty, *Woodrow Wilson: A Great Life in Brief* (New York: Knopf, 1956), is adequate. With the coming of Roosevelt, the biographical field expands astonishingly. Of major importance are Frank Freidel, *Franklin D. Roosevelt* (4 vols. to date; Boston: Little, Brown, 1952–); James MacGregor Burns, *Roosevelt* (2 vols.; New York: Harcourt, Brace, 1956–70); and William E. Leuchtenburg, *Franklin D. Roosevelt and the New Deal, 1932–1940* (New York: Harper and Row, 1963). The best books on Roosevelt's successor are Alonzo L. Hamby, *Beyond the New Deal: Harry S. Truman and American Liberalism* (New York: Columbia University Press, 1973), and Robert J. Donovan, *Conflict and Crisis: The Presidency of Harry S. Truman* (New York:

Norton, 1977). For the Camelot years, Arthur M. Schlesinger, Jr., *A Thousand Days: John F. Kennedy in the White House* (Boston: Houghton Mifflin, 1965), is excellent. No judicious biography of Lyndon Johnson has been published.

Among the notable also-rans there is little of importance to choose from until we reach assessments of Bryan. The ground broken by Hibben Paxton, *The Peerless Leader: William Jennings Bryan* (New York: Farrar and Rinehart, 1929), has been worked over more recently by Paul W. Glad, *The Trumpet Soundeth: William Jennings Bryan and His Democracy, 1896–1912* (Lincoln: University of Nebraska Press, 1960); Paolo E. Coletta, *William Jennings Bryan* (Lincoln: University of Nebraska Press, 1964); Charles M. Wilson, *The Commoner: William Jennings Bryan* (New York: Doubleday, 1970); and Louis W. Koenig, *Bryan: A Political Biography* (New York: Putnam, 1971). For the tumultuous twenties, William H. Harbaugh, *Lawyer's Lawyer: The Life of John Davis* (New York: Oxford University Press, 1973); Oscar Handlin, *Al Smith and His America* (Boston: Little, Brown, 1958); and Richard O'Connor, *The First Hurrah: A Biography of Alfred E. Smith* (New York: Putnam, 1970), are worthwhile. The 1952 and 1956 standard-bearer's style comes across better, perhaps, in Walter Johnson (ed.), *The Papers of Adlai Stevenson* (7 vols. to date; Boston: Little, Brown, 1972–), than in John B. Martin, *Adlai Stevenson and the World* (2 vols.; New York: Doubleday, 1976–77).

Biographies of secondary figures are legion. The best include Edmund and Dorothy S. Berkeley, *John Beckley: Zealous Partisan* (Philadelphia: American Philosophical Society, 1973); John A. Garraty, *Silas Wright* (New York: Columbia University Press, 1949); Robert W. Johannsen, *Stephen A. Douglas* (New York: Oxford University Press, 1973); Irving Katz, *August Belmont: A Political Biography* (New York: Columbia University Press, 1968); Joseph F. Wall, *Henry Watterson: Reconstructed Rebel* (New

York: Oxford University Press, 1956); and Joseph B. Gorman, *Kefauver: A Political Biography* (New York: Oxford University Press, 1971).

Historians believe in looking at the sources. Reading one issue of Horace Greeley's New York *Weekly Tribune* for August, 1860, tells us more about the temper of the times than a dozen secondary accounts. So every informed American citizen must read *The Federalist* and James Madison's *Notes* on the debates at the Federal Convention of 1787 or pay the penalty for political ignorance. Unless we have a grasp of our first political endeavors, the shape of current events and the *raison d'être* of our parties have little meaning, and we tend to be overly discouraged by temporary setbacks. The doleful messages of David S. Broder, *The Party's Over: The Failure of Politics in America* (New York: Harper & Row, 1972), and Henry Fairlie, *The Parties: Republicans and Democrats in this Century* (New York: St. Martin's, 1978), bespeak a shortsightedness that must be overcome. In the United States the dialogue of freedom has always included a raucous shouting of party slogans and creeds. As our loyalties to parties have been nurtured, we have added strength to the democratic process. A reading of the Declaration of Independence, written in the Whig-Republican-Democratic tradition, is always worthwhile.

Index

Index

Index

Thoreau, Henry, 79–80
Tilden, Samuel J., 139; nominated by
  1876 convention, 125; apparently
  elected president, 125; commission
  decides against, 126
Tillman, Benjamin R., 158; attacks
  Cleveland, 148, 149; joins national
  committee, 150
Time, 185
Times (Kansas City), 153
Times (New York): exposes Tweed
  Ring, 130, 134; comments on 1928
  campaign, 188; reports Wall Street
  collapse, 191
Times-Democrat (New Orleans), 154
Tocqueville, Alexis de. *See* De
  Tocqueville, Alexis
Treaty of Ghent (1814), 38
Tribune (Chicago), 122, 151, 152,
  185, 199, 205
Tribune (New York), 98, 134, 136,
  153
Tripoli, 22, 23
Truman, Harry S., 185, 201, 203, 204,
  205, 208, 232; nominated for vice-
  president, 200; succeeds Roosevelt
  in 1945, p. 200; criticized by party
  leaders, 205–206; 1948 nominee for
  president, 206; "Give 'em hell"
  campaign, 207; popularity ebbs,
  209; compared to Jefferson, 230
  231
Trusts, 127, 144, 157, 160, 173; as
  1900 campaign issue, 155, 156;
  Clayton Antitrust Act passed, 171
Tweed, William Marcy: Tammany
  Hall boss, 127; corruption exposed,
  130
Tyler, John, 76; nominated by Whigs,
  72; seeks party nomination, 77

Underwood, Oscar, 165, 173
Union (Washington), 91
Union of Soviet Socialist Republics
  (USSR): cold war with United States,
  200, 203, 209, 213, 214, 220, 221,
  232
Union party, 114–15
United Nations (UN), 200, 201, 209

United States Telegraph (Washington),
  51

Vallandigham, Clement, 113, 114;
  spokesman for Peace Democrats,
  110; drafts "war-failure" plank,
  114; killed, 122–23
Van Buren, Martin, 35, 41, 45, 46, 47,
  48, 49, 51, 56, 57, 60, 68–69, 69–
  70, 72–73, 82, 87; joins Jackson,
  51–52; favors New York-Virginia
  link, 54; plans Jackson's
  nomination, 59–61; nominated as
  vice-president, 62; nominated for
  president, 67; opposes Texas
  annexation, 77; accepts Free-Soil
  nomination, 88–89
Vandenberg, Arthur, 200
Vietnam War, 220; draft resisted, 221–
  22; divides Democrats, 223
Vilas, William F., 146
Virginia, 20, 43, 47, 71, 75, 79, 121;
  Richmond Junto, 31, 72; rejects
  Free-Soil party, 88; seat of conservatism, 215
Virginia and Kentucky resolutions,
  14–15, 17, 23, 52; used in later
  campaigns, 74, 95

Wade, Benjamin, 115, 117
Wagner, Robert F., 185–86, 197
Walker, Robert J., 88, 102
Wallace, George, 223
Wallace, Henry A., 195, 203; dropped
  from 1944 ticket, 200; nominated
  by Progressives, 206
Walsh, Thomas J., 176
Washington, Booker T., 173
Washington, George, 8–9, 10–11, 16,
  36, 54; disdain of parties, 3, 11;
  favors Hamilton's policies, 8
Washington Temperance Society, 64
Watchman (Circleville, Ohio), 111
Watterson, Henry, 125, 145–46
Weaver, James B., 129
Webster, Daniel, 40, 59, 92
Weed, Thurlow, 75, 86
Welles, Gideon, 109
West Virginia, 116, 210, 216

253